THE UNIVERSITY OF
WINCHESTER

Martial Rose Library
Tel: 01962 827306

To be returned on or before the day marked above, subject to recall.

D1492809

The publisher gratefully acknowledges the generous support of the Joan Palevsky Literature in Translation Endowment Fund of the University of California Press Foundation.

André Bazin's New Media

ANDRÉ BAZIN

Edited and Translated by Dudley Andrew

UNIVERSITY OF CALIFORNIA PRESS

University of California Press, one of the most distinguished university presses in the United States, enriches
lives around the world by advancing scholarship in the
humanities, social sciences, and natural sciences. Its
activities are supported by the UC Press Foundation and
by philanthropic contributions from individuals and
institutions. For more information, visit www.ucpress.edu.

University of California Press
Oakland, California

Library of Congress Cataloging-in-Publication Data

Bazin, André, 1918–1958.
  [Essays. Selections. English]
André Bazin's new media / André Bazin ; edited and
translated by Dudley Andrew.
    pages cm
  Includes bibliographical references and index.
  ISBN 978-0-520-28356-5 (cloth : alk. paper)
  ISBN 978-0-520-28357-2 (pbk. : alk. paper)
  ISBN 978-0-520-95939-2 (e-book)
    1. Television—Philosophy.   2. Motion pictures
and television.   3. Motion pictures—Philosophy.
I. Andrew, Dudley, 1945– editor of compilation,
translator. II. Title.
    PN1992.55.B37   2014
    791.4—dc23

                                          2014008944

Manufactured in the United States of America

23 22 21 20 19 18 17 16 15 14
10 9 8 7 6 5 4 3 2 1

In keeping with a commitment to support environmen-
tally responsible and sustainable printing practices, UC
Press has printed this book on Natures Natural, a fiber
that contains 30% post-consumer waste and meets the
minimum requirements of ANSI/NISO z39.48-1992 (R 1997)
(*Permanence of Paper*).

Contents

Editor's Note: About This Collection   ix

Introduction: André Bazin Meets the New Media
of the 1950s   1

PART ONE. THE ONTOLOGY AND LANGUAGE OF TELEVISION

1. The Aesthetic Future of Television   37

2. In Quest of *Télégenie*   44

3. Television Is Unbeatable for Live Coverage   48

4. Was It Live? Preserve Our Illusions   51

5. The Talking Head: Must the Commissaire Stand
on His Head for TV?   54

6. Television Is Neither Theater nor Cinema   57

7. At the Venice Film Festival, TV Shares the Screen   60

8. Voice-Overs on TV: Let the Animals Talk   63

9. Looking at Television   67

PART TWO. TELEVISION AMONG THE ARTS

10. Long Live Radio! Down with the 8th Art! 75

11. A Seat at the Theater 79

12. False Improvisation and "Memory Lapses" on TV 82

13. To Serve Theater, Let Television Adopt
Some Modesty 86

14. Respect the Spirit of Theater First and Foremost! 90

15. TV and the Disenchantment of Theater 92

16. Art on Television: A Program
That Loses on All Counts 95

17. Reporting on Eternity: TV Visits the Musée Rodin 99

PART THREE. TELEVISION AND SOCIETY

18. A Contribution to an *Erotologie* of Television 105

19. Censors, Learn to Censor 116

20. You Can Now "Descend into Yourself" 119

21. Television, Sincerity, Liberty 121

22. Information or Necrophagy 124

23. Television as Cultural Medium *and*
The Sociology of Television 126

24. Do We Really Need Those Serials? 133

25. A Superb Clown Made Incoherent by TV 136

26. TV Can Popularize without Boredom or Betrayal 139

PART FOUR. TELEVISION AND CINEMA

27. Television and the Revival of Cinema 145

Contents / vii

28. Television and Cinema 153

29. Is Television a Degradation for Filmmakers? 157

30. Some Films Are Better on the Small Screen
Than the Large 160

31. Should Television Be Allowed to Chop Films to Pieces? 163

32. From Small Screen to Widescreen 167

33. Sacha Guitry Is Confident about TV, Just as
He Was about Cinema in 1914 171

34. Jean Gabin Gets TV's "Sour Lemon" Prize 174

35. "The Glass Eye" Will Reveal a New Hitchcock 177

36. Hitchcock on TV 180

37. Renoir and Rossellini: Two Top Recruits for Television 182

38. Renoir and Rossellini Debut on TV 184

39. Cinema and Television: An Interview with
Jean Renoir and Roberto Rossellini 187

40. About Television: A Discussion with Marcel
Moussy and André Bazin 204

PART FIVE. CINERAMA AND 3D

41. New Screen Technologies 215

42. Cinerama: A Bit Late 220

43. Cinerama, a Disappointment 227

44. Cinema in 3D and Color: Amazing! 232

45. A New Stage in the Process: Math
Equations for 3D 235

46. Will a War in Three Dimensions Take Place? 243

47. The Return of *Metroscopix* 248

48. *The House of Wax:* Scare Me . . . in Depth!   251

49. The Real Crime on *La Rue Morgue:*
They Assassinated a Dimension!   254

50. The 3D Revolution Did Not Take Place   258

PART SIX. CINEMASCOPE

51. Will CinemaScope Save the Cinema?   267

52. CinemaScope and Neorealism   288

53. CinemaScope: The End of Montage   292

54. The Trial of CinemaScope: It Didn't Kill
the Close-Up   294

55. Massacre in CinemaScope   299

56. Will CinemaScope Bring about a Television
Style in Cinema?   308

PART SEVEN. FINALE

57. Is Cinema Mortal?   313

Appendix: A Selective Reference Guide
to 1950s French Television   319

Index   327

Editor's Note: About This Collection

CORPUS AND ORGANIZATION

The fifty-seven pieces that comprise *André Bazin's New Media* (some a page long, others full-blown essays) were written in the six years between the fall of 1952 and the author's death in the fall of 1958, except for the article on radio (chapter 10), which came out in February 1951. They were selected from the nearly 2,600 xeroxed items maintained in the Bazin archive at Yale University because they all address image formats that challenged the standard cinema of the day. Some articles have slipped through this filter; for instance, the words "television" and "CinemaScope" appear in a number of his film reviews, but often so casually that I set these aside. "CinemaScope" is even in the titles of his reviews of Nunnally Johnson's *Night People* and Anthony Mann's *Man from Laramie,* but neither review interrogates the format sufficiently for me to include it.

I also excluded several primarily descriptive pieces on the spectrum of television programming, because the shows they discuss (sometimes in detail) are now long forgotten, and the ratio of critical ideas to mere chronicle dips below a threshold of analysis Bazin otherwise maintains. Doubtless my own preoccupations also played a role here. For instance, I did not include two articles that looked into sports reporting (including the race at Le Mans), because I found them more informational than analytic. Such pieces, always witty and well written, will certainly interest scholars of media and of Bazin. Let us continue to work toward the moment when all his writings are available to be readily examined. Meanwhile I believe I have collected here more than 90 percent of his writings relevant to the new media of the 1950s, and that all his major concerns stand out in this volume.

A chronological organization of these pieces would carry a few benefits; so too would organizing them by journal (hence readers should always examine the place and date of publication listed at the end of each item). However, I chose to classify these writings by media, theme, and topic so as to best coordinate Bazin's continuing concerns. This results in some overlap and redundancy, as a new event (Cinerama arriving in Paris, for example) would be treated in columns he wrote for two or three different journals during a single month. He would naturally take up many of the same points and sometimes deploy the same analogies. In fact his account of Cinerama published in *Radio-Cinéma-Télévision* is close enough to his *L'Observateur* piece that only the latter is included here. But that is an exception, since generally Bazin varied his emphasis and language even when writing on a single film or topic, and comparing these related pieces turns out to be fascinating. It also clarifies his ideas.

Unsurprisingly, Bazin treated television as quite separate from the big-screen formats that were being introduced with fanfare at the same time; and he recognized that many readers of the popular new weekly *Radio-Cinéma-Télévision* might seldom go to the movies, preferring to remain at home. And so he wrote regularly about the small screen. Choosing again to group these forty TV pieces by topic, I came up with rubrics that are variants of the rubrics Bazin laid out for his collected film writings, *Qu'est-ce que le cinéma?*, with only the fourth part proving recalcitrant. As for the first three parts, just like cinema, TV has its "ontology and language"; it also needs to find its place "among the other arts," and it exhibits identifiable "sociological" characteristics and responsibilities. And just as Bazin had planned to reserve the fourth and final volume of *Qu'est-ce que le cinéma?* for "Neorealism," the corpus of films that he found most personally challenging and satisfying, so part four here brings together his thoughts on the relation of television to cinema, since the latter, despite all I say in the introduction, was unquestionably what he cared most to experience and think about.

As for "new technologies of the big screen," many of Bazin's comments make it clear that he would have split his writings in the way I have done here, giving pride of final position to CinemaScope, the only format he ultimately believed would persist into the next decade, and the one he found aesthetically viable. As for 3D and Cinerama, he became increasingly sure that both would be extinguished within a few years, even if he also expected them to be resurrected, as indeed they have been. I could not resist adding "Is Cinema Mortal?" as a final drumroll to this collection. A prophetic and splendid essay, it shows Bazin in amazing command of media ecology and evolution during a transitional period. Written in 1953, when he had seen scarcely more than a few examples of what Hollywood was throwing his way and what the French were trying to make of the small screen, he projects far into the future. I label this a "finale," even if he penned it in advance of most of the essays to which it stands as a conclusion. And what a conclusion it is!

THE TEXT, THE TRANSLATION, THE NOTES

Except in one instance (chapter 14), each article is translated in its entirety. I reproduce Bazin's italicization and his quotation marks around key words. His original French is reproduced in brackets when his meaning seems truly enigmatic or when a pun is involved. These brackets could have mushroomed; I kept them to a minimum. Titles of some articles have been shortened or lightly altered, and most subheadings have been excised, since his editors, more than he, exercised control over these para-textual features. When the wit of an article title signals Bazin's presence, I have made an effort to reproduce this effect, but I find it more important that each title point clearly to the article's topic. As for subheadings, these are the province of publishers, each magazine striving for an identifiable *mise-en-page* that often mandated their use for visual effect, even when an argument didn't need them. I retained those that I believe clarify a piece.

It was Grant Wiedenfeld and Michael Cramer who, while preparing their contributions to *Opening Bazin,* ventured translations of a few of Bazin's writings on TV and technology. Reworking these in an idiom designed to serve the author, I realized that I could proceed to translate all Bazin's articles that I found pertinent to these topics as I systematically went through the archive. With limited translation experience but knowing the issues and the vocabulary to the bone, I checked my drafts with Madeline Whittle, who has assisted me on other projects, and who was essential in keeping this one on track and accurate. So in tune were our co-translation sessions that I entrusted her with the first drafts of a number of the essays that I then verified and adjusted into the rhythm I expected the whole work to maintain. In a final careful run-through, I clipped difficult sentences or phrases and sent them to Jeremi Szaniawski, a native French speaker, asking him for clarification or for variants. He was unfailingly generous, swift, and illuminating. On a couple of occasions Tom Conley and Steven Ungar enjoyed extricating me from syntactical conundrums. I thank all of them, especially Madeline, but I alone am responsible for the translations.

Well beyond its first decade, France's single TV channel broadcast only a limited number of hours per day. Hence Bazin returned more than once to certain programs or personalities that reappeared weekly or at least intermittently throughout the six years of his vigilance. Many of these are identified in the appendix, which eliminates redundant notes after the chapters and serves as a highly selective reference guide to early French television. The editor's notes at the end of each article aim to identify or clarify other issues or names that arise therein. Most titles of films and books are given in their original language with a translation or gloss in the notes or in brackets at their first appearance.

One troublesome title is that of the periodical often referred to simply as *L'Observateur*. In fact it was founded in 1950 as *L'Observateur politique, économique et littéraire*. It changed its name but not its editorial position to *L'Observateur d'Aujourd'hui* in November 1953, then to *France-Observateur* in April 1954. A decade later it would become, and remain until today, *Le Nouvel Observateur*.

A very few of these selections have appeared previously in English. Bazin was actually introduced to British readers just after his death, when *Sight and Sound* translated a somewhat truncated version of the interview he conducted with Roberto Rossellini and Jean Renoir about their television ventures. I have filled in all the lacunae and amended the original in places to produce an integral English text of this important interview. This volume's most substantial essay, "Will CinemaScope Save the Cinema?," has come out twice previously in English, the first time in *The Velvet Light Trap* (1985), ably translated and annotated by Catherine Jones and Richard Neupert. Before I looked at their translation or at a later one, I started from scratch, checking my results only at the end and adding notes missing from the earlier versions. Overall, my aim has been to provide Bazin's scattered pieces with a single voice that is consistent and recognizable, and which I hope has affinities with Bazin's highly consistent, wonderfully flexible, and often quite beautiful French.

In the 1950s, while Bazin was in Paris writing these essays, Sam Becker (1923–2012) was teaching and researching the very same things in Iowa City, where he directed the university's Television Center. Later, as a legendary scholar and department head, he supported my research on Bazin and opened the door to a fulfilling career. He would have been proud of this volume; it would have provoked warm, even heated discussions between us. My efforts here could be dedicated to no one else.

André Bazin Greets the New Media of the 1950s

DUDLEY ANDREW

It took the expanded media environment of our twenty-first century to get me to look beyond André Bazin's film theory to see what kind of media critic he might have been. How did he come to terms with all the threats and changes to cinema that arose just as he started the journal he is most associated with, *Cahiers du Cinéma?* I have been first among those who take him to be the patron saint of cinephilia, an organizer of film clubs, the man behind the auteur theory that came to dominate *Cahiers* and raised the prestige of cinema as art. But in fact, anyone who looks closely can tell he was a born cultural critic, intent on clarifying the most prominent or fascinating phenomena around him. After World War II, cinema was unquestionably the most prominent and fascinating of all, clearly the era's most crucial and sophisticated cultural manifestation. As daily film critic for France's largest circulation newspaper, *Le Parisien Libéré*, and as regular contributor to *L'Ecran Français*, the popular weekly for real film lovers that had been born in the Resistance, his job and his pleasure was to raise the level of discussion about what was playing in the more than three hundred movie theaters in Paris.

Thanks to his legendary curiosity and broad educational background, he took every opportunity to instruct himself and his readers on topics that any given film, or the cinema as a whole, might bring up, topics not just about the movies but about technology, science, art history, and so on. Those opportunities became far more frequent after 1950, when he was recruited to write regularly for two periodicals that were just being launched and that are exceedingly prominent to this day: *Radio-Cinéma-Télévision*, which is now *Télérama*, and *L'Observateur politique, économique et littéraire* (later called *France-Observateur* and then *Le Nouvel Observateur*). In the title of the first of these, cinema finds itself sandwiched between two rival media. As for *L'Observateur*, from the outset it has been a wide-ranging cultural news magazine with the visibility of *Newsweek* but the sophistication of *The New Republic*, only even more to the left. Today the *Huffington Post* may come closest to its stance and coverage. Readers expected extended film reviews from Bazin but also articles on trends in the entertainment industry.

Bazin's first pieces for each journal appeared in September 1950, during a long forced respite from his daily cinema-going that was occasioned by a serious bout of tuberculosis. Writing from his new suburban home and addressing an educated general readership, he declared that he treasured this opportunity, first to assess cinema among the arts, and second to analyze its response to the political and technological crises of the time. The crises were American in origin, coming to France on the heels of the divisive Marshall Plan and, in the realm of cinema, the hard-to-swallow Blum-Byrnes accord, which dismantled most protections for French films against the Hollywood juggernaut. And Hollywood needed Europe more than ever following the 1948 Paramount divestiture decree, when, suddenly, the major studios lost their exhibition wing. Independent and foreign producers now could break into the formerly closed U.S. market. As the majors scrambled to keep control, long-term alliances broke down. A free-for-all ensued, exactly the moment for entrepreneurs to come up with attention-grabbing schemes. Evidence of this is all over the pages of American newspaper ads after 1950, promising spectacles "never before seen on screen," while upstart distributors flirted with censorship as they promoted risqué movies from Germany, Sweden, or Italy.

The usually fiscally conservative studios also turned their engineers loose, looking to gamble on the format of cinema itself, understanding that, given their tremendous advantage in capital, they could still control exhibition after altering its format: why not make the movies gargantuan? Why not surround spectators with stereo sound and even put them into the midst of images projected in three dimensions? Already lagging behind Hollywood in color, all other producers would take years to catch up to these new technologies. Of course Hollywood also had the nightmare of television in view. A minor threat in 1948 (when there were still under 50,000 sets in operation, 80 percent of them on the East Coast), TV was growing exponentially as a formidable, unstoppable rival for the affection of the mass audience. Against television's convenient, low-cost home viewing, Hollywood realized it had better offer increased spectacle. And so, after years of low metabolism in research and development departments, "new" inventions suddenly rolled out of the labs. With predictable fanfare, Hollywood promised to renew not just the movies, but the cinema experience.

Bazin, who traveled twice to South America, never tried to visit the U.S. This may have secured his often-praised critical distance, but it also meant that he surely missed elements and details that could have contributed to a larger account of things. He didn't monitor drive-in theaters, for instance, which were unknown before 1950 but grew to nearly a quarter of all the screens in the country by the 1960s, and which competed head to head with TV for the newly mobile suburban audience. One can only imagine his anatomy of this social phenomenon and his analysis of the genres that thrived on screens set in front of enormous parking lots. But to my knowledge, he could not have found a single drive-in in France.

Drive-ins would be difficult commodities to export overseas; besides, they were developed by the seamier side of an already highly scattered exhibition wing of the industry. But films and technology are readily exportable, and these are in the hands of producers and distributors. In their fight with TV, the major studios needed to expand to Europe and beyond, not just to amortize the costs of their research and development units, but to pay for the greater expense of movies made in new formats, including ballooning publicity costs. Elaborate campaigns prepared the way for premieres of new formats at film festivals and in key theaters in many European metropolises. Bazin had a front row seat from which to watch Hollywood's gaudy response to its TV crisis, but he was never in broadcast range of American TV, which would have allowed him to better measure the strength of its threat. His deep concern lay not with America, of course, but with the effect of its entertainment war on standard cinema the world over. And what about the future of TV in France, which was being born as he wrote his essay? For better or worse, it lagged behind the United States and operated under complete governmental supervision. What should it look like and how might it affect French cinema? Might there be a Parisian entertainment war too?

A large and extremely attentive readership followed his reports and essays, which mix historical information, technical explanation, aesthetic speculation, and cultural opinion. A critic by profession, he was expected to pronounce on the quality of what was available on screen, no matter the size or type of screen. But he was reluctant to pummel the first efforts of any new form, because, ever bearing the attitude of an evolutionary scientist, he was fascinated by all early expressions emerging from a new cultural configuration, including those that were likely to fail to develop.

Bazin never questioned evolution, accepting not just Darwin on biological species but Malraux on the arts. Having experienced his first talkie when he was twelve, he facetiously entertained the notion that the cinema was maturing at about the rate of a human being, though a bit slower. After the war, it was striving mightily to achieve adulthood, while being pulled this way and that by hormones and social pressures it scarcely understood. This was nothing like traditional arts such as painting and theater, which took millennia to arrive at a range of consistent genres. Traditional arts were born with human civilization and will expire only when it does. They may reach notable high points—classical periods—and they may undergo the vicissitudes of history that enervate them for a time, but we can count on their survival as long as there are people around who care about words, stories, drawing, shaping, or playing games of imitation.

By contrast, there's nothing natural about the technological arts that began appearing in the nineteenth century. Aimed at mass culture, their paramount value must be measured far more by their social function than by their aesthetic achievement. Cinema, clearly the most potent art of the twentieth century, has an amazing capacity to capture, express, or process contemporary experience, even if, on the formal level, it could hardly be expected to reach the depth and significance of its noble predecessors. No one should denigrate cinema if in its first decades a very large part of celluloid and projection time was given over simply to providing things on screen that people cared to see conveniently (like boxing matches, variety acts, stage plays, and exotic places and peoples). Original concoctions on film, including adaptations from novels and oft-told stories, amount to a cinematic surplus, so to speak. Just half a century old when Bazin began his career as critic, genuinely innovative filmmaking could not be expected to often reach the level of sophistication that is more routine in the other arts; but by the 1950s Bazin believed that the most advanced cinema (the "nouvelle avant-garde" of the time) had taken on its shoulders the concerns and sensibility of the period, sharing these especially with the novel. No matter what your assessment of the traditional arts in the postwar era (when action painting, theater of the absurd, and the nouveau roman were causing their own stir), you had to credit the most ambitious postwar films as operating in the same cultural terrain as painting, theater, and the novel. The cinema had evolved to a point where it deserved the high-flown critical attention Bazin and others were paying it in journals like *Esprit* and *Les Temps Modernes*.

Yet as an industrial art, cinema is subject to technological and economic forces that mock any idealist notion of aesthetic evolution. Bazin writes fondly of Hollywood, realizing how terribly vulnerable it is, despite the way it so brashly puffs out its chest. He imagines some crisis or miracle in the world of economics and technology that may extinguish Hollywood and cinema in toto, or more likely, change it into some new medium, scarcely recognizable to his generation of critics. Never sentimental,

Bazin will not retreat to a notion of "pure cinema" impervious to the marketplace. He may personally have looked forward to the more arty films, that 5 percent forming the aesthetic leading edge in each year's march of 3,000 or so movies made worldwide, but cinema depended on being a world phenomenon and a mass art. To him this was non-negotiable. And, as much as he hated to admit it, cinema probably depended on economic and political concerns hostile to art.

This was patently true of French television, which he watched wriggle to survive in the harshest of incubators, a frigid climate drifting to France from the Hollywood entertainment wars and the Cold War. The trumped-up homegrown programming that he followed nightly on the single ORTF channel that served all of France continually provided him with ideas about media as a whole, about the inevitability yet unpredictability of its evolution. He wanted television to succeed and to do so on its own terms, but he knew the terms would never really be its own. He took a more cynical tone when addressing the other new media of the day, since these came to France as imposed by Hollywood's determination to alter the cinema experience for its own gain. The public and the art form might gain as well, but that seemed a secondary issue to those making decisions. A lot was at stake for France with television and even more was at stake for cinema with CinemaScope, Cinerama, and 3D. Let's begin with TV.

TV: THE HOMELY BABY IN THE IMAGE FAMILY

Years ago, in a dramatic personal moment that I've written about, I discovered a page of Bazin's typed notes neatly folded inside his personal copy of Sartre's *L'Imaginaire*.[1] I was instantly drawn to the way these notes suspend cinema as a medium between past and present, with photography as a frozen record of the past on one side and television as a live extension of sight on the other. Cinema's distinct ontology, he intimated, derives from its being an image that, eerily, is both from the past and alive: life deferred indefinitely, re-animated at every projection. Today it is not cinema but his mention of television that fascinates me, and his premonition in these notes of what it might become. Ruminating in the 1940s, Bazin could only deal with TV as a thought problem, but by the 1950s it had become a genuine problem, with ramifications in every sphere he cared about: the artistic, the cultural, the political, the educational.

Bazin tucked this page inside the section of *L'Imaginaire* called "The Family of Images," in which Sartre distinguishes paintings from memories, caricatures, hallucinations, and so forth. To this "image family" Bazin adds photos, films, and broadcast television—the newborn baby of the family. Whereas cinema inevitably projects images that lag days, weeks, or years behind the moment when they were recorded, television can be said to depend on the liveness of present perception. All viewers reached by a broadcast "participate" simultaneously in one and the same event. This essential difference may have become smudged over the decades, since the institution of television increasingly replays events recorded earlier, something Bazin already considered in his page of notes. And nearly right away, in the 1950s, entire movies would often show up on TV. But as the coronation of Elizabeth in 1952, as well as the routine of sports matches, nightly news, and (for us) the Olympics, the Oscars, and other live broadcasts attest, TV is *essentially* distinct from cinema. André Bazin's philosophy of the image can be found within that distinction.

But we must be careful; Bazin was not prepared to pronounce on the essence of cinema, let alone TV, or to come too quickly to a definition of *télégénie* equivalent to the *photogénie* that critics in the 1920s rhapsodized. Indeed, TV was the new example that let him recognize that instability must also be the state of cinema, though to a lesser degree. He realized that the new technologies—and he used this term—needed time to steady themselves, since their forms could still be in flux and their social functions had hardly been tested. This was even truer of a completely new medium like television than of technologies like CinemaScope that he deemed supplements of the already established cinema system.

Since television was effectively starting from scratch, one should not hastily circumscribe its essence. Nor should one immediately impugn its chances eventually to contribute even to intellectual culture in the manner of the other arts. After all, the pundits of 1908 who had ridiculed the cinema for its baby talk had to eat their words twice, first in the 1920s, during the efflorescence of the silent screen, and then more recently when sound cinema, against all prognosis, had proved the film auteur to be "the equal of the novelist."[2] Might the same be true a few decades hence with regard to TV? Bazin wasn't sure; he claimed that the priority of utility over expressive creativity was evident in radio, a medium he was fond of, but which he took to be, in the main, a site where one could encounter creativity produced elsewhere, more like an orchestra hall than an orchestra. The same was surely truer for TV, even with the addition of the visual dimension, for at the time he wrote, French TV was limited to a single channel, and this hampered the experimentation and competition that gave radio at least a range of avenues. Bazin, who scoffed at the 1920s refrain "Ça c'est du cinéma," rebuked anyone ready to say, "Ça c'est de la télévision."[3]

Approaching television as he did all phenomena, through its evolution, Bazin predicted an optimistic tale of development, but no instant gratification. One couldn't expect TV to achieve eloquence and maturity in a single decade if it took cinema half a century to do so. Indeed, for this to happen, TV would have to focus so completely on a single avenue of progress that it would sacrifice other possible aesthetic and social routes. Bazin didn't mind seeing it drift. In fact, it wasn't drifting enough to suit him. Operating on but a single channel was an immediate impediment. Another impediment, he went on to argue, came from technology itself, which actually works against the future it lays before us. Every technological invention seems futuristic when it first appears, but its bulky machinery then weighs down its flight. Just look at cinema. Its advances have been miniscule given the amazing changes that have occurred in civilization since its invention (Bazin mentions automobiles and airplanes, and he could have talked about social revolutions too). He was shocked to be watching two-hour feature films in 1952 just the way his parents had in 1918, the year of his birth. Where were the innovations that science had made in other spheres? His favorite whipping boy was Thomas Edison, whose quite arbitrary choice of 35mm as the standard gauge hampered the development of larger gauges that might have genuinely improved exhibition. Except for sound, films looked and acted very much the way they had for decades. Bazin also repeatedly mentions the retardation by a quarter century of Henri Chrétien's 1926 anamorphic lens (the Hypergonar), the squelching of Abel Gance's Polyvision, and the fact that a variable-shaped screen—such as the one Eisenstein proposed in

"The Dynamic Square" and which Bazin supported—was infeasible.

But why infeasible? Not just because of capitalism, he wrote (since the Soviets showed no interest even in implementing what inventors had already come up with). Technological status quo must be the default of every mass industry, and it certainly was a drag on cinema for decades. Once the world's 30,000 screens had been outfitted for sound, once thousands of exhibitors and projectionists had grown accustomed to their routine, even excellent supplements had a terrible time making a go of it, including the one process that had some economic punch behind it, Technicolor. Bazin was fatalistic and disappointed about the mediocre color and 3D processes that won out in the 1950s after having taken so long to be implemented at all. Just as Edison's sacrosanct 35mm standard doomed a superior variant, the VistaVision system, so TV was almost certainly stuck with the mere 625 lines (525 in the United States) that were mandated for it in 1938. Even if some 2,000-line version had suddenly become available, it would not have been implemented, since this would "render obsolete all of the current broadcasting and receiving equipment. From this perspective, it is reasonable to think that TV as we know it will last for a long time just the way it is." Bazin recognizes that color TV may in fact be on the near horizon, but he predicts—rightly, it turns out—that it will come about via a transition that "will be smooth and that ... will not overturn TV any more radically than it did cinema."[4]

In sum, Bazin felt that while we should not essentialize the medium, a "provisional essence" could be detected because, for the foreseeable future, television's possibilities would be limited by the hardware in place as well as by strict institutional conditions (in France, a single channel under state supervision and censorship). He characterized this provisional essence in several general articles and in the many reviews of programs he watched, often from his sickbed, when he couldn't get to Paris for the movies or to work in the office at *Cahiers du Cinéma*.

IMAGES EN DIRECT: TV IS "NOW"

Although for its first decades its content was controlled by impersonal institutions (the state in France, three powerful networks in the United States), television was sold as a friendly medium, a domestic one. Its size, its familiar position in the living room, and its utility in providing news and weather reports, often via the kindly voice of an attractive *speakerine,* immediately distinguished it from going to a movie theater and paying for something that promised to be extraordinary. Bazin wrote often of TV as the replacement for the hearth around which the family gathers to be warm and comfortable while watching—often inattentively—images that have been scrupulously sanitized. But far more critical to Bazin than this important though local social function was TV's genuinely universal difference from cinema: its default tense is the present tense. Television addresses every viewer within its broadcast range in the now, no matter where they are. Bazin couldn't get over the fact that a science program he watched let him see through a telescope the very moon whose light was streaming at that moment through the window beside the TV. He turned his chair from TV to window to verify that it was the same object, in its current phase. (Characteristically, he quipped that the moon and stars were not quite present, however, since they are available to us only via a more primary medium, light, which takes its own time. The stars we see on TV or out our window are no longer exactly there.)[5]

Bazin relished the drama and risks of live broadcasts. A daring live TV science program shows the exploration of a diseased lung, in real time, through an invasive bronchial procedure. What if something goes wrong, we ask as we watch? In cinema, what may have gone wrong on the shoot has been eliminated. Not so on live TV, where we suffer now with those who suffer now, and where we share some of the patient's marvel at looking at his own lung at the very moment it is keeping him alive.

Let's repeat. Bazin was no purist. As radio had demonstrated prodigiously, prerecorded material can often enhance a live broadcast, but Bazin cautioned that it ought to be recorded under "live conditions," so that its more finished style wouldn't clash with the roughness of the live portion, which, at least in those first years, served as TV's baseline, and which it seems he had a taste for. Hence, he came down hard on that astronomy program when it intercalated images of a couple of planets that clearly had been taken earlier, all the while pretending that the on-camera astronomer had just swiveled his telescope. Television owes the public an attestation about the status—the tense—of what is sent out and received in the present.

These issues arose most frequently in teleplays, the medium's most ambitious genre and one Bazin kept up with closely. If TV were going to become an art, everyone assumed it would be through the creative adaptation of good theater or through original dramas written for it. Bazin investigated this hope by triangulating TV with cinema and the stage in a large entertainment arena. Ontologically hybrid, a broadcast teleplay can deliver at least some of the selected perspectives and shot changes available to cinema, but it does so in the present tense of a play put on at a legitimate theater. Bazin writes about British experiments with four cameras that permit the "switching" of points of view within pure continuity; the "TV switcher" is completely distinct from the film editor who assembles an illusion of continuity from fragments. If prerecorded segments are called for by the script (or by a particularly audacious director), these can be carefully intercalated, but spatial contiguity should be maintained. He applauded this strategy in one play adapted for TV that took place in a sailors' dive by a wharf. The set and dialogue implied there to be a barge presumably docked just outside. Scenes on the barge had been prerecorded on film, and unrolled seamlessly after being cued by the movement of the actors as they walked offstage and out of the bar, thus preserving continuity while giving the actors (and the TV cameramen) a few minutes' break before action resumed back on the live set. This program existed only in a single unbroken ninety-minute block on TV. It was not a movie that could be shown again, and it was more than a play, since its action extended outside, beyond the wings of the stage. In Bazin's rather conservative appraisal, there are limits to this, however. For instance, it would not have done to cut to some scene in the city. The filmed barge should really serve as a contiguous extension of the barroom stage setting.

With Sartre's *L'Imaginaire* no doubt in mind, Bazin meditated on the mode of existence of the teleplay, wondering how its actors can hold up in a kind of ether. There is no audience as at the theater. There is "the public," we want to say, but it exists as a statistical sum of individuals watching at the same moment but in ignorance of one another. In fact the actors perform before the cold eye of one or several lenses on television cameras. What if they slip up? At the theater they can be prompted by a complicit or generous audience member sitting somewhere in the first rows, but on TV they are naked and alone. This accounts for the double chagrin Bazin claimed he felt when, especially in the first years of TV dramas, slip-ups were common. He felt ashamed for the actor but also for his own impotence. At the cinema, by contrast, the editor restores everyone's potency simply by inserting "take two" and smoothing over the scene. A well-made film is hermetic, something we admire without its knowing we are there (this is Stanley Cavell's central insight cuing the title to his book *The World Viewed*); meanwhile, a TV program, even a well-made one, shamelessly addresses an invisible "public" without whose experience and memory it evaporates when the half hour is up. Hence TV's often ingratiating and pathetic address to the eyes of spectators that it can't be sure are attentive or even there. Nightly newscasts and variety acts, the staples of early TV, clinched this realization.

Now most variety shows on TV even today include an audience that we hear applaud and occasionally see. The TV spectator can be given the role of witness or invited guest, who looks on while an event unfolds. In one of his most endearing pieces, Bazin marvels at being invited, like everyone else who tuned in, to a swanky Parisian charity soirée that included famous people among its diegetic guests (if they can be called diegetic, since the event was not being recounted but lived). These guests were garbed in expensive evening attire and possessed the gestures of courtesy proper to the haute bourgeoisie. Among the celebrities attending was Charlie Chaplin. Bazin claims to have been doubly pleased, first because he was able to be present for an occasion the likes of which he had heard about all his life but never would have witnessed without TV, and second because, once the variety acts began that were the announced "spectacle" of the evening, he was able to enjoy not just the jugglers and singers, but the reactions of the attendees. The payoff came when the producer switched cameras to focus occasionally on the guests. The high point of the broadcast, at least in Bazin's estimation, was a moment not even the most distinguished guest present got to see: Chaplin reacting to the mediocre routine of a clown hired to entertain him and everyone else, indeed the entire nation.

Television interpellates each individual viewer through its chief psychological draw: intimacy. In America, viewers feel the personal solicitations of advertisers; in France, interpellation is evident each time the *speakerine* talks you through the evening's lineup of shows. Bazin found her to be the figurehead of the ship of television that cruised straight into your living room; she greeted you and expected a greeting in return. He recalls having restrained himself from going up to TV personalities he would encounter on the Paris streets because he felt they had become friends and that his greeting was a necessary courtesy. This has nothing to do with the fandom that cinema fosters.

The small screen's familiarity makes it friendly in this way, or so it felt in France in the 1950s. We get to know people we'd never get close to on the big screen, or wouldn't trust because the film director and editor would have processed them for us. Perhaps thinking of *Farrebique,* which he had once lauded as an exception to the rules of propriety in French cinema, Bazin praised a specific television reportage on peasants that he had anticipated would be dull, since peasants, by profession and habit, tend to be neither loquacious nor eloquent.[6] Yet listening to them for thirty minutes gave him fresh insights into their work and their social values. More important, he liked these men and felt connected to them. In its first years, television occasionally provided a glimpse of the new forms of social understanding and cohesion it is capable of fostering. Here Bazin should have noted that TV, far more than cinema, is a national institution, regulated by the state. Programs are broadcast to the nation and the people we watch are more often than not our fellow citizens. Would Bazin have felt as comfortable inviting into his home some peasants from China or, more problematic for France at the time, from Indochina? Just how domestic has TV remained in our own era?

But his point had much more to do with the immediacy of meeting these French peasants in real time, knowing that they were breathing and talking right then on the other side of his TV set. He wrote: "What counts for the spectator is not so much what he sees but the fact that he sees: what counts is *la présence.*" That's why Bazin was seldom bored by TV, unless it tried to overreach itself and "make cinema." He loved interview shows where a single person held forth without a cutaway and simply addressed the spectator in dialogue, with a proxy host who asked questions: an author presenting a book, or a police commissioner talking about his efforts in the community. Sure, he says, you might find more excitement if you ran off to the cinema to see a movie adapted from this novelist's work, or to a gangster film dramatizing police procedures, but if you really had the novelist or the commissioner coming over for dinner, don't you think you'd rather stay home and listen to their genuine voices and stories instead? If TV brings such people into our homes, go to the movies another day and enjoy their presence *now*. "People have the right to sit before the camera and simply talk, just as we would have the pleasure of hearing them 'in real life.'"[7]

These hopes for a virtual community of tele-spectators suggested an ethical dimension that Bazin believed could have a salutary rebound effect on the new medium's older brother. So when he trumpeted Sidney Lumet's film *12 Angry Men* when it took the Golden Bear at Berlin in 1957, he immediately pointed out that as good as Henry Fonda was, his performance had de facto been trumped by that of Robert Cummings, who originated the role in the 1954 live teleplay. Bazin ruminated that TV might be the perfect vehicle for a script that turns individual viewers into jurors addressed by the bar and then by other jurors. It ought to be watched at home alone, where you are forced to make up your own mind about the situation, and on the spot, without the moral comfort of a crowded movie theater.

But of course Bazin was glad the film had been made, if only because he was out of broadcast range for the teleplay.[8] Also, Lumet bucked the trend of technological bravura, attesting to the enduring appeal of black and white dramas. Indeed, TV's ever-growing audience enticed some film producers and several top-level auteurs to get behind smaller subjects and to experiment with a "direct" approach, as in the first years of neorealism. "Eureka," shouted Jacques Rivette when he saw Rossellini's *Viaggio in Italia* (*Voyage to Italy*) in 1954. "'I have made a discovery': there is a television aesthetic.... I learned [this] just recently from an article by André Bazin.... Rossellini's films, though film, are also subject to this *direct* aesthetic with all it comprises of gamble, tension, chance and providence."[9] Rivette also characterizes this film as like a "sketch" by Matisse, achieving equilibrium, then falling off balance momentarily before rising to a new equilibrium, and always with his charcoal or crayon on the page in a gesture of linear fluidity. When Rivette concludes that *Voyage to Italy* is the first feature film to master the "essay," he mentions Montaigne, Gide, and Audiberti (saying that the essay today has buried the novel); but I would add Alain, the tremendously popular French philosopher of the early years of the century, whose thousands of short *propos* (two-page essays) were written, it is claimed, at one sitting, with no recourse to rewriting, crossing out, or editing, just the forward movement of a continuous idea.[10] This is the direct; this is continuity; this is the TV aesthetic.

The TV genre that shared the most with Rossellini's film was the social problem program, the slice-of-life drama shot in a single location over a brief period of time. Paddy Chayefsky was the first master of this form (Bazin, however, found *Marty* melodramatic and overrated). Marcel Moussy emerged as France's best writer working in this vein at the time. He produced a series of engaging TV programs on juvenile delinquents called *Si c'était vous* (If it were you). When Bazin interviewed him at length in *Cahiers du Cinéma* in 1958, Moussy declared television to be the neorealist medium par excellence. I suppose he was thinking of the way perceptual flow in live situations usually involves periods of dead time. Moussy always left his dramas open, after an hour's meandering had been set in motion by some specific premise. He looked for material that could be performed by citizens acting just like themselves. He wanted each individual viewer to face up to a moral quandary that the writer hadn't rigged and whose solution wasn't obvious. Bazin conducted his interview just as Moussy was putting the final touches on the script he prepared with François Truffaut for *Les 400 Coups* (*The 400 Blows*), a film famous for featuring an ordinary boy playing someone like himself, improvising an encounter *en direct* with the psychologist, and running toward the beach before turning back to look at his director and at us in perhaps the most famous open-ended ending in cinema. In an oft-cited instance of pathos or cosmic irony, Bazin died the first day *Les 400 Coups* was in production. But his belief that television could rejuvenate French cinema was about to materialize. Thanks to its speed, improvisation, and sheer presentness, TV had administered a *choc en retour,* a rebound effect, that kicked French cinema off on an adventure of risk and frankness known as the New Wave.

The boldest and frankest contributors to the New Wave were surely the ethnographic cineaste Jean Rouch and the sociologist Edgar Morin. Bazin knew them both and especially admired Morin, who penned a beautiful eulogy for Bazin in 1959.[11] In 1960 they shot the first *cinéma verité* feature, *Chronique d'un été*. This label has caused no end of argument, but not its near relative, *cinéma direct,* which characterizes one of the chief impulses of the New Wave, as well as an emergent American documentary movement. Rouch and Morin were proud to be at the fountainhead of *cinéma direct.* Behind it lay the values of *la télévision en direct* that Bazin had promulgated all decade long.

CINEMA'S SPECTACULAR RESPONSE TO TV

The headlines and advertisements in *Variety* in the first half of the 1950s are uncannily familiar. Today, IMAX, 3D, and 48-fps projection entice a public to experience something different from the video entertainment that is increasingly accessed on personal (often minute) screens. Back then it was CinemaScope, Cinerama, and (again) 3D. Just as Bazin had a lot to say about TV, usually termed "le petit écran," so he wrote frequently about these new technologies of film exhibition, including various types of widescreen ("le grand écran") and 3D. He felt it his obligation (and surely it was his pleasure) to explain to the layman just how these systems functioned technically, sometimes using diagrams as aids. One can still learn from him such things as the difference between the two types of 3D (anaglyph and polarized), the absolute screen-width onto which an image that has been squeezed through an anamorphic lens can be released, and the relation of angles of projection to veridical perception.

The breadth of his interests is breathtaking, particularly in comparison to the undiluted cinephilia that was the creed of his confreres at *Cahiers du Cinéma*. They prided themselves on writing only about films and their auteurs, whereas Bazin might use the occasion of reviewing a film to delve into issues relating to its technological substrate, for his criticism and theory were continuous with, and rested upon, an understanding of what today we would call media ecology. For instance, his article on *Blackboard Jungle* (1955) looks at Richard Brooks's modest aesthetic achievement, but only after first identifying the pressure put on Brooks to conform to the new technological regime of widescreen and the old moralistic regime of censorship.

Many of Bazin's articles reviewed no film at all but delved directly into the causes and possible outcomes of the technological changes that were looming and that might alter the world's chief entertainment ritual, disrupting the "movies as usual." Writing for a broad public, he naturally favored its interests, as well as those of the artists whose work the public paid to see, rather than the interests of the industry, whose motives, often transparently crass, it was his job to explain. He went after exhibitors mercilessly, arguing that their "inertia" (he used this term more than once) resisted every new idea, seeing it as a potential threat, thus retarding the evolution of the medium and the growth of the art. France's theaters, to a far greater degree than those in the United States, have always been owned and run by individuals or small businessmen, rather than vast chains. Bazin could praise the operations of a particular exhibitor for trying to present films for optimal viewing, but he generally excoriated the more abundant penny-pinchers, who were primarily concerned with simplifying their routine and selling more ice cream.

One of his earliest overviews deploys a quasi-Marxist vocabulary of "revolution," "conjunction," and "disruption," as he compares the current conditions to those that led to the changeover to sound.[12] With enough access to capital to unilaterally renovate the medium just when it suits them, deploying inventions that may have been around for some time, Hollywood studios make momentous decisions with their stockholders, more than their directors or even their public, in mind. Only this explains the delay in the exploitation of sound, which could have been rolled out well before 1927, or the far longer delay that kept widescreen processes at bay until 1952. No doubt Bazin's often difficult relationship with Communist film historian Georges Sadoul kept him especially alert to the economic undercurrent of technological innovation, but he always held that cultural and commercial history are crucial to understanding how cinema functions. Technology never simply appears; it is called into existence by circumstances, even if its availability precedes those circumstances. The historiographic debate he held with Sadoul (and that continues to this day) was more than academic. Bazin made his readers recognize that they were living in a tumultuous media storm, the outcome of which was worth speculating on, even if there was little that critics and filmgoers could do to change things, particularly if they lived outside the United States, where the future most likely would be decided.

Bazin may have believed in an impersonal "evolutionary" force that works via its own logic, but generally he wrote as if those who mandated and retarded change (producers, distributors, exhibitors) were rational agents who knew that ultimately they needed to keep or expand their public. And that public was losing its taste for movies, with attendance dwindling everywhere year after year from 1946 on. You couldn't put the blame only on television, for the results were the same even in areas untouched by that medium. Whatever the reasons (and Bazin assumed they were legion), change would most likely come about when a major studio felt its imminent demise but still could muster enough funds to gamble everything, the way Warner Brothers did in 1928. In the early 1950s, bets were thrown down on 3D, on Cinerama, and on various widescreen formats. Paris was a high-profile testing ground for each of these, since no revolution could succeed unless it spanned the globe. Bazin had a good perch from which to monitor this high-stakes poker game.

3D: THERE WILL BE NO REVOLUTION

The author of "The Myth of Total Cinema" doesn't let us forget that most of those who contributed to cinema's birth "saw in a trice the reconstruction of a perfect illusion of the outside world in sound, color, and relief."[13] Yes, 3D was part of the original "idea of cinema," thanks to the popularity of stereophotography. Well before Jonathan Crary, Bazin claimed stereoscopy indispensable to the "idea of moving pictures" because both forms involve a visual synthesis that occurs in the mind, rather than in the eye. With hopes for 3D endemic at the origins of cinema, it isn't surprising that there were attempts to engineer and exploit its development, something that occurred briefly in the 1930s and then much more insistently in the 1950s. Bazin had no doubt that it would return in force eventually—which it certainly has. In 1952, upon seeing it in action for the first time, Bazin let himself dream of its future: "If one day 3D cinema evolves beyond a trivial scientific curiosity, as it will likely do, directing the garden hose to spray the audience will not be enough to astonish us. The distant future of 3D cinema will see a leap as great as the one from *L'Arrivée d'un train en gare de La Ciotat* to the train engine sequence in *La Bête humaine.*... Let us nimbly take this new and decisive step toward total cinema."[14]

From the beginning, though, one could not write about this new format without focusing on its chances of succeeding, for from the outset it was a very uncertain venture. Predictably, the need for initial success dragged producers of 3D into obvious genres like the horror film. In Bazin's day, special moments of special effects were the primary attraction of any movie made in 3D, such as *Mystery of the Wax Museum,* a film that seems to have charmed if not actually frightened him. Actually, the fifty-two 3D films made during the 1950s represent several genres. But few 3D films crossed the Atlantic, and only a very few of these were shown in their 3D version. The reason? Bazin pointed to the inconvenience to the exhibitor of having to distribute glasses that the public found uncomfortable. More troublesome were the two interruptions of the show required to reload the single set of dual projectors most theaters possessed, since this jolted the spectator out of the very illusion they had paid to experience. So all but one or two dedicated exhibitors shied away from showing the 3D version when given the option of showing a film flat. And that option became available early on, even for films whose value depended on effects that were lost in normal projection. Although he couldn't think of a 3D film to genuinely commend, Bazin felt that as long as movies had been made with this format in mind, the public needed to be given a chance to vote on 3D at the box office.

Bazin was especially disappointed not to be able to experience in its intended format a genuinely dramatic fiction made by a great cineaste, like *Dial M for Murder,* but its 3D version was pulled by the studio even before it was given a chance in the United States. While he waited in vain for something truly valuable to appear in three dimensions, Bazin, who had been delighted by Norman McLaren's stereoscopic animations, must have ruminated on the aesthetic potential of the format. What might it mean, for instance, to someone for whom the cinema was a "window on the world"? Indeed, in 1953 he explicitly returned to this metaphor to praise another new technology, CinemaScope, saying that its screen worked much more like a "hole" cut out of a wall than like a picture "frame" on the wall. Agreeing with Cocteau that the screen is a "keyhole," he rejoiced to have it enlarged via widescreen.[15]

Shouldn't 3D, then, be seen to open that window, letting represented objects enter our space and inviting us to pass through the window into the volume of the universe beyond? But of course, windows are terribly noticeable features in any room; so unlike CinemaScope, which, if you sit close enough, can erase all sense of the theater, surrounding your sight the way the stereo sound that has always been integral to this format surrounds your ears, 3D restricts you to the square (why not call it a box) toward which you direct your bespectacled eyes. Indeed, those glasses themselves isolate you from your neighbors and force you to concentrate on the viewing box; they train your view, punishing you with dizziness should you turn your head to glance at the exit sign, say, or at anything outside the borders of the screen. In 3D the window frame is particularly prominent. And this contributes to the impression of a diminishment of scale that Bazin recognized and that even today spectators experience. We peer

at characters as if they were in a box that contains them, swallows them. The range of lenses, angles, lighting, and focus (including trans-focus) that is available in standard cinematography helps directors let actors dominate a flat screen, whereas actors appear smaller, more like puppets or mannequins (Bazin says "Lilliputians") when projected into a third dimension.[16]

Ads claim that in 3D, objects will invade the theater space, growing so large as to nearly strike the viewer's eye, but Bazin was certain we would quickly become habituated to such moments, or tired of the few genres where such things occur in motivated ways. The format would need to take hold across genres, and directors would need to learn how to organize dramatic space on sets that the viewer looks *into* rather than *at,* as through a door that we aren't quite invited through. He didn't expect this to come about anytime soon. Writing about it several times across a span of a few years, he came to the conclusion that 3D was commercially doomed, at least for the moment. He would not have been surprised to see it resurface in our era; you can be sure he would have looked for a "conjunction" of causes, and especially for a certain economic panic in an industry ready to gamble on *Beowulf* and *Avatar.* And he would have been right.

WIDESCREENS

Bazin understood all along that extending the width of vision was likely to win out over deepening it into a new dimension. And he treated these formats as if they were in a knock-out competition, believing that the industry could not support too many competing spectacles without losing the identity of what the cinema was. Besides, there was only so much money in Hollywood, and the complete conversion of filmmaking into widescreen on the one hand and 3D on the other would be prohibitive (since 3D wouldn't be ready for widescreen until well into the next decade). Between the two, Bazin preferred widescreen for the added freedom it provided directors to move their actors and camera about, and the freedom it afforded spectators to survey the screen rather than be locked into the more rigid 4:3 format. Great width even provides its own illusion of depth, he argued.

And so Cinerama, the first and most spectacular of the widescreen processes, initially enthused Bazin. But with its three-camera rig needing to be carefully set up and synchronized, Cinerama was so clumsy and expensive to deploy that only three titles had reached Europe when he wrote about the format in 1955, and all told, only eight would be made by 1962, when *How the West Was Won* came out as its swan song. With so much money at stake and so many requirements for each rare title to fulfill, producers literally called the shots after employing whole committees to arrive at serviceable scripts. Struck by the aerial tour of the United States in *Cinerama Holiday,* Bazin declared himself impressed by the format's "realism of space," which immerses viewers in a nearly unframed world, but he found little in the films to surprise him. In his understanding of it, realism must surprise as well as impress.

Bazin considered Cinerama even more of a novelty than 3D, a curious attraction audiences were likely to experience once or twice but not return to as they returned to the movies week after week. In this it had much in common with such spectacles as sound and light shows or the Ringling Brothers Circus, or, as he pointed out, with the stage show at the Folies-Bergère, all of them twentieth-century counterparts of the dioramas and wax museums of the previous century. Such urban attractions are tied to exclusive exhibition sites, where astonishing effects are orchestrated throughout a few serviceable scripts, fewer than one per year in Cinerama's decade of existence. Naturally this rate of production inhibits the refinement and improvement of a new aesthetic.

Cinerama forced Bazin to come clean about his artistic allegiances. We know that he took cinema to be a hybrid, owing something to each of the arts, but he had no doubt that its chief inheritance comes from the theater and literature, particularly prose fiction. Influenced by Sartre in this regard, he found the most culturally relevant arts in the modern era to be those that provide narratives developing in social and natural space, where various points of view can be tried out, put in dramatic opposition, and adjudicated. Cinerama, especially as its entrepreneurs exploited it, limits rather than expands these aesthetic and cultural possibilities; its machinery weighs it down, despite the experience of buoyancy it offers the spectator. Bazin never failed to note that Abel Gance had devised this format for *Napoléon* back in 1927. An inventor in all senses of the word, Gance was not afraid to use his Polyvision for moments of spatial montage, each screen sometimes holding a separate shot. Leave it to Hollywood, Bazin declared, to banalize so radical a technology.

Bazin would remain a proponent of CinemaScope until he died (he must have encouraged Truffaut's decision to make use of it in *Les 400 Coups*). Perhaps he took it more seriously than the other new media because it alone had a chance to become widespread. In one of his characteristic analogies, he compares the film industry to a pyramid standing on its head, with the world's thousands of screens at the top and its few dozen producers clustered at the point on the ground. Keeping this system from toppling over is the trick. As new technologies rise up from decisions made down at the point, they need to spread out evenly across the world's screens to maintain equilibrium. CinemaScope did exactly that.

From the standpoint of the art he hoped would keep evolving to become ever more sophisticated and humane, Bazin recognized that CinemaScope returns to reality some of the respect that the standard frame literally cuts off, while it hands to cineastes additional ways to bring out the value and significance of whatever reality concerns them. Editing and geometrical composition remain available, but they needn't dominate, as they must on the small screen of TV. Indeed, CinemaScope may jolt film aesthetics with a healthy shock, renewing the close-up (since its use will be rarer and thus more insistent in widescreen) and making us wonder if montage is really as essential to film's grammar as once was thought.

Bazin's views about widescreen actually varied from year to year. He recognized some real drawbacks, worrying about the imposition of this format on directors who work better in the Academy ratio (1.37:1). He never wanted all films to be shot in what he understood was a trendy shape. He felt that theaters ideally should be equipped to accommodate whatever shape a director found best for the material. Understandably, this posed a challenge to a great many theater owners who built their movie houses around a 4:3 screen. Bazin was adamant that these theaters had no business screening films made in CinemaScope. There were plenty of films still coming out in the Academy ratio.

Some of his most scathing articles expose the (literally) cheap tricks by which many theater owners retrofitted their halls for the new processes. With a little math (which he always loves to display), he calculates how large a theater's back wall really needs to be to accommodate true CinemaScope projection, and he claims that 80 percent of theaters in Paris take the shortcut of simply halving the height of the screen and masking the image until it appears to be widescreen. Bazin lets you know how much of the image has been lopped off, noting that as a result, cinematographers resort to implanting a second rectangular template in their viewfinders to help them keep crucial details and compositions in play, knowing that their full image will not be viewable everywhere. Isn't it the same today, with video assists providing up to four different templates to let directors know how their work will appear, not just at the best theaters or the multiplexes, or even in cable or DVD release for television, but when streamed onto PCs or iPhones? The notion that some portions of the image can be deemed "extraneous" appalled Bazin.

Bazin extolled the possibilities of a larger image, believing, along with Eric Rohmer, that the medium's mission was not to "signify" things but to "show" them; the larger the image, the more might be revealed. Widescreen could encourage viewers to use their eyes more actively in daily life. That is why he remained frustrated with the 35mm limit that had been arbitrarily imposed on an entire art form at its outset, before anyone could object. What if painters were required to work within frames of a certain shape or size? Well, this is the case for filmmakers. Of course, one can blow up a 35mm image to any size desired, but it barters luminosity and definition as it grows. Bazin favored VistaVision because it doubled the area of the celluloid image, allowing for a far denser and a much larger one too, if you had a powerful enough projection source.

But why should Bazin, who seldom sides with spectacle, beg for a larger image? First, out of respect for the mass audience for whom cinema equals spectacle. We deserve any improvements that science and engineering can bring to what motion pictures offer the senses. However, Bazin has another agenda in mind, his usual one: realism. First he argues that of all the CinemaScope films he has seen, documentaries have made by far the best use of the new process. And then, counterintuitively, he looks for a new generation of neorealist films that should be shot in CinemaScope. He mentions that Antonioni's 1953 *I Vinti* would have gained a lot in widescreen, given that its value owes little to either montage or the plastics of its composition. What makes the film so powerful, he says, is the will of the author to reveal more, something that a wider screen could only enhance. Heretically, he even hints the same about Bresson's *Journal d'un curé de campagne* (*Diary of a Country Priest*).

Bazin would later claim that neorealism finds a perfect home on the small screen; this suggests that any size image can benefit neorealism, which, we should remember, he took to be an ethic first and an aesthetic second. Bazin ultimately stood against apparatus theory; technology has a history, but it need not determine the uses people make of it, or the consequences of those uses. Absolute screen size is aesthetically indifferent. What counts is the inventiveness of the filmmaker in helping his or her subject find its most revealing form. The properties of the art, including the size and proportions of the screen, should suggest how a given film ought to develop; screen dimensions may help decide what aspect of a subject deserves emphasis. So one might expect televisual neorealism to record unembellished the daily actions of ordinary citizens, in real time, while neorealist filmmakers working with celluloid and anamorphic lenses could situate their human dramas in more telling environments, where humans create a moral world within a natural and cultural surround. And so while producers have pressed CinemaScope into service for obvious genres like the western and the musical, the format should not be deemed compulsory for any particular type of film. Its use should be indicated case by case, as individual projects in preproduction are fashioned into what promises to be their most eloquent shape.

This, finally, is Bazin's message to our own era, in which new media greatly multiply the complexities already at work in the 1950s. While digital platforms and formats may be more numerous and more intricate than anything he had to deal with, Bazin would have known how to locate and celebrate artistic expression arising out of—indeed, because of—new technological and commercial constraints. His ecological perspective aims to circle in on the artworks for which, putatively, the system exists. The tension between system and work is endemic to the arts, whether traditional or postmodern. A symptomatic analysis of the most challenging films and TV series not only evokes the three-dimensionality and breadth of various media situations, but suggests that human understanding can sometimes transcend, and should never ignore, those media and their situations. Nothing is more modern than cinema; yet to remain in tune with its own form of modernity, cinema will need to take risks. Writing about the new media of his own age, Bazin understood that his chief mission, as well as his supreme talent, lay in identifying works of cinematic art that could shed light on the context out of which they arose.

May every film scholar, young and old, shuttle, as did Bazin, between intricate analyses of films (new ones and old) and investigations of the multiple force fields within which those films are made and viewed.

NOTES

1. Dudley Andrew, "The Ontology of a Fetish," *Film Quarterly* 61, no. 4 (Summer 2008), 62–67. French translation in *Trafic* 67 (2008).

2. André Bazin's concluding phrase in "The Evolution of the Language of Cinema," in *What Is Cinema?* (Berkeley: University of California Press, 2004 [1968]), 40.

3. See chap. 5 (originally published as "Le Commissaire Belin, doit-il faire les pieds au mur?," *Radio-Cinéma-Télévision* 155 [4 January 1953]).

4. See chap. 1 (originally published as "L'Avenir esthétique de la télévision: La T.V. est le plus humain des arts mécaniques," *Réforme* 548 [17 September 1955]).

5. See chap. 3 (originally published as "La télévision est imbattable dans le reportage 'en direct,'" *Radio-Cinéma-Télévision* 177 [7 June 1953]).

6. See chap. 2 (originally published as "A la Recherche de la télégénie," *Radio-Cinéma-Télévision* 270 [20 March 1955]). Bazin earlier wrote about peasants in cinema in "Farrebique ou le paradoxe de réalisme," *Esprit* 132 (April 1947).

7. See chap. 5.

8. In 2003 a full kinescope of this live show was discovered, so we have an opportunity not afforded Bazin to compare the two versions, but his point remains. The live TV version was directed at "you out there" in a way that cinema cannot replicate.

9. Jacques Rivette, "Letter on Rossellini," in Jim Hillier, ed., *Cahiers du Cinéma: The 1950s* (Cambridge, MA: Harvard University Press, 1985), 197–198.

10. Robert D. Cottrell, "Introduction," in Alain, *Alain on Happiness* (Evanston, IL: Northwestern University Press, 1989), xiv.

11. Edgar Morin, "Eloge du cri," *La Nef* 24 (January 1959), 86–88.

12. See chap. 46 (originally published as "La Guerre de trois dimensions, aura-t-elle lieu?," *L'Observateur politique, économique et littéraire* 153 [16 April 1953]).

13. André Bazin, "The Myth of Total Cinema," *What is Cinema?* (Berkeley: University of California Press, 2004), 20.

14. See chap. 45 (originally published as "Un Nouveau Stade du cinéma en relief: Le relief en équations," *Radio-Cinéma-Télévision* 131 [20 July 1952]).

15. See chap. 51 (originally published as "Le Cinémascope sauvera-t-il le cinéma?," *Esprit* 207–208 [10 November 1953]).

16. See chap. 48 (originally published as "*L'Homme au masque de cire*: Fais-moi peur ... en relief!" *Le Parisien Liberé* 2733 [27 June 1953]).

PART ONE

The Ontology and Language of Television

1

The Aesthetic Future of Television

It is always imprudent to claim to imagine the future of a mode of expression that depends directly upon technical progress and is subordinate to the magnitude of its dissemination. Without going back to Louis Lumière, who told Georges Méliès that his invention had no future, you only need to read what was written about cinema around 1925–27. Critics and aestheticians considered it to be a specifically silent art, and the notion of a talking cinema seemed to them to be technically dubious and aesthetically contradictory. So without losing sight of such precedents, which ought to foster humility, let us still risk speaking about the future of television. Unquestionably, unforeseen technical variables could deeply modify the givens of the problem. Color will end up becoming standard, as might 3D, even if its recent failure leaves one thinking that the public had little use for it, at least when, against its nature, it is forced to emerge within the frame of a screen. Let's not forget that television does not exist in itself, any more than cinema does: it is nothing but perhaps a provisory form of contemporary spectacle. So one can hardly speak of it as one does of theater or painting, whose essences, beyond technology, remain human, hence eternal. In contrast, what should we say of a film rebroadcast in theaters on the big screen from a central broadcasting unit—would it still be cinema, or rather TV?

Nevertheless, one should not let oneself be paralyzed by a futurist romanticism that is largely denied by the comparison with cinema and radio. If technology is a factor in revolutionary and unforeseeable progress some of the time, it is also, at other times, an unshakeable ballast. If one considers that the cinema was invented before the airplane and the radio, and that we are now in the atomic age, one will admit that its technical changes have been minimal in relation to those of our civilization. It is easy to theoretically imagine a cinema very different from the one we continue to content ourselves with, but at least half of the hypothetical innovations would necessitate the relinquishing of the current standard of 35mm, fixed more than fifty years ago, rather arbitrarily, by Edison. In the same way, the perfection of the TV image is limited by its linear structure. There is good reason to predict that even if certain technical innovations allowed for the practical emission of a standard of, say, 2,000 lines, these inventions would remain in the laboratory stages where they would be unable to do what is economically untenable, i.e., render obsolete all of the current broadcasting and receiving equipment.

From this perspective, it is reasonable to think that TV as we know it will last for a long time just the way it is. The only plausible progress for the years to come is the standardization of color, but one can admit that the transition will be smooth and that it will not overturn TV any more radically than it did cinema. Surely more important than its material progress will be the dissemination of TV, as additional indispensable relay stations are created. Let us then consider the aesthetic future of

TV from its current technical state while assuming dissemination almost as great as that of radio.

TV IS NOT AN ART

At the risk of disappointing the reader, I will first declare my skepticism as to the importance of the artistic revolution implicated in TV. More precisely, TV seems to me, like radio, to be an acquisition of great importance as a technology of reproduction and transmission, and it is in these that its principal vocation lies. If there exists a "radiophonic art," it does not seem to me to be at all comparable in originality to the traditional arts or even to a major "modern" art like the cinema. Radiophonic "specificity" does not seem sufficient to be the foundation of a true art, as it only plays around the margins. It is at most a supplemental factor in the aesthetic perimeter of the traditional arts that are transmittable by sound. In other words, the importance of radio seems situated more on the level of the psychology or sociology of art than on that of formal aesthetics.

It is true, nonetheless, that the addition of the image changes many things and could make TV a major art with varied and subtle resources, like cinema. But that image, as I said, is relatively imperfect, and in all likelihood will remain so for a long time. This imperfection and the image's small size do not allow us to consider TV as a plastic art. The question is already debatable with regard to cinema, and even more so with TV. We do not ask that the image be beautiful, but simply that it be legible, and for this to be possible TV has to get rid of tiny details and characters framed from too far away.

Should one complain about this? I think not; indeed this technical problem seems to me rather fortunate. Because of it, TV is condemned from the start to simplicity. Humility must be the main virtue of the TV director. He should not, of course, lack imagination, but all of the inventions of mise-en-scène must tend toward sobriety and efficacy. A clearly constructed and well-lit image—this should be the plastic ideal of televisual mise-en-scène. Beyond that, I would like directors to keep in mind that the qualities one expects from a theatrical performance on TV are the same as on a stage: we need good casting, actors who know their roles perfectly, who are imbued with them, and who have rehearsed a sufficient number of times to not be preoccupied with the blocking. When these ordinary but essential conditions are fulfilled (too rarely, alas!), the performance has already succeeded, no matter what style of mise-en-scène is adopted.

This does not mean, however, that televisual mise-en-scène is a matter of indifference. Directing is adequate when it satisfies the traditional qualities of theater and the physiology of the television image. But it is better still when it takes into account television's psychology. I will not venture a definition of this psychology, but it includes at least one indisputable aspect, namely the intimacy experienced by the spectator with the characters who appear on screen. This intimacy can even become troubling, to the point of implying reciprocity. As for me, each time I meet one of the presenters of the TV news or even a TV actor in the street, I have to suppress a spontaneous urge to shake their hand, as though they knew me from having seen me daily in front of my screen.

THE INTIMACY OF TV

Transposed to the domain of televised theater, this remark means that intimacy is the privileged style of television. Practically speaking, this should be translated into a mise-en-scène that relies more on the actor than on the décor; and this could take us to the limit case of a mise-en-scène composed entirely of close-ups. Perhaps this approach would only be tolerable in drama or tragedy, since comedy requires more distance. Undoubtedly, great care must be taken with this approach. In any case, the notable experiment by Cl. Vermorel (*Jeanne d'Arc* and *Andromaque*) and the more recent, less systematic one by Marcel Cravenne (*Le Malentendu*) had enough success to allow you to believe that this is one of the rare laws upon which television directors may rely.[1]

Its application to theater, however, is but a particular case of a more general idea, that of "live transmission." Clearly this intimacy I speak of is as much linked to temporal presence as to spatial presence. In principle, this phenomenon is common to both radio and TV, but the perfection of sound reproduction makes the difference between the live and the recorded virtually indiscernible, except on certain news reports. On TV, however, there's generally no technical reason to prefer the recorded, and furthermore we don't yet have recording techniques perfect enough to make live and recorded material indistinguishable. Without a doubt this will come one day, and it will then be necessary to preserve in recordings the spontaneity of *the live*, since a great part of the charm of the TV image would disappear if one had the impression of finding oneself in front of a rebroadcast film. Cinema, thanks to montage, cheats with time. The aesthetic morality of television is, on the contrary, one of frankness and risk.

We are talking about aesthetic morality, but also morality *tout court*. From this point of view, television is perhaps the most moral of all the mechanical arts. Even if "tele-theater," "telecinema," the "tele-varieties," or even the television news are hardly in the end more than an adaptation of other arts or means of information through the intermediary of TV, there is one domain in which TV outdoes all other arts, including the radio, namely that of human testimony, that is, individual revelation. One of the best TV programs is that of Jean Thévenot, on which he asks personalities from the arts, medicine, or letters to speak about themselves in front of the camera. Addressing the "average Frenchman," it shows that kings and shepherds, geniuses and simpletons are equal before television, in the same manner as we are all equal before death. This demonstrates that the TV camera is an extraordinary revealer of the human. Even if the mystery of *photogénie* is hardly ever mentioned today in regard to cinema, that of *"télégénie"* merits the reflection of both the psychologist and the moralist. It would doubtless be too simple, even ridiculous, to accord television the authority of the angel of the Last Judgment to separate the good from the bad. It is clear that certain people who are congenial in daily life would never "pass" on TV, and particular physical traits can be favorable or effectively disqualifying; but it is equally certain that "télegénie" is not a question of beauty, dexterity, or intellectual ease. Still, it always reveals, if not one or several moral qualities, then at the very least a certain human authenticity. One of the most revealing series from this point of view was that of Roger Louis dedicated to rural France. There, in every instance one saw real farmers discussing their professional problems. Now this is not a profession where verbal eloquence reigns, yet these people always spoke straight away and with a kind of authority that was fascinating. Indeed, even beyond the economic questions under discussion, this conversation constituted an astonishing human document.

From this example one can imagine what immense and inexhaustible treasure is offered to TV. Such human revelation is perhaps its only specific function, its only truly particular vocation, but it is sufficient to justify its existence. Television maintains, first of all, a quotidian intimacy with life and the world, such that it penetrates every day into our living rooms, not to violate our privacy, but rather to become part of it and enrich it. Even more precisely, TV, in the infinite variety of its revelations, favors man. Each time a human being who deserves to be known enters into the field of this iconoscope, the image is made richer and something of this man is rendered to us.

NOTES

From "L'Avenir esthétique de la télévision: La T.V. est le plus humain des arts mécaniques," *Réforme 548* (17 September 1955). *Réforme* is France's official Protestant weekly journal, appearing since 1945. During the 1950s it was an eight-page tabloid format with as many as three pages devoted to cultural articles and reviews.

1. Claude Vermorel (1906–2001) was a novelist, playwright, and scriptwriter who often dealt with historical and classical material (e.g., he was assistant director on Abel Gance's 1935 version of *Napoléon*). For Marcel Cravenne as for other television personalities and shows, see the appendix.

2

In Quest of *Télégénie*

Each week the small screen of our set brings us some new confirmation of one of the few truths that one might inarguably pull from the first years of television. We are still wondering what the style of televised theater or variety programs or documentary journalism should be. But we can be sure about one thing: we are rarely disappointed by the pleasure of simply seeing and listening to an engaging personality who has something intimate to tell us. This doesn't mean that this always succeeds automatically; there surely are reasons to try to define the conditions that foster "télégénie." We will have to come back to this someday, but already it seems certain that these conditions are fulfilled in a wide range of personalities. The past few weeks you could find utterly opposed examples of such types, first on Roger Louis's rural show *D'hier à aujourd'hui* [From yesterday to today] and then on either *Lectures pour tous* [Books for everyone] or *Trois objets, une vie* [Three objects, one life].

Roger Louis's program, instructive and useful though it may be, is probably not too attractive to spectators who are not directly involved with agricultural issues. It is usually composed of two distinct parts: the first is a short documentary (shot, by the way, with aplomb and taste), and then comes a round table where Roger Louis talks with what are most often the farmers and rural technocrats we've just seen in the film. Now as paradoxical as it may seem, it's this second half that most draws our attention and holds it. While it always feels as if you've seen the film somewhere before, you listen with real curiosity to these people who come to discuss their lives and work with precision and competence. This challenges the prejudice that assumes farmers to be taciturn and timid. For three years now, Roger Louis has brought before his TV camera dozens of such people from all corners of France. I don't recall having seen any of them stammer, let alone have stage fright, something that happens even to professional speakers. It's undoubtedly true that Roger Louis calls on a rural elite whose professional intelligence as well as their charm—their spirit of initiative—is clearly demonstrated by the film, but this simply shows that it's the human qualities, including sincerity and technical competence, that are the decisive factors of this "télégénie," which is shown here to operate in a social arena that cinema itself has found to be practically inaccessible. In fact we know that the major difficulty of documentary films about farmers lies in the near impossibility of getting them to talk in a genuine and natural way. And this is just what Roger Louis is able to do, week after week, in a television studio.

The next example, which lets me address the other end of the "télégénie" spectrum, was provided by Louise de Vilmorin, whom we watched three separate times this week on the programs of Jean Thévenot and then Dumayet and Desraupes, where she gave us a joy bordering on awe.[1] This time we found ourselves in the realm of poetry and fantasy personified. Even if we were familiar with the writings of Louise de Vilmorin, we couldn't possibly imagine that there had been a time when we loved this work without knowing its author; if I had to be deprived of one or the other, the work or its author, I believe I wouldn't give up seeing Louise de Vilmorin again on television, and I am certain that she is from now on the indispensable friend of tens of thousands of bewitched TV viewers. Now, in movie theaters over the past few years we have certainly seen a growing number of films about celebrated men, like *François Mauriac* by Roger Leenhardt or the *Gide* of Marc Allégret; but beyond the fact that the aim of these films is synthetic and nearly necrological (assembling maximum documentation about aging artists), it's quite clear that celebrity is the criterion.[2] In any case, such films are rare, while each year television lets me get to know several hundred faces that are new to me or are made new again through the test of direct—live—contact. (For renewing a face, I am thinking of that of Montherlant captured without his knowing it by a camera he wasn't looking at or had forgotten was there, whereas in fact he was posing for posterity.)[3] What counts most in television is no longer the social level, or the glory, or the intellectual value of the subject. It is primarily its human interest. The cinema will never film a biography of my concierge or my grocer, but on my TV set they can be admirable and astounding. Just as we stand equal before death, all men are equal before television.

NOTES

From "A la Recherche de la télégénie," *Radio-Cinéma-Télévision* 270 (20 March 1955).

  1. Louise de Vilmorin (1902–1969) was a wealthy writer once engaged to Saint-Exupéry. Her 1951 novel *Madame De...* became a film masterpiece by Max Ophüls. She was very close to Jean Cocteau and,

through him, to Truffaut. Her final years were spent as André Malraux's companion.

2. Roger Leenhardt, film critic and Bazin's predecessor at *Esprit* (the leftist Catholic monthly journal begun in 1932 and still prominent today) was also a documentary filmmaker. His half-hour film featuring the great novelist François Mauriac (1885–1970) appeared in 1953. In his early years Marc Allégret was André Gide's companion, making *Voyage au Congo*, a feature documentary about their 1925 adventure. He went on to an important career as a director, discovering such stars as Simone Simon. In the last year of Gide's life he made *Avec André Gide*, to which Bazin devoted one of his most important articles, collected in volume 1 of *Qu'est-ce que le cinéma?*

3. Henry de Montherlant (1895–1972) was a premiere playwright and essayist who also wrote highly successful novels before World War II. He would be elected to the Académie française in 1960. His elitist, often right-wing sympathies have hurt his reputation, except in France, where he is considered a stylist *sans pareille*.

3

Television Is Unbeatable for Live Coverage

Having attended, out of professional obligation, a few swank charity events like the Bal des Petits Lits blancs is enough to make one grateful to TV for letting us participate in these ordeals as fully as—indeed even better than—if we were there, and without the hassle. The spectacle offered to the participants of the Bal des Petits Lits blancs was rather mediocre, but what the TV viewers experienced was far superior, because while the guests were watching some poor music hall numbers, we were watching the guests. Those privileged with fortune or fame paid a great deal to be there, but the TV viewer had the greater privilege of comfortably watching them make an uncomfortable spectacle of themselves. A dog can stare straight at a bishop! Since I have a TV, I do not see what I would have gained from being an actual guest at this soirée, but I see quite well what I might have lost. In the room, I would not have been able to follow nearly so well the reaction on the face of Chaplin as he watched the clown's skit; it was certainly much more compelling to know (what am I saying?—to see) that Charlot was laughing at this clown *at this very instant,* than to be in the room and to have laughed about it with him.

I confess to never having been invited to the Princess de Faucigny-Lucinge's, nor, for that matter, to the home of any other princess, but for anyone who has read Marcel Proust, this is a universe whose reality is not in doubt. I marvel at having penetrated it the other evening with an ease that surprises me. Because we were her guests, we had intimate access to those admirable salons. As if we had done this all our lives. Like those polarized glasses that let light pass in only one direction, the TV screen transmits presence one way, and always in our favor. The princess had 100,000 invisible guests in her salon.

. . . AND A TELESCOPE FOR THE MOON . . .

The latest rendezvous that I want to marvel at is that which Stellio Lorenzi arranged the other evening with the moon. J.-L. Tallenay will speak in much greater detail about this excellent program, but I would simply recall for my purposes the extraordinary instant when we saw the moon appear live, *en direct*.[1] Objectively, there wasn't any difference between this image and what I would have obtained in some retransmission of a simple astronomical photograph, but it was the moon just as we would have seen it at that instant through the eyepiece of a telescope, the "same" that we could see through our window if we turned our heads. And so I am stunned that the director a bit later committed the error of mistakenly introducing an equivocation about the status of the photos of the planets that Etienne Lalou was supposedly looking at through the eyepiece.[2] Without a doubt, the savvy TV viewer would have understood that these were faked and that the camera wasn't pointing at the heavens; the live feed is too crucial a resource for TV to permit playing around this way, for at least in the sphere of journalism, the spectator always has the right to be sure if he is in the presence of what he sees, even if the event in question took place two or three million light years before. I hope that TV won't forget to verify for us the next lunar eclipse.

THE SPECIFIC DOMAIN OF TV

The only real superiority of TV over cinema, and a fortiori over every other means of expression, resides in the live transmission of the image: this is something no one has ever questioned. However, it would be excessive and futile to say that retransmissions always represent a drop in quality and loss of audience interest. Just as with radio, certain TV shows would gain more than they lose from being prerecorded. It's enough if, during shooting, the essential conditions of direct filming are maintained (the continuity of acting in particular), so that what is excised are only those technical incidents that are telltale defects, like cameras or crew getting into the field of view, things that are surefire indications of direct retransmission. But genuine live broadcasting incontestably reasserts its rule in news reporting, which remains the "specific" domain of TV. Next week the broadcast of Elizabeth's coronation ceremony will surely demonstrate this.

NOTES

From "La télévision est imbattable dans le reportage 'en direct,'" *Radio-Cinéma-Télévision* 177 (7 June 1953).

1. Jean-Louis Tallenay was the pen name of Jean-Pierre Chartier, founding editor of *Radio-Cinéma-Télévision* and a close friend of Bazin's all his professional life.

2. The French term for eyepiece, *lunette,* connotes "little moon."

4

Was It Live? Preserve Our Illusions!

I've complained enough, right up to a couple weeks ago, about the horrid quality of kinescopes, so I'm relieved at the decisive improvement in this process visible recently in certain broadcasts (notably the compilation taken from *En direct du fond de la mer* [Live from the bottom of the sea]). It seems now that before every French TV program we will have to wonder if it is or is not prerecorded. Let's not hide either the tremendous benefit or the great danger here.

There's a benefit because, at bottom, it is rare in fact to find compelling reasons for actual live broadcast. As I've often underscored regarding dramatic programs, most of the time it is the continuity of shooting that gives the play the sort of tension associated with "live" broadcasts, not veritable simultaneity (what is before the camera reaching our antennas at the same moment). This has been accepted for a long while on radio, and there's no reason for it not to be the same for TV, except under certain circumstances.

Those circumstances concern the need to avoid the great risk of transforming TV into ersatz cinema. Kinescope should not be used as a kind of filmed broadcast, but rather as a way to bring together the advantages of live passages with those of prerecorded material. This also applies to a comparable if less important process, the playback. Undoubtedly, playbacks are employed to reassure vocal artists who are anxious about their deep bass notes or their high C. Playbacks have come into vogue as a tool that seems prepared to control the extent of its use.

For example, in my view the excellent "Méli-Mélo" that Tchernia and Chatel brought us went astray only in its *découpage*, which incurred not the advantages but the drawbacks of intercalating live and prerecorded material: haphazard framing and montage on one side, and on the other, the flagrant impossibility of imagining some of the numbers being sung live (notably that of Les Frères Jacques).[1] Let them use as much kinescope or film as they like, but we should be told or at least made to understand this. I'm not saying they should lie to us; on the contrary, I would like them to have the honesty to tell us later on what was live, what prerecorded.

It's the same with playback, which, however, is unacceptable in something like *A l'Ecole des vedettes!* What if participants on *Cabaret du soir* didn't even deign to risk actually singing in front of the camera; that would certainly not honor this program. Still, if they do [use playback], let them at the very least have the decency to hide it better from us.

NOTES

From "Sauver nos illusions," *Radio-Cinéma-Télévision* 408 (10 November 1957).

1. "Meli-Melo" (Mishmash) was a song made famous by the group Les Frères Jacques, a hugely successful quartet of singers who toured the world for nearly four decades (1945–1982) with their mix of mime and comedy, including operetta. They were associated with Jacques Prévert and Joseph Kosma's songs, and later with Serge Gainsbourg. They staged Raymond Queneau's *Exercices de style* in 1949.

5

The Talking Head: Must the Commissaire Stand on His Head for TV?

Television, watch your right; television, watch your left. You can start to hear it said that "television is" this or that, just the way people used to say "Ça c'est du cinéma" or "Ça ce n'est pas du cinéma." I employ the past tense here because the phrase is scarcely utilized anymore, and critics have become more modest and reticent when it comes to cinematographic aesthetics, since actual films too often have mocked their laws and prophecies.

So let me highlight a current danger: that film people who are or will soon be quite interested in television may bring to this newborn art the aesthetic sectarianism that they no longer display in matters of cinema. I sometimes hear television treated with the kind of authoritative condescension (fundamentally, with the contempt) that in 1908 a distinguished class of people trained in literature and theater felt they needed to display when they discovered cinema stuttering and assumed the duty of teaching it to play tragedy.

Is this the same as saying we should renounce providing a formal education for the latest enfant terrible of modern technology? Hardly, but at least let's make an effort to apply practical pedagogical methods by taking into account its nature, its age in 1952, and its physical and intellectual attributes. Television is not cinema. What's more, it is false to say that it came *after* cinema, just as it is to say that, aesthetically speaking, cinema came *after* theater and the novel. Like film, TV has been obliged to pass through stages of growth that run from infant cries to adulthood. To want it to immediately pick up from cinema is to reason against nature, while perhaps also violating television's nature, which we should try to guide as well as patiently discover. We will certainly have many chances to illustrate these remarks; the following one is enough for today.

Too often you hear condemnations (sometimes right on TV) of "programs where you watch someone talking to the camera," under the pretext that television, like cinema and theater, ought to be a spectacle. "I'll let this happen for things like the sports reports, where something's going on, but not the gabbing back and forth between Commissaire Belin and Goldeti, or those literary debates that take places under Thévenot's whip."[1] Such judgments only amount to prejudice. They unconsciously imply an unfortunate analogy with film. And it is debatable whether cinema is in every case a spectacle, or even whether it is an art of the "image." Applied to TV, such views are misguided. Television's fundamental psychological pleasure doesn't reside in the notion of spectacle at all, but in the illusion of ubiquity. The TV screen is not a white, neutral surface but the retina of a magical eye that can watch, from behind, events our senses cannot perceive. What counts for the spectator, therefore, is not so much what he sees but the fact that he sees it: what counts is *la présence*. In other words, Commissaire Belin doesn't need to stand on his head to justify being on camera. When one of your friends returns from a long voyage and you invite him to dinner so he can relate his adventures with the cannibals, you wouldn't dream of comparing the pleasure and advantage of hearing such tales straight from his mouth to an evening at the cinema. In pressing the TV's "on" button, the viewer does nothing other than invite Commissaire Belin, or Pierre Sabbagh and his explorer, to dinner, or ask Thévenot and his critics to have coffee. Unless you prefer to consider yourself the guest. Either way. People have the right to sit before the camera and simply talk, just as we would have the pleasure of hearing them "in real life."

NOTES

From "Le Commissaire Belin, doit-il faire les pieds au mur?," *Radio-Cinéma-Télévision* 155 (4 January 1953).

1. Bazin is almost certainly referring to Jean Belin, an experienced police commissioner who had recently published a memoir that was translated into English as *Secrets of the Sûreté* (New York: Putnam, 1950). For Jean Theévenot, consult the appendix.

6

Television Is Neither Theater nor Cinema

We have often reproached dramatic television programs for having, in the name of laudable but vague experiments in mise-en-scène, lost sight of the basic demands of every theatrical spectacle. These include rhythm, the correctness of the actor's movement on the stage, and above all the full possession of the role by the actor, that is, the initial grasp of the text. And so it is with particular delight that the other night we could sense the presence of the angel of television during a dramatic program that in principle did not signal that it would be exceptional in the least. This was *Sixième étage,* a play by Alfred Gheri that is of ingenious construction but that is, from the literary point of view, mediocre.[1] It sports a melodramatic and sentimental plot that will not go down in posterity: a banal love story whose only originality is that it takes place on the seventh floor of a tenement, so that it brings to the witness stand, so to speak, half a dozen picturesque tenants, quite closely studied. But very quickly a certain charm comes into play that makes this one of the most unpretentious and successful pieces we have seen in quite a while. It gives us a glimpse of several highly instructive rationales for televised theater.

Sixième étage is a work lying somewhere between a play and a film scenario. As to the former, it sports both unity of action and a dramatic line; for the latter, it emphasizes the importance of realist details, a careful social setting, and a certain variety in its décor. Also, television has a particular way of dealing with actions: more freely than theater, but less varied than cinema. These limits are naturally defined by the technology of live broadcast, which can safely do more than theater but less than cinema. Yet *Sixième étage* brings up an additional law. The action gains from unrolling in a variety of settings while doing so with perfect unity of action: we are sometimes in the hero's room, sometimes on the landing, sometimes in a second apartment, but always on the seventh floor. Such unity in variety is especially appropriate for the TV viewer, who ends up unconsciously considering himself an invisible extra tenant. You might suspect that such intimacy is able to develop over the course of an action that requires changes in location and a temporal discontinuity, just the way it usually occurs in novels and films.

Doubtless, the possibilities of Gheri's play would have remained virtual without the intelligence of Marcel Bluwal's mise-en-scène, the simplicity of which is equaled only by its efficacy. An ideally laid-out set allowed three cameras to cover naturally and without interruption the three places where the characters meet. The frequently irritating problem of actors' movements and of entrances and exits is resolved in the simplest and most elegant way, without slowing down or breaking the rhythm of the mise-en-scène. Finally, and most important, with each of the three cameras having ultimately found its best spot in this readily intelligible space, the spectator knows from the outset and at every moment, right up to the conclusion, just where he is.

The prospect of being oriented this way, realistically yet with clarity, is actually rarely granted us. I can't tell you how much it matters to the credibility of televised shows. If I have little to say about the value of the acting and the exceptional realism of the sets, it is because these precious qualities are in a certain sense standard, and I have wanted to underline instead those qualities that seem essential to televisual mise-en-scène.

NOTES

From "Au *'Sixième étage'* la television n'est ni du théâter ni du cinéma," *Radio-Cinéma-Télévision* 223 (30 May 1954).

1. The title of this play literally means "sixth floor," which in French apartment buildings and hotels is actually the seventh floor, generally the one with the least expensive rooms. Alfred Gheri (1895–1972) was a prolific playwright, *Sixième étage* being unquestionably his most memorable work. Written in 1937, it was first adapted to film in 1940. Other adaptations followed, one in film, several for TV.

7

At the Venice Film Festival, TV Shares the Screen

Let's abandon the Lido for just one evening and take the "motor-boat" over to Venice.[1] However, this is only so we can rejoin the festival, because thanks to television, the festival this year is endowed with ubiquity. This is an event worth talking about because Italian TV, only recently born, is using the occasion of this thirteenth Venice festival to indulge in a demonstration that will put it in the avant-garde of European television. For about a half hour each night, four electronic cameras capture the opening of the screening from outside the Palace on the Lido, inside the hall, and even inside the luxurious theater. Simultaneously, 1,300 spectators seated a few kilometers away in the Rossini (a truly beautiful ultra-modern movie theater) are able to gaze upon this event as if they were there.

If you are even slightly up to date with TV issues, you can understand how this event opens up tremendous possibilities. The migration of the TV image from the tiny individual screen to the large screen set up for cinema spectacles still poses a major technical problem, one that is decisive for the development of television. Small individual TV sets keep us back in the era of "Vitascope," so to speak, and of other image-boxes that preceded the cinema that we now know.[2] But blowing up the image means running into practically insurmountable technical difficulties, since the luminosity needed for projection onto a screen of many square meters is enormous and hardly compatible with the fluorescent phenomenon of the original TV image.

In France you might be able to see TV projections on screens averaging two to four square meters, convenient for small groups at most, whereas the surface of the image here in Venice is larger than fifty square meters, which is just about what would cover the screens at either the Rex or the Normandy.[3] The brightness is definitely sufficient and is comparable to that of normal cinematographic projection. It is achieved by reprocessing the initial small fluorescent image through a parabolic mirror, using the same principle as in an astronomical telescope, though as if the telescope projected the stars on the sky, instead of observing them. The secret lies in the enormous electrical energy—some 90,000 volts—put in service of the initial image, rendering it quite luminescent, as well as in an excellent optical system. Still at issue is the visible presence of the installation in the screening room, but the projector has been reduced to a cylindrical apparatus hardly larger than a strong sunlamp. Only two balcony seats needed to be taken out.

Certainly what I saw was not always perfect: the image's contrast and its stability sometimes left plenty to be desired. But these faults have nothing to do with the enlargement process, for they stem from the emission itself, and so are correctible. Moreover, when the transmission was good, the image's quality became impressive, exactly comparable to that of the film image. Originally the festival considered broadcasting not just live coverage of the opening of the evening's show from the Lido, but also the film itself. This plan was abandoned, however, as everyone reckoned there would be reduced interest, since the Rossini could show the film [on celluloid] the next day. But already telecinema on the big screen appears possible. Might this be the cinema of tomorrow?

NOTES

From "Grâce à la télévision, le Festival est doué cette année d'ubiquité," *Le Parisien Libéré* 2485 (10 September 1952).

1. The Venice Film Festival always takes place on the strip of beachfront known as the Lido, which can only be reached by boat from Venice. Hence, Bazin is leaving the festival location to go into the city proper, where in fact he will still be at the festival via live broadcast.

2. Bazin would seem to mean the kinetoscope here, for the Vitascope was Thomas Edison's first moving-image projection apparatus, replacing his single-viewer kinetoscope box. Edison did not in fact invent the Vitascope, but he bought the rights to it and it became immediately popular in 1896.

3. The Rex and the Normandy were the largest picture palaces in Paris in Bazin's day. They remain in operation today.

8

Voice-Overs on TV: Let the Animals Talk

Animal life is an inexhaustible subject and an infinite source for TV programs. [Producer] Frédéric Rossif has proved this with his makeshift methods. So we turn with interest to his new venture, *Caméra en Afrique*, which pleasantly, instructively, and in tune with the summer season, will fill up some of your vacation, a quarter hour at a time. Those responsible for the programs, M. A. Denis and his wife, already have a number of hunting films to their credit, the best known of which is *François le Rhinocéros*. I can't tell the extent to which that little film was shot for TV or if it is only a montage assembled for the small screen. The large number of close-ups seems to indicate, in any case, a concern to satisfy the perspective of TV.

It's not in fact the images I want to critique but once again the commentary. I have too often protested on these pages against the way that Claude Darget expounds on *La Vie des animaux* [The life of animals] not to render him indirect homage, this time at the expense of Stéphane Pizella. Indeed I don't think the latter has found a tone that's any more suitable. His commentary may be relatively discreet, descriptive, and vaguely explanatory, but most often I find it useless. Occasionally he verges on nonsense, when, for example, he marvels that little crocodiles aren't afraid of the water or that Mme. Denis might be kind enough to set them free (instead of killing them with her stick, I suppose).

You could say that I am making too much of a quite secondary aspect of a program whose worth lies in its images. Perhaps I am particularly sensitive to the subject of animals, but really it is the general issue of commentary on TV that is the source of my irritation. Before the war, rare was the documentary that sported a decent commentary; the stupidity of the text and voice accompanying the making of spaghetti, let's say, or some trip across the canyons of Colorado, contributed verve, like cabaret numbers. Over the last dozen years, it must be said, things have changed, and today one can watch documentaries whose soundtracks carry not a single word. Or others, like *Dimanche à Pékin,* where the text is just as important as the image, with which it engages in a rigorous and vital dialogue.[1] In any case, cinema is finally done with the tepid water coming from the tap of some garrulous and arrogant speaker who multiplies the pleonasms between screen and commentary. Are we going to see those faults that have finally been purged from cinema find refuge in TV, while the latter, evidently ignorant of the experience of its older sibling, falls prey to the same errors?

IMPROVISATION: IS IT INEVITABLE?

Surely the problems of commentary on TV are quite different from those that present themselves in cinema, but for reasons that are mainly contingent. A film commentary can be just as carefully developed as the montage of its images. It is the product of a writer who meditates and takes his time. On the other hand, the regime of TV makes improvisation nearly always the rule. Indeed, we might wonder to what extent this results from complacency, or whether it might not be possible to devote more time to readying programs for broadcast. Here, it's the working methods that are up for debate.

But whether improvised, semi-improvised, or carefully rehearsed, TV commentary should respond to certain requirements. Commentaries that accompany films of a documentary nature ought to be inspired by the restraint that has been adopted by cinema. They should also be competent and effective, for example, providing the names of the animals instead of going on ecstatically about their fur or their speed, which everyone can see. But overall I confess I prefer the insolent ignorance of Claude Darget, who narrates *La Vie des animaux* like a wrestling match, to the basic science of Stéphane Pizella, who teaches us nothing we didn't already know.

A certain redundancy, at most, is admissible, to the extent that TV, not having the visual clarity of cinema, can sometimes make us grateful that the narrator helps us perceive what we are looking at. From this perspective, an ideal commentary is of the sort that usually accompanies films in the series *Magazine des explorateurs* [Explorers' magazine]. The verve and the casual improvisation in this show never exclude precision, competence, and utility. It is true that in this case the narrator is also the auteur of the film, but this exceptional conjunction indicates nonetheless the ideal toward which TV narration should be heading.

NOTES

From "La Parole est aux animaux: Reflexions sur le commentaire à la T.V.," *Radio-Cinéma-Télévision* 392 (21 July 1957).

1. *Dimanche à Pékin* (Sunday in Peking) was directed by Chris Marker. Bazin reviewed it very favorably in *France-Observateur,* 6 December 1956, and again on 27 June 1957.

9

Looking at Television

Two excellent books devoted to television have just been released, almost simultaneously: *T.V.*, by Jean Quéval and Jean Thévenot (Editions Gallimard); and *Regards neufs sur la T.V.*, by Etienne Lalou (Editions du Seuil).[1] It is significant that these two books are appearing at the same time, and in 1957, for there can be no doubt that in France, as around the world, a general synoptic elucidation of TV has only become possible, not to say valid, in the last year or two.

In France, in any case, 1956 did indeed appear to be decisive. Jean Thévenot explains the history of French television along these lines: "1932–1935: early milestones; 1935–1939: attempt to launch; 1939–1945: active dormancy; 1945–1948: delays, doubts, and disarray; 1948–1953: takeoff; 1953–1956: rising development." Of course for real takeoff our material infrastructure must reach saturation, in terms of transmitters and regional stations as well as individual TV sets. With our 500,000 receivers, we still lag far behind America's 35 million sets, or even Britain's 6 million.

Any increase of these numbers obviously depends, first, on the enlargement of the provincial districts reached by French airwaves, which currently cover only a third of the national territory. Ultimately, though, we appear to have crossed a decisive threshold, even if just three or four years ago our TV was in its heroic pioneering period.[2] The quality of its technology has been stable for an even longer time, so that the heart and soul of its future now depend on the government's administrative and economic policies. On this point, the consensus among Thévenot, Quéval, and Lalou is striking.

However, French TV is now able to take stock of itself profitably, due more to its artistic status than its technical development. For any viewer who has kept up with his four hours of daily programs more or less continuously over the last five years, I think there can be no question that the first stage of trial and error, of uncertainty, and of aesthetic experimentation, ended with the period 1954–1956. It is striking that the year 1956 did not deliver any truly novel programs. While it may be that from a technical point of view, the development of our TV is now merely a matter of transmission, on the artistic front we are observing a clear leveling-out, even a tendency to regress from where we were at the end of the 1955 season. In this way, critical assessment has had the leisure of looking back with some distance on innovations it saw emerge over the course of the preceding years.

Although virtually confined to a discussion of French TV, Etienne Lalou's book nevertheless constitutes an excellent introduction to TV in general—especially in its first two chapters, which are devoted, first, to a psychology of TV, and then to its history and to a technical explanation of the "miracle" of the small screen. Next comes a critical analysis of programming in its current state—which, as I mentioned, has been more or less stable for the last two years—and then a chapter on the means of production, which allows us to go behind the scenes, as it were, followed by a final section given over to constructive criticism about future prospects.

I do not think that Lalou's *Regards neufs sur la T.V.* makes Quéval and Thévenot's book redundant. There are, however, two matters in which their overlap is significant. First, in their criticism of what is aired (more succinct in *T.V.*), Quéval and Lalou largely agree about the major programs, despite differences in their taste—and, with just a few minor adjustments, I cannot help but agree with them too. According to both books, the three best regular shows are *Lectures pour tous* and *En Votre âme et conscience* (both of which were justly awarded the annual TV critics' prize) and, of all the variety shows, *Music-Hall Parade.* On this, the verdict was unanimous: that's a good start. There was less agreement over certain other shows that are nonetheless celebrated for their high quality, such as *Ciné-Panorama* and *Edition Spéciale.* The discussion is more open ended with respect to the many other variety shows (*36 Chandelles* [36 candles], *Joie de vivre,* and the game shows: *Télé Match, Echec au public* [Public failure], etc.).

It is on this subject that I most often feel the need to challenge the opinions of Quéval or Lalou, who sometimes differ. Lalou, especially, seems to start from an idea that is seductive in principle but somewhat utopian, if not demagogic, in its applications. He believes that it is still possible to resolve the contradiction between education and entertainment. For him, the most "entertaining" shows should also be instructive, and the best educational programs should entertain. This might makes for a worthy ideal, but wanting to make it a reality at any cost could be dangerous: by hoping to make shows about serious subjects "fun," you run the risk of merely sanitizing or distorting them. This is not to say that such a program has to be boring. But criteria for boredom are not the same as those for amusement. Lalou implicitly acknowledges this when he rightly praises the extraordinary medical shows that feature endoscopies of human organs. Here no concession was made to vulgarize science. *Lectures pour tous* is not an "amusing" show either, but it is fascinating. *En Votre âme et conscience* [In all honesty], on the other hand, illustrates Lalou's thesis. It is perfect, and we must rejoice in it while still remaining skeptical about the synthesis that can occur between entertainment and quality. What's more, Lalou, like Thévenot, vigorously rejects the idea of a concession to commercial TV; for without criteria other than to please and entertain, inevitably the worst wins out.

Returning to game shows, Lalou, for example, seems to have a slightly naïve, optimistic idea as to the nature of the success of the famous Italian show *Quitte ou double* [Double or nothing] when he sees it as the result of the public's taste for erudition and the acquisition of knowledge. I think we are dealing instead with a less idealistic sociological phenomenon by which *Quitte ou double* is aligned much more closely with the abominable *Reine d'un jour* [Queen for a day] than with the pedagogical games of the Ecole nouvelle.

I am surprised that, unless I missed it, none of the authors cites a show that, while modest in scope, has had success from which lessons can be drawn: I am referring to *Gros plan* [Close-up], filmed reports whose subjects are chosen by actors or stars. It would be interesting to show why—in spite of the medium—TV's innate truthfulness has turned these little investigations into something fascinating, while attempts at the same genre in cinema are always split between vulgarity, lies, self-importance, and stupidity.

As for programs that feature live reporting, the authors once again are unanimous in praising them, taking them to be the central pillar upon which the entire makeup of TV programming rests. There is complete agreement as well—but this time more critical—with regard to *Journal télévisé*, a show which was, during the early heroic years, the pride of French television, but which, if it is not a source of embarrassment, nevertheless represents a major site of the contradictions and weaknesses of French TV. Everyone knows where the trouble comes from. There are two main sources: first, the lack of financial means that would allow the show's reporters to be everywhere they need to be to record the news; second, and more important, the scandalous dependence of radio and television news reporting on the "powers that be."

In this critical area, which engages current events directly, the fundamental vices of RTF's administrative and political regime are most clearly on display.[3] The convergence of Quéval, Thévenot, and Lalou's criticism on this point is eloquent. Everyone knows perfectly well what the score is. The incoherence of an absurd, antediluvian administration, totally inadequate to the new problems created by TV, renders certain reforms and improvements inconceivable in advance. TV is like Kafka's castle on the one hand and Father Ubu's kingdom on the other—the most absurd of these fathers having turned out to be a socialist. The solution lies in the autonomous administrative and political status of television.

Under these conditions, the fact that French television programs do not have even more defects, relative to their many good points, testifies to the imagination, the tenacity, and the enthusiasm of the men, most of them very young, who have been the pioneers of the system. But, lest we harbor illusions, the genius of invention will run dry, and we are arriving at a moment where the health of the institution must take over from the virtues of individuals. The time has come when the ground, once it is fully cleared, can receive and benefit from the intellectual seeds of inventors, novelists, filmmakers, dramatic authors, poets ... artists who have until now remained in a state of wary uncertainty. Radio has long benefited from their collaboration. But this would require favorable material and moral conditions. Such is the price that must be paid, however, to ensure the future of French TV.

NOTES

From "Regards sur la télévision," *France-Observateur* 381 (29 August 1957).

1. Jean Quéval (1913–1990) was a prolific writer and translator and a founding member of the avant-garde literary group Oulipo. He served as critic for *Mercure de France* in the 1950s, when he also wrote books on Marcel Carné and Jacques Becker. For Jean Thévenot and Etienne Lalou, consult the appendix.

2. Bazin uses "heroic period" to mean an early era that established TV but that has passed, something like the age of Homer for the dramatists who lived in Greek democracy and drew upon him.

3. RTF (Radiodiffusion-Télévision Française) was baptized in 1949 as the national institution governing all broadcasting in the country. It would become ORTF in 1964.

PART TWO

Television among the Arts

10

Long Live Radio! Down with the 8th Art!

I beg those of my colleagues who are the radio specialists at this journal to pardon me for imprudently crossing the fence that separates our gardens as I go stomping around in their flower beds. But this fence is fragile and radio does have certain analogies with cinema. Also, the circumstances that have kept me from patronizing movie theaters for quite a few months have brought me close to my radio; this leads to comparative criticism.[1]

The purpose of this article grew out of the following remark, whose weakness, I readily acknowledge, is that it is perhaps too personal: dramatic or literary broadcasts that are labeled "radiophonic" (whether originating from a radio play, fantasy, novel, or film) disappoint me nine times out of ten. Listening to them requires attention sustained to the point of exertion, and it just doesn't pay off. Everything happens as if the radio were standing like a screen between the works it transmits and us. I should add that these stories are usually so curiously put together that a single instant of inattention costs you the thread, and you are doomed thereafter to grope through the labyrinth. Should your milk boil over at the other end of the apartment and you need to relight the gas with your neighbor's igniter, you are lost.

I would draw the following conclusion from such experiences: I have more and more faith in radio, but less and less in the 8th art.[2] More precisely, I believe that in radio just as in cinema, there can be a sin of idealism [*angélisme*]—a fantasy of strict specificity, of purity, of autonomy—which is heresy, other than in purely experimental work.

It would take too long to discuss the principles of an independent radiophonic art parallel to cinematographic art. I admit these exist. But that's just it: we know where the mirage of pure cinema leads—to those experimental works that today have only historical interest and are found only at the *cinémathèque*. A film made up entirely of superimpositions could be pure cinema, but it would have every chance of remaining invisible to the public. If we can already glimpse an "evolution" of cinema, all evidence points to its heading toward less "specificity." The way things are going, today's filmmakers more and more relinquish the idea of treating cinema as a goal, whereas they more and more use cinema as a means of recording works that could originally seem quite foreign to the screen. Superimpositions, accelerated or slow motion, and rapid montage (and all the distortions that cinema alone can subject reality to) have practically been abandoned today. The idea of the original scenario seems on the way to disappearing; anyway, what one might call "original" is a tale that could as well be made into a novel or a play. Nor do I believe this evolution to signal a falling off; on the contrary, we now recognize a truth that has gradually established itself through long experience: there is no such thing as a "cinematographic" play or novel, only dramatic and fictional works that are more or less well adapted. The eternal laws of dramatic action, the psychology of characters, and the moral values put in play are far more important in this business than cinematographic art. More precisely, this latter is just the necessary means serving the end—which is the work. All the artistry of the filmmaker should go toward making us forget him. In the same way, and I would say a fortiori, there are no "radiophonic" works. Anything with such a designation would likely make for a poorly constructed play or a novel with phantom characters, since the creator's attention would have been diverted from his essential goal by what are secondary and subordinate technical matters. But there can be a radiophonic adaptation of *Hamlet* or a *Madame Bovary* made for the airwaves [*mise en ondes*] whose artistic interest is perhaps no less than when these works are staged for cinema. Some time ago the radio studio workshop produced a series of adaptations from novels that I am very sorry has been discontinued; and one of the most convincing of Pierre Schaeffer's experimental works on his *Rue de l'université* was the pure and simple recording, some years ago, of Marcel Proust's *Fin de la jalousie,* read by Pierre Fresnay.[3] I found it heart rending; but no matter what one thought of it, it was the real thing, pure radio.

NOTES

From "Vive la radio, à bas le 8ᵐᵉ Art," *Radio-Cinéma-Télévision* 58 (25 February 1951).

1. Bazin had been hospitalized with tuberculosis in the summer of 1950 and by winter 1951 was convalescing at home.

2. In France, especially in the 1920s, cinema was known as the 7th art, hence radio, in the opinion of some, might be the 8th.

3. Pierre Schaeffer (1910–1995), one of the founders of concrete music and a major postwar figure in experimental radio, was simultaneously

an engineer, broadcaster, scientist of communication and acoustics, and composer. Evidently *Rue de l'université* was one of his regular programs. A translation of his important 1952 book, *In Search of a Concrete Music*, was published by the University of California Press in 2012.

Pierre Fresnay (1897–1975) was one of French cinema's greatest actors, most memorable for his role as le Capitaine de Boeldieu in Jean Renoir's *La Grande illusion*.

11

A Seat at the Theater

While the first night of Jean Masson and Jean Antoine's new TV broadcast, *Place au théâtre* [A seat at the theater], was no doubt a success, you were allowed to wonder if it were a fluke. But the second broadcast was even better, so we've been reassured. Like most shows that effectively group together a series of variety acts, the premise of the first installment was a bit artificial. Time will tell. We much preferred the October 12 rendition of an excellent popular melodrama (performed by Rolla Cordion's carnival troupe) over the appearance of the new stars of the Grand Ballet de Monte Carlo that opened that October 26 broadcast.[1] It's true that the camerawork was quite mediocre; still, the very idea of a *Club des amis de télévision* [Club of friends of television] isn't bad. This "club" is made up of artistic people, Parisians, some of whom are there to present a recent "discovery" worthy of appearing on our screens. This is an original way to renew the classic theme of the "testing ground."

Be that as it may, the core of the program came at the end, when four actors had to improvise a sketch on a theme or character provided by the public. You can imagine that this would include the most bizarre requests. Jane Marken trying to be a "madame" (this wasn't very original), Jeanne Moreau a sausage, Robert Hirsch a singer, and Robert Manuel an impresario. All of this happened of all places on the Great Wall of China while referring to the theme "four characters in search of an author."[2] I should say in passing that such improvisation is not commedia dell'arte, which presupposes instead a detailed backdrop, based on old conventions. But that doesn't matter, since the result is excellent and it is perfectly "television."

Indeed, improvisation is a sort of theatrical game, and it assumes, even more than "serious" theater, the awareness of complicity between the actors and the audience. Throughout the game, everyone, on the stage and in the room, is conscious of being involved in the same amusing adventure. The actors watch each other, being at the same time audience onlookers, authors, and actors, while the public is itself a bit author and actor. Despite the size of the auditorium, this complicity creates an intimacy, and intimacy is already present in television. Televiewers quickly identified with the audience at the Théâtre de l'Etoile and were even aware of their superior position over those glued to their seats; being right beside the actors on stage, they could observe far more closely their creative hesitations. Our enjoyment wasn't without a touch of emotion—true theatrical emotion!—when we saw Jeanne Moreau resist an overwhelming desire to laugh in front of her partner. Finally, and above all, the perpetual creation that gives rise to dramatic play seems to have been invented especially for live television. We have often opposed cinema to theater on the notion of the physical and temporal presence of the actor. But television is the presence of theater with the ubiquity of cinema.

NOTES

From "Place au théâtre: Surtout quand il convient admirablement à la télévision,"*Radio-Cinéma-Télévision* 199 (8 November 1953).

1. The Grand Ballet of Monte Carlo was founded in 1947 by the Marquis de Cuevas. It relocated to France in 1950 taking the name of its founder. A highbrow company, this was the first Western dance group that Rudolf Nureyev would later appear with. Characteristically, Bazin prefers a popular melodrama performed by a carnival troupe.

2. Of the performers mentioned, everyone will recognize the name of Jeanne Moreau (born in 1928), who had appeared in a half dozen small film roles by 1953 and was a recognized stage presence. Jane Marken (1895–1976) was a beloved character actress whose appearance in over a hundred films began as early as 1912. She played the mother in Renoir's *Une Partie de campagne* (1936) and showed up in *Les Enfants du paradis* and many classics. Robert Manuel (1916–1995) debuted on the Paris stage in 1933 and became a member of the Comédie-Française, during which time he also acted for TV and in many films (he had a major role in *Rififi*). Robert Hirsch (born 1925), now an award-winning member of the Comédie-Française,didn't make his first screen appearance until 1951 but went on to appear in many films and TV series, and continues to appear in them today.

12

False Improvisation and "Memory Lapses" on TV

I have already proposed some remarks to my readers aiming modestly to contribute to a description of what could be called *télégénie,* in the sense in which Louis Delluc spoke of *photogénie.* And I will resume these reflections one of these days, whenever my daily TV viewing suggests new ideas.

Last Sunday I admired the supremely refined ease with which Madeleine Renaud and Jean-Louis Barrault (along with André Brunot) performed the poems that they had chosen for their *Impromptu du dimanche* [Sunday impromptu].[1] It struck me straightaway that this program constitutes the first success of false improvisation. By this I mean "scripted improvisation." Nothing is normally worse on TV; we have seen many programs that purport to adopt this tactic fall apart or quickly abandon it.

Take, for example, the *Cinémathèque imaginaire* of Marcel L'Herbier, or the little character sketches that Pierre Dumayet keeps trying out with great courage in *Lectures pour tous,* despite the stumbling of his actors week after week.[2] Decidedly, TV appears to tolerate only pure, sincere improvisation, without any trickery, or else the recitation of a perfectly memorized text: in other words, either conversation or theater. However, Madeleine Renaud and Jean-Louis Barrault know how to speak directly to the spectator while alternating their voices, without reading, as you would speak to a friend; the text was undoubtedly highly rehearsed, but it appeared to flow naturally. Nevertheless I am convinced that this is only an exception that confirms our rule; only their tremendous familiarity with the public can explain it.

Quite paradoxically, it was in delivering a fable by La Fontaine that André Brunot faltered. Oh, it was hardly anything major, and Brunot knew how to acknowledge the blunder gracefully and with intelligence. However, this little snag gave me a fright, for I always find that when actors falter in their texts, it affects me so much more on TV than in the theater. Also I feel relieved and comforted when a play is interpreted by actors who know it thoroughly, as was the case with *Marius* and *Fanny*. I don't hesitate to say that this latter program was even better than the film, better even than the play on stage.[3] I believe J-L Barrault and his company have shown me the reason for this.

On the little TV screen the person who looks at us is supposed to talk to us face to face, person to person; he or she is among us. This is where that feeling of intimacy that presides over *Impromptu du dimanche* comes from. But let this interlocutor stumble and lose the thread of his discourse, and the falseness of this illusory situation is brutally revealed, because we can do nothing for him and he, many kilometers away from us, finds himself alone, if not disabled, in front of soulless recording machines. In contrast, at the theater, an actor who has a memory lapse knows that the prompter is nearby. Moreover, the audience, clued in to the situation, is not a blank pitiless mirror set in front of his breakdown. Its collective mood and the quality of its silence are, for the actor who knows how to play it, a possible resource.[4] Ask the juggler who blows his number but starts over again after a quick wink to the public. On TV, nothing of the sort; the incapacitated actor not only makes us suffer for him, he makes us suffer our impotence. Just at the instant he is so close to us, he becomes once again the inaccessible prisoner of the electronic tube that gave him birth!

NOTES

From "Fausse improvisation et 'trou de mémoire,'" *Radio-Cinéma-Télévision* 274 (17 April 1955).

1. Jean-Louis Barrault and Madeliene Renaud were the most celebrated married couple in French theater from the 1940s into the 1980s. They also appeared in several exceedingly famous films. André Brunot was a member of the Comédie-Française who appeared in a score of films.

2. Marcel L'Herbier, preeminent director from 1917 until after World War II, turned to directing TV shows, including the one Bazin mentions here, in 1953. For Pierre Dumayet, see the appendix.

3. *Marius* and *Fanny* are two of Marcel Pagnol's beloved plays, written in 1928 and 1931 respectively, then adapted to high acclaim in 1931 and 1932. Evidently French television presented them in the mid-1950s.

4. Bazin made a similar point in his famous essay "Theater and Cinema," where he mentions TV in a footnote:

> Television naturally adds a new variant to the "pseudopresences" resulting from the scientific techniques for reproduction created by photography. On the little screen during live television the actor is actually present in space and time. But the reciprocal actor-spectator relationship is incomplete in one direction. The spectator sees without being seen. There is no return flow. Televised theater, therefore, seems to share something both of theater and of cinema:

of theater because the actor is present to the viewer, of cinema because the spectator is not present to the actor. Nevertheless, this state of not being present is not truly an absence. The television actor has a sense of the millions of ears and eyes virtually present and represented by the electronic camera. This abstract presence is most noticeable when the actor fluffs his lines. Painful enough in the theater, it is intolerable on television since the spectator who can do nothing to help him is aware of the unnatural solitude of the actor. In the theater in similar circumstances a sort of understanding exists with the audience, which is a help to an actor in trouble. This kind of reciprocal relationship is impossible on television.

From *What Is Cinema?* (Berkeley: University of California Press, 2004 [1968]), 97–98.

13

To Serve Theater, Let Television Adopt Some Modesty

The other week, Jacques Chabanne's regular theater series presented *Candida* by George Bernard Shaw. No question, *Candida* is an admirable, well-constructed play that never stops surprising one with a consistency you might qualify as classical in its dramatic invention, while from other angles it is extremely modern. However, we have seen other good plays staged for TV; so the choice of program doesn't explain by itself the exceptional theatrical pleasure I'm not alone in having felt this time. Should we attribute this to the cast? Definitely the actors were selected with meticulous care: Alfred Adam, Brunot, Eugène Macheaukis—but we have seen equally brilliant casts before. So was it Max de Rieux's direction?[1] Rarely was it more than neutral, not ever venturing beyond the three walls that are the convention in theater.

But that's just it; this economy of means could be the key to the mystery, revealing that there isn't any mystery. *Candida* has given us a rare pleasure because it is even rarer that on television you are allowed to see a good play, perfectly cast with actors who give the impression not only of knowing their lines intimately but of having taken possession of their roles from the inside, and who play them exactly as they would in the theater ... and, I want to say, under forthright direction. In short, we have finally recognized in our pleasure the very quality that a good evening at the theater affords us.

In art as elsewhere, we must beware of generalizations. I would never deny that television can renew the theatrical event, or say that experiments in TV staging are necessarily useless. For example, I think that what Claude Vermorel did with *Andromache* points in a particularly interesting direction, and indeed other directions are possible.[2] But from so unexpected and simple a success as *Candida* I draw a double lesson.

First, I must keep restating for television the two heresies that cinema runs into when it takes on theatrical material. In effect there exists "filmed theater," which is nothing more than the mere photographing of a play; this has been rightly panned. But bias for the reverse position, whereby everything must be done to "detheatricalize" a dramatic text, is perhaps even more insidious, since it uses Art as its excuse. The real difficulty is for cinema to actually "make theater" and thereby find its true success. However, while the cinema is a mode of reproduction that thus distinguishes itself from its model, television is from the outset a method of transmission like radio. As such, even more than cinema, it should limit its goal to a really good display without deformation. Of course, you can rethink TV's mise-en-scène inside out, based on its technology and psychology. But I fear that even talent would not be enough to accomplish this. But who will alert us to the damage caused by the prejudice for the fourth wall and for candid "outdoor" scenes, which is the equivalent of "cinema at all costs," the undoing of so many filmed plays. In *Candida*, we never left the single set, nor even got a glimpse of the fourth wall.

Conversely, we did see some excellent actors in perfect tune with their roles, speaking their lines in just the right rhythm, without any worries. Maybe this was because they weren't being led around the playground weighed down by an intricate mise-en-scène overloaded with useless exits and unnatural staging. In any case, they had rehearsed enough so that all in all they wouldn't have performed the play any better if this had been the twentieth night on some Parisian stage.

I apologize for such a lengthy discussion to get only this far, but the simplest truths are not always the most obvious. Whether televised or not, theater is theater before anything else, that is, a dramatic illusion created by actors who bring a text "to life." All problems of mise-en-scène must be secondary to this primary requirement: televised theater absolutely partakes of staged theater, and this is something that, sadly, it has all too often forgotten.

If you need confirmation of this thesis, I'm happy to bring up the terrific program *Place au théâtre,* the key to which, as everyone knows, involves a sketch improvised by professional actors on a basic idea that the public itself provides.[3] This show's success is more pronounced each time it airs, so that I see in it something typical about TV's triumphs—because TV recruits new awareness for traditional theatricality, not presuming to transform it, but only to allow us to participate in the experience even better than does the most privileged of the paying public. A stage, three pieces of scenery, plus some actors; that's all that's needed for theater to be yours via your television.

NOTES

From "Télévision doit apprendre la modestie," *Radio-Cinéma-Télévision* 211 (31 January 1954).

1. Max de Rieux (1898–1963) was a silent film actor who turned director in 1927. In the 1940s and 1950s he staged mainly operas and operettas, sometimes arranging them for TV. He returned to film direction in the early 1960s before his death in a car accident.

2. Claude Vermorel (1906–2001) was a novelist, playwright, and scriptwriter who often dealt with historical and classical material (he was assistant director on Abel Gance's 1935 *Napoléon*).

3. See chap. 11, where Bazin reviews this program.

14

Respect the Spirit of Theater
First and Foremost!

This past month brought us some theatrical broadcasts on television that, while not equally successful, were at least quite enlightening and well worth revisiting. [*Bazin goes on to review a New Year's Eve variety show and an operetta—Offenbach's* La Belle Helène—*for the propriety of their acting, direction, and costumes, finding in both cases that the dimensions of the television screen had not been sufficiently taken into account. He then continues here by addressing a third program.*]

But one perfectly on-point program, *Chemise*, by Anatole France, directed by René Lucot, unfortunately proved that ingenuity in *découpage* and in handling "stagecraft" devices do not make for good television when theatrical verve and a sense of dramatic timing are missing.[1] In the first place, Anatole France's script could not provide enough tension to produce any effect. The scenes follow one another but are not linked in true theatrical progression. René Lucot's directorial shrewdness and his abundant visual ideas are no use, since all these effects fall flat in the absence of dramatic tension.

Thanks to examining three theatrical broadcasts of a seemingly comparable style, we can glean once more a lesson that has been repeated many times here. Certainly television has its own laws and we'll never sufficiently take them into account, but first and foremost, it is foolish not to respect the fundamental laws of theater that television may modify but should not destroy. When the essential is respected, some weakness in direction is a less serious problem than an otherwise perfectly polished broadcast from which the spirit of theater is absent.

NOTES

From "D'abord respecter l'esprit du théâtre," *Radio-Cinéma-Télévision* 316 (5 February 1956).

1. Anatole France (1844–1924) was the Nobel prize–winning novelist and man of letters. *Chemise* is not one of his most notable plays.

15

TV and the Disenchantment of Theater

I do not plan to return to my critique of *Chevaliers de la Table ronde* [Knights of the Round Table], intelligently directed by François Chatel, except to develop one of the thoughts that this show, though disappointing, inspired in me.[1] It is extremely difficult to translate to television the conventions that produce theatrical magic.

Whatever we may think of the mise-en-scène of this Jean Cocteau play, at least one thing went irreparably wrong —the costumes. Not that they were objectively ugly or poorly designed with respect to the style of the work, but they failed probably because they were conceived from a theatrical point of view, whereas the television camera submits them to an ordeal for which they were not made. Theater's sense of detachment and the conventions of its stagecraft permit certain liberties, allowing a stylization that the lens pitilessly destroys. What we see on the small screen is no longer the clothing of dreams, but rather bizarrely cut-up fabrics whose very material—including felt and jersey—we can identify; we can even make out the stitching and count the fasteners. What I'm suggesting about the clothes is equally true of the props, as is clear in the case of the miserable little flower that springs up in its white wooden box.

Now it seems to me that the proximity of the camera is not the only reason for this disenchantment, since the use of black and white is also an important factor in ruining the balance devised by the set designer. We know that in theater, colors abolish the substance of things and contribute to making us accept conventions. When the colors vanish, the mask falls, and the set and costumes return to their primary material reality. Cinema, however, has been coming up against these very problems for a long time, and it has learned how to resolve them. The style of costumes on the screen, including the techniques of fashioning them, takes into consideration the constraints of *photogénie*.[2] Jean Cocteau, with the help of Christian Bérard, knew how to illustrate this transposition better than anybody.[3] In his great film, the Beast's costume and mask admirably stand up to the close approach of the camera. It is true that cinema has both the resources and the time to concoct additional "spells," primarily through lighting.

The working conditions of live broadcast television, in particular the straightforwardness of its lighting, make certain illusions impossible. I am certainly not claiming to provide or suggest solutions to the problem that I pose; I am just bringing its existence to light and underlining its importance. An entire dramatic repertoire will remain virtually forbidden on television so long as directors and designers do not come up with a style of costume, and, more generally, with a full technique of transposition, adapted to the direct and mercilessly close perspective of the small screen.

NOTES

From "Théâtre désenchanté," *Radio-Cinéma-Télévision* 431 (20 April 1958). Bazin had been close to Jean Cocteau since 1947 and knew about the latter's quest for enchantment; hence the title of this review.

1. This play by Cocteau was first staged in 1937.

2. Bazin calls on this 1920s term, which refers to the specific manner in which cinematography lifts objects out of their ordinary state. Here he suggests that cameramen and designers understand the effects of light, color, and texture on the resultant image.

3. Christian Bérard (1902–1949) was an accomplished set designer for theater when Cocteau asked him to work on *La Belle et la Bête,* his most famous project. Cocteau's *Orphée* is dedicated to him.

16

Art on Television: A Program That Loses on All Counts

It pains and troubles me to come down hard on an obviously ambitious program on an artistic subject, directed by a cultured, intelligent, and conscientious man, and produced from a challenging angle for a medium as popular as television. If I have decided to go ahead, it is because I am reproving not only the latest show by J.-M. Drot, but, retroactively, and through these "Problèmes d'un jeune artiste d'aujourd'hui," the already prolific series *L'Art et les hommes* [Art and mankind].[1]

For a TV system like France's, with but a single channel and limited airtime, the essential problem of programming is obviously to satisfy contradictory demands by finding a way to reconcile them as much as possible. First is the need for a variety of subjects and goals. There must be programs that offer pure entertainment that is consciously popular, capable of amusing everyone; still, we have the right to expect that such shows offend neither good taste nor intelligence, that they be neither silly, ugly, nor crude, and that their presentation be conceived in a style adapted to the resources particular to television. This remains the vexing problem of the variety shows, about which one cannot say that they have yet found a truly satisfying response, apart from Margaritis's productions.[2]

At the other end of the spectrum, if I can put it that way, those responsible for programming have been admirably concerned to find subjects that educate without inducing boredom: documentary, scientific, and finally, artistic programs. Looking only at the latter group, let me distinguish between those that are literary (*Lectures pour tous*), those that are musical (*Musique pour vous*), and those that are pictorial, which will be my focus today.

In principle one could argue that the directors of these shows share two essential problems that must be resolved: one from the technical point of view, the other from that of the audience. At issue, first of all, is the fact that television brings something specific—something new and inimitable—to the knowledge or understanding of the art it summons up. This is exactly what Dumayet and Desgraupes successfully brought off in *Lectures pour tous,* which is not only an excellent program of literary criticism *on* television, but *via* television. It is also crucial that, no matter how elevated its intellectual bearing, the program be able to hold the attention of a wider audience than merely the one comprised of specialists or enthusiasts interested in the art in question.

All the same, let us not delude ourselves: it is normal, inevitable, and even legitimate that in the absence of specialized channels, as on the radio, certain shows will interest only a fraction, large or small, of TV viewers. Those who have never read a novel can hardly watch *Lectures pour tous* attentively, and I confess that my own musical incompetence often leads me to switch off *Musique pour vous*. And so we must applaud twice as loud when, like last week, we are offered a poetry reading that is as satisfying, from the point of view of both quality and popularity, as that of J.-M. Tennberg.[3] But that is a limit case and an exception; we should be less demanding. What counts is that the show should make for original television, and that, while reaching beyond connoisseurs, it should nonetheless satisfy their legitimate intellectual demands.

It is precisely in this task that J.-M. Drot has, it appears to me, decidedly failed. Having taken charge almost singlehandedly of the plastic arts sector, he seems, first of all, to have done scarcely more than adapt for TV the various formulas of the so-called "film on art," without much originality or pleasure. These formulas are no doubt diverse, and some might be usable again with modifications, but most have already stretched their limits in cinema. If they still manage at times to seem successful as movies, it's because commercial film, in addition to color, allows for greater care in shooting and editing. Hence TV has lost the battle in advance on this terrain and should aim to pull off something other than rushed, botched films.

I might reproach J.-M. Drot still further from the point of view of strict pictorial criticism, for his work is highly dissatisfying. Apart from the arbitrariness of choosing a painter like Bernard Marre to illustrate the "problems of a young artist today," I think the program's approach to the problem of abstract art was artificial, intellectual, and wrong.[4] It provided an illusory solution, satisfying the need for logic but never getting to the core of things. The solution consisted in showing what could in figuration serve as a pretext to abstraction—that is to say, precisely what in abstraction remains concrete and therefore is excluded from it. This is hardly art criticism; at most it is a superficial and pretentious illustration of scholarly data on the functioning of the imagination.

Thus these programs seem to me to lose on both fronts [*perdre sur les deux tableaux*]. Of very dubious value from the strict point of view of art criticism, they cannot disguise the tedium they induce except in the eyes of TV viewers impressed by the ambition of their aims and the morose solemnity of their tone.

NOTES

From "Art à la T.V.: Une emission qui perd sur tous les ... tableaux." *Radio-Cinéma-Télévision* 458 (26 October 1958). The original title is a pun: "Une émission qui perd sur tous les ... tableaux" is an idiom meaning "a program that loses on all fronts," but *tableaux* also means "paintings."

1. "Problems of a young artist today" is the title of the specific program in the series that Bazin is reviewing here.

2. Gilles Margaritis (1912–1965) was a circus performer and music-hall impressario remembered best as the peddler in Jean Vigo's *L'Atalante*. See appendix.

3. Jean-Marc Tennberg (1924–1971) was a popular actor and poet who made many appearances on TV in the 1950s. Bazin analyzed the rapport between his vocal delivery and its appearance via television in "Jean Tennberg," *Radio-Cinéma-Télévision* 365 (13 January 1957). He claims that Tennberg's "recitation is a veritable spectacle; however the actor stands before us, if I dare say so, in formal attire but without gloves and in an abstract place without décor, against a bare white backdrop. The result is stunning; I think I've never felt as I did here the existence of a specific televisual space, determined on one side by the camera lens and on the other by the proportion of the small screen. When Tennberg moves, the studied effect is quite different depending on whether the movement is lateral or in depth." Bazin also brings up Tennberg in *Radio-Cinéma-Télévision* 457 (19 October 1958).

4. Bernard Marre (born 1924) was exhibiting abstract designs in the 1950s; his reputation has not grown since.

17

Reporting on Eternity: TV Visits the Musée Rodin

Stellio Lorenzi's "Visite au Musée Rodin" [Visit to the Musée Rodin] constitutes one of those rare programs in which you can experience the new thrill of "pure television."

As with pure poetry of course, television's grace is bestowed only on those who earn it, first of all, by honestly serving their subject.[1] The exceptional qualities of Stellio Lorenzi's program are perfectly definable. We can easily imagine the splendid film for which this TV visit to the Musée Rodin might serve as something like the dress rehearsal.[2] The auteur threw himself into his subject, coming up with a preliminary layout that is not inferior at all to the kind of *découpage* made for a film. He understood how to group the presentation of the sculptures into consistently valid categories, whether historical (Rodin's beginnings), thematic (hands), or logical (the various stages of the monument to Balzac). Best of all, this presentation never confined itself to description, to just turning its light on the stone or the bronze; the framing, the camera movement, and the montage were wedded to the movement and rhythm of thought.

Finally, the commentary added a dimension to the image. Without sidestepping the explanations necessary for a decent presentation of the artworks, and without ever lapsing into poetic esotericism, the commentary was as self-effacing as possible in confronting the literary texts that had more or less directly inspired Rodin: Dante, Baudelaire, Villon ... and this juxtaposition not only made for the most effective of commentaries by way of contrast, but also, reciprocally, it enriched the texts themselves. Added to this was the intelligence of a musical score selected in the same spirit, for example the organ playing over the sequence of hands, or the chorale for *Les Bourgeois de Calais*.[3]

My praise here would apply just as well to the "film" that Stellio Lorenzi might direct using the same *découpage* (and it would be a shame if he doesn't make such a film). Now—and this is the stunning lesson of such a program—this live report, instead of reducing the quality of the spectacle, actually makes it more effective than the most polished film. This is an observation much more paradoxical than one would at first have thought: that "live" television is of interest only if the subject of the reportage has duration, if it concerns an event that is temporal in nature. One can never attend the same football match twice; and even a theatrical play is not entirely identical to itself on each performance. But the plastic arts are exactly arts that are not temporal, and it is hard to see what could be added to these marble and bronze forms by the substitution of the television camera for the film camera, which has all the advantages of the former and none of its drawbacks.

This may well be the case; yet our gaze alongside Stellio Lorenzi's on this petrified humanity was hardly timeless [*intemporel*]. The bumpy tracking shots of the Orticon camera, the groping attempts to frame, the simple, brutal illumination of the spotlights, the slight hesitations of the montage, all this made us participants in the show's creation. I do not mean to say that the technical imperfections of live shooting constitute a spectacle in themselves—such a claim would be absurd. I would even add that these imperfections work favorably only on account of the care taken in the show's production. Live television may distinguish itself technically from telecinema by only indeterminable differences, enough for us to have the feeling of living with the image, of discovering it at its birth. The contrast between theater and cinema is often based on the physical presence of the actor, perpetually renewed on the stage but fixed once and for all in film. Television gives rise to a new notion of presence, void of all visible human content—nothing, in short, but the presence of the spectacle to itself [*la présence du spectacle à lui-même*]. A tracking shot, in television, never passes through the same place twice. No two framings are alike, any more than there are identical leaves on trees. Let us savor the image that we will never see twice.

NOTES

From "Une Reportage sur l'éternité: La visite au Musée Rodin," *Radio-Cinéma-Télévision* 148 (16 November 1952).

1. "Pure poetry" in France is associated with Stéphane Mallarmé and became a watchword after Abbé Brémond's famous lecture with that title and Paul Valery's short reply "Sur la poesie pur" (both from 1925). *Cinéma pur* was used the next year by Henri Chomette, René Clair's brother. Bazin was never favorably disposed toward the term and would soon write a key essay with the title "Pour un cinéma impur."

2. From 1947 into the mid-1950s, the film on art was a genre Bazin particularly revered. This TV program thus seemed to him to line up alongside Resnais's many shorts (on van Gogh, on Picasso's *Guernica*), some of which were also "visits."

3. Rodin's most well known sculpture, *The Burghers of Calais*, is a group.

PART THREE

Television and Society

18

A Contribution to an
Erotologie of Television

In trying to define the factors pertinent to an erotology of television, it's convenient to compare it to cinema. The clearest difference between the two is the size of the image. Now, beyond the fact that its reduction on television is an accidental phenomenon that will disappear (at least on big-screen TV), to me, this is not one of the determining factors. Furthermore, the smallness of the screen is a debatable fact and always relative first of all to the spectator's angle of vision. I'll agree that a large screen viewed from very far away is not exactly the same as a small screen viewed close up from the same angle, but the fact remains that a photogram of a film is not perceived as a scaling down of the given scene: the mind adjusts by itself. More important than its dimension, perhaps, are the defects to which technology irremediably condemns the television image. The fleeting composition of the image makes the spectator an incurable myopic who hasn't the option of looking more closely, since he would wind up seeing what's there even more poorly.

It seems clear right away that this imperfection is ambiguous: indeed, insofar as a certain manner of obstructing the gaze is a well-known law of eroticism, the blurriness of television may serve our purpose, deliberately or accidentally. But it can also be counterproductive, for instance when the precision of a game of hide and seek is central, as in American films whose erotic efficiency is based on nuances of the censorship code. The exact placement of the neckline on a blouse, the significance, intensity, and position of that shadow a few centimeters above it, are often what does the trick entirely. What would be left of this in a blurry image with poor contrast? It follows that suggestiveness on television can only come from the lack of clarity of what is shown, rather than from the precision of what is hidden.

But here again, technological factors seem to me of quite secondary importance. We will reach significant conclusions not by studying differences in the plastic quality of the image, but by examining psychological factors and social impact.

Live broadcast must come first on the list of what is particular to television. Indisputably, our awareness of the simultaneity of an object's existence with our perception of it constitutes the pleasure principle specific to television and the only thing it offers that cinema cannot. There is no reason such an awareness could not serve erotic sensations. Obviously our feeling is not the same when, let's say, we're in front of the image of a nude woman on a film screen as when faced with the reflection of a real woman transmitted to us via a series of mirrors. Let me note in passing that this proves that the real presence of actors is not what constitutes the basis of theater; rather, what counts is their integration in an interplay. Every day television offers us live displays that are not anything like theater. Those American spectators who had the good fortune to not blink at the precise moment when, during a live program, the strap of a dress broke, unexpectedly uncovering a breast in close-up, witnessed a specific moment of erotic television: the time of a naked breast between two changes of camera. Such spectacles are rare and one cannot reasonably count on them. Still, I believe that the mere live presence of human beings on screen carries an emotional factor that needs only a shade to become erotic, if the subject arises.

In the world of cinema there is no lack of beautiful women, but for some time now, "bathing beauties," or more generally, alluring dancers and the like, have only served as a rhetorical figure on screen, a simple decorative element. I have noticed that there is always something moving and even arousing about seeing a pretty girl in the range of the television camera, although I wonder if this feeling will pass as it becomes more familiar. For example, in the variety shows of André Gillois or Jean Nohain, you can notice a certain brunette, with the figure of a model, who generally stays discreetly in the corner, waiting to appear as needed: she's the one who hands the prize to the winners of the "find the treasure" game and goes about other menial but elegant tasks. The cameraman never frames her, and she never appears on screen except by chance and always briefly, but this charming figure is like the white chicken who crosses the corner of the screen in some documentary about the tse-tse fly, and which the natives of Bantou-Bantou do not fail to notice, to the detriment of their learning about disease prevention and to the great despair of the missionaries (for more detail see the *Revue Internationale de Filmologie*).[1] Her almost incongruous presence is the very picture of grace selected at random by God (or the Devil) in the thankfully flawed productions of Jean Nohain and André Gillois.[2] I am, alas, convinced that such incidents will be become progressively more infrequent. Those filmological missionaries now pay attention to white chickens; in the same way, maybe reading this article will alert the creators of *36 Chandelles* or *Télé Match* to disruptive elements in their programs that they were not aware of. Still, the unexpected will remain prominent in live broadcasting, and the opportunely useless, unforeseen, or absurd presence of some charming person in the frame of the camera will surely be more frequent than a broken strap.

My example, though, fails to be convincing because the object in this case is enjoyable, even clearly desirable. It must be proven that eroticism can arise from presence alone, as it can in a painting's pictorial quality (and not from the beauty of the model). Dare I take the extreme example of the coronation of the queen of England? You can be sure I would not have the bad taste to say that this might suggest any impure thoughts, but in the end a quite sublime eroticism accompanies the myth of the princess, as evidenced in so many popular tales (and as well exploited in *Roman Holiday*).[3] Television allowed us to live a few hours of intimacy with a queen, and I do mean her intimacy, first because television divided the spectacle into millions of individual images, but most of all because it reconstituted their duration. Despite the poor resolution of the image, one could discern, with troubling indiscretion, the progress of the fatigue that came over the face of Elizabeth. It was an extraordinary instant when, with the enormous crown hiding her feminine hairdo, the face, with its drawn features, suddenly began to resemble that of the dead king. And it did so in such a way that in itself, royalty changed it.[4]

No doubt, then: television's "live-ness" [*le direct*] constitutes a determining factor in its erotic possibilities, this term being taken, as you will have understood from the outset, in its broadest sense. But the "presence" of the object relates only to the form, or the support, if you will, of the feeling. We still need to define the content, and here sociology necessarily intervenes. Due to its technological and economic basis, television is fundamentally condemned to being watched by families. The size of the image limits optimal viewing to the normal number of family members, that is, from two to five or six spectators. Since the way it is used generates TV's programming, there ensues a virtual censorship that limits television's audacity to a level comparable to the kind of cinema directed toward family audiences. We should, however, give French television its due, noting that it does create programs "for adults" while suggesting that children go to bed first; still, since this can't be enforced, any licentiousness remains of a rather intellectual nature and hardly affects the mise-en-scène.

One should not assume, however, that the family nature of television is limited only to its subjects: *ad usum Delphini*.[5] In the last resort, it is less because of children that virtual censorship was instituted than because of their married parents, that is, because of the psychosociology of the conjugal couple. I can think of no better example than that of the figure of the *speakerine*.[6]

If television were cinema, the ideal *speakerine* would be someone more or less like the music hall presenter: a pretty girl in a bathing suit, agreeable and spirited. Of course you can imagine options that are more intimately persuasive, in the genre of the "White Tooth Smile," for example, but the *speakerine* quickly installs herself in the mind of the television viewer as a figure from his private life: *a person whose daily visits must be suitable for the whole family, especially for the wife.* This amounts to suggesting that the male viewer must have no guilty conscience about wanting to see the *speakerine* enter his dining room day and night, since this would quickly create awkwardness, even domestic disorder. In other words, the *speakerine* must inspire the sympathy of the husband but not the antipathy of the wife.

This psychological requirement eliminates certain types of women I call "a-conjugal," which includes, precisely, the greater part of the feminine ideals of the movie screen. The *speakerine* must be pretty and gracious but in no way lead the viewer toward imaginary adultery. With this in mind, French television possesses two superlative *speakerines*, Jacqueline Joubert and Catherine Langeais.

About the first, I readily grant that both her physical qualities and what shines through of her character identify her as a perfect wife. Pretty, energetic, with a confident but not provocative grace, she has the authority and assurance that mark a good hostess, capable at once of working outside the home while also keeping house, raising beautiful children, and still keeping an eye on her femininity. Of course such an ideal figure raises the danger of irritating any wife who might imagine her husband making a comparison. And I have noticed that Jacqueline Joubert's popularity is not unanimous or complete among women. But in general, rather than envying her, the female viewer identifies with this ideal of conjugal femininity, unconsciously considering herself to be the Jacqueline Joubert of her husband. At the same time, she would not mind the presence of Joubert herself, since this is the type of woman one marries, one whose romantic life could only be that of the most transparent morality. If, despite everything, the husband has impure thoughts, he clearly is getting his money's worth, in a virtual sense. To make things even more perfect, Jacqueline Joubert is married to Georges de Caunes, as all viewers know (and can almost see).[7] She takes great care to keep us more or less directly up to date with her family life. This is not the same as the famous American series *I Love Lucy*, in which the protagonists seem to give us daily confidences about their conjugal life; instead it is a discreet sketch of such a life, adapted to the French temperament and to the needs of the role of the *speakerine*. Thanks to allusions to her family, Jacqueline Joubert is a friend of the family, a friend whose husband is named Georges and whose son is named Patrick. Her regular presence at the hour when the family is gathered before the television set is thus congenial, modest, and exemplary.

The case of Catherine Langeais is altogether different, yet she too is perfectly satisfactory. Perhaps less obviously pretty than Jacqueline Joubert, but nonetheless gracious, Catherine charms primarily by the intelligence that her beauty conveys. She has a bit of the "blue stocking" about her, which makes her perfect for presenting "intellectual" shows, such as those about bridge or chess. She is, if you will, a strong-headed woman, and if not the ideal spouse for the average French tele-viewer, for other reasons she is at least someone you could invite over to the house. The feelings that she inspires must include admiration from women and respect from their husbands. Furthermore, she is one of those who puts a man in his place with tact, finesse, and firmness. You can tell that she would never inspire indecent desires, spite, or jealousy. Unlike Jacqueline Joubert, we know nothing about her private life,* this discretion being consistent with her character.

Let me excuse myself in advance for what I am going to say about the third, Mlle. Jacqueline Caurat. I ask that, where

---

* I have learned while correcting page proofs for this article that Catherine Langeais is going to marry her colleague Pierre Sabbagh. However, I hope that for the needs of my thesis she will be just as discreet about her marriage as she has been about her engagement.

appropriate, the reader, and she herself, not forget that I am speaking here only of the fluorescence of the cathode ray tube and of the psychological phenomena that crystallize around it: any correlation between my personal feelings and what I feel I can write as a television critic can only be accidental. Bearing this in mind, let me contrast Mlle. Jacqueline Caurat to her colleagues; she is a troubling figure. She was doubtless chosen for her professional qualities and her charm, but perhaps this charm was not analyzed prudently enough. Mlle. Jacquline Caurat is what one could call a spicy brunette. A fetching beauty spot underlines the vigor of her undeniably sensual smile. It is not that her comportment is the least bit immodest—on the contrary, a slight timidity clearly testifies in her favor—but I am not sure that this timidity might not give the viewer certain ideas that Jacqueline Joubert and Catherine Langeais discourage in different but clear-cut ways.

Perhaps we must deduce from this that cinema is in fact much more social than we normally admit or, better, that its individualism is dialectically linked to its mass character. In the darkened cinema, I have the feeling that the starlet incarnates my dreams because she incarnates the identical dreams of the several hundred people who surround me. But with the *speakerine,* who talks to me every day and looks me in the eyes, even if I know that her image is repeated on hundreds of thousands of little screens resembling the facets of an enormous fly's eye, I am conscious that it is I who am looking at her. All she has in front of her eyes is a metal box, a machine that delivers her instantaneously to my gaze. This extraordinary power, which brings me control over her, entails something indecent by its very nature, something that cannot bear that the one who is delivered to us this way should lay herself open to our imagination by provocation, or, in what amounts to the same thing, by passivity.*

It is easy to experience the imaginary reciprocity of the television image. Frequently it happens that on the street or at a reception I approach someone I think I know, or I pull back my offer of an inopportune handshake at the last minute, finding myself in the presence of people I have never seen except on television. This mental illusion is particular to television; it doesn't exist in cinema. Poor at remembering faces, when standing before someone who looks familiar, I often ask myself whether they are from my school days or from my stint in the army. To this list I now need to add "from television."

Let me conclude. From our example of the *speakerine* we can see how much the eroticism of television is restricted by the psychology of its live broadcast and the sociology of its home consumption. But when it comes down to it, all restrictions are ambiguous and engender their own compensations. Chaste by necessity, television takes from that very chastity the principles of its erotology.

P.S.: It remains to dream up a kind of television that, adhering to its psychology, is liberated from its sociology. In matters of eroticism, such TV would far surpass the most specialized (i.e., niche) cinema.[8] But one can hardly imagine, at least for the pres-

---

* The media reported on the misfortune of one of the English *speakerines* who received menacing letters from a TV viewer. The anonymous correspondent demanded that she give up television under pain of death. Everybody who has enough experience with television will admit along with me that this is far too believable given the typical impulses of compatriots of Jack the Ripper. With the young woman's physique alone being enough to arouse the desire of the consumer in question, we can easily imagine that the latter might reach an intolerable state of exacerbation. I repeat that this specific reaction to live television is not conceivable in cinema.

ent, clandestine television. I will advance just one suggestion in support of this absurd hypothesis. On television you sometimes have to sit through "interludes." This is the name for snippets of films where nothing happens except some gratuitous action: a fire burning, fish in an aquarium, a windmill in the breeze, the hand of a potter shaping clay, and so on. These little inserts amuse the eye between two programs when the second is late in coming. Along these lines one can imagine a striptease number, one complex enough to extend beyond the time of the longest intermissions, so that the appearance of the expected show would interrupt the striptease at an unforeseen moment, but of course always too soon. Still, one time, by chance, one may see a bit more. Then perhaps one day, even ...

NOTES

From "Pour contribuer à une érotologie de la télévision," *Cahiers du Cinéma* 42 (December 1954).

1. Bazin is recalling two rather racist studies: John Maddison, "Le Cinéma et l'information mentale des peuples primitifs (notes sur les travaux du Colonial Film Unit du Gouvernement Britannique)," *Revue Internationale de Filmologie,* volume 1, nos. 3–4 (October 1948), especially pp. 307–308; and "Cinéma pour Africains" in volume 2, nos. 7–8 (October-December 1951), 277–281.

2. The reference to grace is an allusion to Saint Augustine's way of characterizing Adam and Eve's original sin as a *felix culpa*, a happy fault, because it resulted in the coming of a divine savior. Here the mistake in the framing brings with it the lucky glimpse of grace, a beautiful woman.

3. *Roman Holiday* (1953) was directed by William Wyler and starred Gregory Peck and Audrey Hepburn.

4. "Tel qu'en lui-même la royauté le changeait." Bazin here varies Mallarmé's famous last line of his "Le tombeau d'Edgar Poe": "tel qu'en lui-même enfin l'éternité le change."

5. This phrase, literally "for the Dauphin's use," refers to the cleaned-up classics that Louis XIV's son, the Dauphin, was allowed to read.

6. An institution of French TV from the outset, the *speakerine*, always an attractive woman, announced the evening's programs at intervals each night.

7. Georges de Caunes was a highly visible figure on early French TV who married the *speakerine* Jacqueline Joubert. Their son, Antoine, has become an even more visible TV personality in recent years.

8. Bazin writes only "le cinéma le plus specialisé," meaning pornographic films aimed at a small sequestered audience, as opposed to television's ubiquitous broadcast.

19

Censors, Learn to Censor

I am certainly not one of those who would reproach television for offering nothing but shows viewable by children, on the pretext that the small screen is intended for family viewing. Sentencing television to this kind of servitude would amount to forbidding it any artistic development. It is perfectly natural and legitimate to take parental responsibilities into consideration, and thus to warn parents that certain spectacles are only suitable for adults.

Given this observation, I am at full liberty to criticize the conception TV seems to have of its own responsibilities in this area. For, ultimately, it must also take into account a certain minimum set of contingencies. It takes a lot of nerve, for instance, to dispassionately announce, between four and eight o'clock in the evening, that the next program is highly inappropriate for children, and even more so when such a program airs on a Saturday or a Sunday in the late afternoon. But it happens! Such was the case when, on October 11, *Ecole des Parents* (highly inappropriate for children) was scheduled for 7:30 in the evening.

What are parents supposed to do at that hour, then: put their children out on the street, or lock them in the cellar?

These silly matters would be less irritating if it weren't also the case that such an adult program, deemed inappropriate for children but aired at an hour when children have not yet been sent to bed, may be followed by a perfectly family friendly show. But what I find perhaps even more regrettable are the vagueness and arbitrariness of the censorship criteria applied to TV. Often everything plays out as though the announcer were instructing parents to be wary, without knowing herself what would justify such a warning—as though she were giving it at random, in order to protect herself against eventual recriminations! It follows, then, that viewers are utterly surprised at the mildness of the reasons behind such sternness. These observations are especially applicable to films.

TV is fortunate in that theoretically it does not depend on any legal censorship: it ought to be able to exercise a more flexible and intelligent self-censorship than that which is applied to cinema. As far as youth is concerned, the legal ban on children under sixteen years of age hides a psychological error: indeed, it confuses moral criteria, especially sensitive during adolescence, with psychological criteria affecting childhood proper. For example: a horror film that would be intolerable for a ten-year-old kid can be safely shown to a boy of fifteen; but *Le Blé en herbe* [*The Game of Love*],[1] acceptable viewing for a child who understands none of it, is not appropriate entertainment for young adults.* It would thus be wise and fitting to inform parents

* On Sunday, November 17, at 5 PM, there was a broadcast of *Canon City,* an extremely violent film not appropriate for the children who would normally be home at that hour. On the other hand, at 8:30 the same evening, they aired *Miquette et sa mère* [Miquette and her mother, a 1950 comedy by H.-G.

(possibly via an agreed-upon coding system) of the seriousness and, in particular, the reasons for the warning. So it would be up to the heads of families to decide what measures ought to be taken. And let's also mention that there is no surer means of discrediting a form of censorship than by applying it without good reason and indiscriminately.

NOTES

From "Censeurs, sachez censurer," *Radio-Cinéma-Télévision* 411 (1 December 1957). The French title puns on a French tongue twister, "Un chasseur sachant chasser est un bon chasseur."

1. This 1954 film by Claude Autant-Lara is an adaptation of the sensational 1923 novel by Colette.

Clouzot]—not advisable viewing for the adolescents who had every opportunity to see it—whereas it might have been screened during the afternoon, for children, without any cause for objection.

20

You Can Now "Descend into Yourself"

The noise made by Etienne Lalou's latest program, *Science de demain* [Tomorrow's science] has reverberated all the way to the major daily papers. Obviously it's a bit late to pick up the echo here, but we can take away a lesson that goes beyond the current news.

We have already called attention to some of the scientific programs on TV that include live transmissions of phenomena that normally are recorded by photography or on film. But the subject of last night's program was more sensational by far. It featured the live observation from a hospital room of images obtained by a bronchoscope inserted forty centimeters into a patient's windpipe, then of various human and animal X-rays. From a scientific point of view the importance of such an experiment is obvious (teaching, remote diagnostics, etc.), and it surprised even the scientists themselves, who noted that looking at the televised image was sometimes more convenient or more productive than direct interpretation. But such professional interest alone could only halfway justify a program aimed at the larger public, were it not for the fact that the experiment at the same time constituted a prodigious spectacle. Those who have seen scientific films on the same subjects will be able to gauge the intensification of emotion, and I dare say of beauty, that comes from seeing such things live on TV. To view the X-ray of a beating heart in the cinema is already a marvel; hearing the amplified beating of a human heart on the radio has become almost commonplace. But to simultaneously see and hear the solemn rumble of this vital palpitation was, I assure you, a major moment of "pure television"! The patient, who watched the dark depths of his second right bronchiole onscreen, while at the same time the crystal shaft of the bronchoscope was exploring its opening, will not disagree with me. Thanks to TV, man has become his own Plato's cave.

NOTE

From "On peut maintenant 'Descendre en soi-même,'" *Radio-Cinéma-Télévision* 312 (8 January 1956). "Descendre en soi-même" is a French expression in religion and psychology indicating self-analysis. Pierre Corneille used it notably in his tragedy *Cinna*.

21

Television, Sincerity, Liberty

The reader will perhaps be surprised that the subject of my observations here are programs that appear to do nothing but invoke political opinions. Yet everything that passes across the small screen can be judged from the point of view of the art of TV—that includes the current campaign for the referendum just as much as science programs or dramatic plays. And perhaps even more so, inasmuch as TV has revealed itself to be, first of all, an art of live communication from person to person, face to face. Each evening, every one of us will have been able to consider the reasons for voting "yes" or "no" on the referendum, but we might also judge the way in which each propagandist is attempting to persuade us.

Long ago, in the columns of this journal, Father Pichard argued that TV is essentially democratic, and that, as a means of expression, it is in any case in utter contradiction with the bewitchment of fascist ceremonies.[1] Hitler was thinkable on radio, in cinema, and in the great plaza of Nuremberg, but his sorcery could not stand up under the intimate, live propaganda of the small screen.

Now, I wouldn't presume to exhibit so much optimism, and I am not sure that there aren't some corrupt uses possible for TV's power of conviction (just think of *A King in New York* and the scene of the investigating committee).[2] But it is certain that, without taking the theory to an extreme, TV as a means of propaganda offers, if I may say so, a specific resistance, or, more positively, a moral guarantee that neither radio nor cinema provides.

Why? Because it is essentially a technology made for sincerity. I have often emphasized the particular quality of shows that simply reveal people to us, and it is no coincidence that the best and most durable program on TV is paradoxically *Lectures pour tous*, which truly has brought a new dimension to literary criticism, that of the human being. In just this way, I would venture to say that in these last few weeks TV has brought this dimension to politics. Addressing us eye to eye without special effects, each of these representatives of propaganda was forced to reveal something of himself. However cunning he might be in the rhetoric of his discourse, he could not prevent us from sensing something about his level of sincerity or the conviction behind his words. No longer was it only some idea that counted, but now also the man's relation to the idea, and if this relation did not pass judgment on the idea, it wound up judging the man.

Let us also remember that in America, it was TV that finished off McCarthy.

NOTES

From "Télévision, Sincérité, Liberté," *Radio-Cinéma-Télévision* 455 (5 October 1958).

1. Raymond Pichard (1913–1992) was a Dominican priest who pioneered religious television in France. His ninety-minute program *Le Jour de Seigneur* (The Lord's day) started in 1949. He was a member of

the group that in 1947 founded the periodical *Radio-Loisirs,* to which Jean-Pierre Chartier became a contributor. *Radio-Loisirs* ran for twenty-four issues sponsored by the Dominican publishing house Temoinage Chrétien; in 1950 the latter joined forces with Editions du Cerf and resurrected the media journal with Chartier as editor under the name *Radio-Cinéma-Télévision.*

2. Charlie Chaplin's *A King in New York* premiered in France in October 1957. Its representation of the McCarthy hearings impressed Europeans.

22

Information or Necrophagy

On his program "La Caméra a-t-elle un cœur?" [Does the camera have a heart?], François Chalais questions whether images representing the death of human beings, especially from accidents, have to be made public. Rossif could have profitably illustrated this thesis with images already seen on French TV, such as the [1955] catastrophe at Le Mans or the hallucinatory document that aired last year on *Journal télévisé* displaying Japanese frogmen exploring an underwater glacial abyss, a site particularly favored by suicide candidates. This unforgettable image came back to me not long ago when I ran into its more hallucinatory supplement in color during a newsreel playing at the cinema. After being offered a splendid underwater ride on the backs of individual Rebikoff torpedoes, rather in the style of *Le Monde du silence* [*The Silent World*], the camera haphazardly approaches the remains of an airplane recently fallen into the sea as if it were just another curiosity, a particularly sophisticated detour from the main line of the program.[1] This modern Icarus makes for a strange apparition indeed, but that's not all: for the pilot is there at his post, drowned, his eyes half open. And the camera takes its time, complaisantly lingering on this powerful sight ... before setting off again to reap images of Greek amphora used by some brand of Athenian perfume.

This spectacle, unsettling to say the least, has scandalized more than one viewer. Should it have been censored? It is with some regret that I believe I must respond "yes." Not so much because this phantasmagoric atrocity was inserted into a show that had been cleared for everyone to watch, nor in the name of respect for the dead, but because its unwarranted and casual presentation makes it indecent. What is condemnable is neither the cruelty nor the objective horror of this document (once legitimate social precautions against minors' seeing it have been taken), but rather the absence of any moral or aesthetic justification, without which the image turns us into sheer necrophages, cannibals. The death of a soldier, that of a lifeguard, indeed that of a torero or a racecar driver, is an event that has some meaning, even if it's debatable. The resulting document addresses itself to our minds by way of the ambivalent horror of our senses.

But there are no "exquisite corpses."[2]

NOTES

Originally published as "Information ou Necographie," *Radio-Cinéma-Télévision* 408 (10 November 1957).

1. Dimitri Rebikoff (1921–1997) was a French engineer who in the early 1950s invented an underwater flash and waterproof housing for a camera, called the "torpedo." He operated it while in his manipulable one-person underwater vehicle. He designed the apparatus Jacques Cousteau employed for his award winning *Monde du silence* (1956).

2. A reference to the surrealist game of this name.

23

Television as Cultural Medium *and* The Sociology of Television

TELEVISION AS CULTURAL MEDIUM

The statistical services of French television divide up the weekly programming as follows: out of forty-four hours and forty-five minutes per week, eleven hours and fifty-five minutes are devoted to "news magazines," seven and a half hours to "variety shows," five and a half to the rebroadcast of commercial films, three hours to *Télé-Paris,* two hours and thirty-five minutes to sports broadcasts, two hours to educational programming, two hours to music hall, two hours to religious programming (Protestant and Catholic), one hour and forty-five minutes to children's fare (on Thursdays), an hour and a half to dramas, one hour to classical music, and two hours and fifteen minutes to miscellaneous programming.

This breakdown does not correspond to the one that I proposed—arbitrarily, it's true—at the beginning of this series of articles. After having discussed news and journalistic programming, which I collectively called "Le monde chez soi" [The world at home], I moved on to those programs that I grouped under the heading of "culture," which comprises several shows that the official statistics include in the eleven hours and fifty-five minutes of news magazines. In particular, I have in mind Pierre Sabbagh's *Magazine des explorateurs,* the various "art programs" of J.-M. Drot, and the scientific programming by Etienne Lalou or Roger Louis, to which list I would naturally add the literary (*Lectures pour tous*) and musical programs, leaving aside the educational ones.

A Marvelous Medium of Cultural Diffusion

It has always seemed to me that a major argument against those who hold the mechanical arts that have invaded modern life in contempt lies in the fact that these arts are as much a prodigious means of spreading culture as they are of entertaining. There's no denying that in this respect, the results of [decades of] radio have not been particularly positive—certainly not for those who listen all day long to the bland music of Radio-Luxembourg. But if this ambient soundscape serves no purpose other than to afford a certain psychological relief, where is the harm in it? On the other hand, I never cease to marvel at what I learn when I listen to the French cultural hour while I wash up. Of course, nothing will be gained by those who look for nothing; they won't miss what they don't seek. But anyone with even the slightest bit of artistic or intellectual curiosity will find himself satisfied, indeed expanded, by what radio has to offer: thanks to it, we are steeped in culture.

Television, at least in France, does not present the same drawbacks as does radio (even if, it must be said, it doesn't offer all of the latter's advantages), because except in certain limited parts of the country, the single channel imposes one and only one option on the spectator. However, thanks to its variety, a substantial amount of programming is devoted to cultural values. So our programming can be criticized—and I'm among those to have done so—except in one aspect: aside from a few aberrations, French TV cannot be said to have contributed to inanity or vulgarity.

The current constraint of a single channel undoubtedly compels those in charge to keep down the number of specifically cultural programs. This honorable alibi, however, has unfortunately resulted in certain pretentious, boring, and poorly made programs that don't tend to last. For that matter, the same could be said (alas!) about certain variety shows. There are, however, several fruitful counterexamples; so let me point to three programs in which the seeming austerity of the topic is belied by the execution. These prove that the intellectual quality and cultural value of a show can go hand in hand with its interest as spectacle. I mean to discuss *Lectures pour tous*, *Magazine des explorateurs*, and *Sciences d'aujourd'hui* [Science of today].

Television Is Personal Testimony

It might seem a priori that literary criticism is as nonvisual an endeavor as could be. Yet Pierre Dumayet and Pierre Desgraupes have been able to give it a face. This is because—and we come back to this principle like a leitmotif—television is first and foremost an art of personal testimony. In convoking authors to expound on their books before the camera, Dumayet and Desgraupes may not have discovered the moon, but they have invested in the essential. For even before it is a spectacle, television is a conversation; so it is worth only as much as the people who speak and what they have to say to us. One of the best programs of last year, whose disappearance we will forever regret, was that kind of public confession by a famous personality that Jean Thévenot carried out in *Trois objets, une vie*. Still, even with this same principle in view, *Lectures pour tous* could have been a mediocre series, and it owes what it is to the intelligence and good taste of its directors. As pleasing to the eye as it is to the mind, *Lectures pour tous* proves that a program can be intellectual without giving up its popular appeal.

There is less to say about *Magazine des explorateurs*. There again, the program's interest is founded on the interest of personal testimony. Pierre Sabbagh plays it safe. He does so with warmth and finesse, but perhaps the program would benefit from a greater effort with regard to its mise-en-scène.

But it is *Sciences d'aujourd'hui* that I want to take up as my primary example, since it has provided some of the finest moments of pure television the new art can boast. I am referring especially to Jean Painlevé's programs, in which he has managed to revive, via television, the aesthetics of scientific cinema.[1] Of course we know that Painlevé's achievement is not merely to have resolved the supposed contradiction between art and science, but rather to have developed an aesthetic and poetics of cinema based on the medium's scientific value. On television, this aesthetic could only be based upon the scientific advantages of the live broadcast. Painlevé has demonstrated exactly this over the course of several programs, the last of which, on bronchoscopy, represented a sensational climax.

These films (which are in color, by the way) that treat endoscopy in general and bronchoscopy in particular are no longer a rarity in the arena of scientific cinema. Anyone who has seen them knows that they constitute a powerful spectacle. But how much more moving was this descent forty centimeters into a man's lungs when broadcast live on the television screen. In theory, of course, this display belied television's value as a tool for scientific investigation, and especially for education, but all the same, it made for the most fascinating spectacle.[2]

And I recall something along the same lines from a visit to the observatory, in which we saw the moon "live," enlarged with a telescope. There was, of course, no perceptible difference between this image and the simple broadcast of a photograph, but we knew that we were looking at the same moon that we could have seen, at that very instant, through the window. This knowledge alone was enough to change the quality of the image. Nothing but the moon, but—dare I say it?—live!

THE SOCIOLOGY OF TELEVISION

In last week's column, "Television as Cultural Medium," when mentioning the live broadcast of a bronchoscopy I said that it "belied television's value as a tool for scientific investigation." Of course this should have read "demonstrated" rather than "belied" [*démontrer* instead of *démentir*].

Now, with regard to that article, my colleague Joffre Dumazedier sent me the *Bulletin de la Société Française de Pédagogie* (issue 113), which features the lecture he gave on April 28, 1954, on the pedagogical prospects of tele-clubs.[3] To anyone interested in the sociological and cultural consequences of television, I cannot recommend this article highly enough. From that piece, I have lifted the following passage:

> M. Cassirer, head of television for UNESCO, announced that today there are about 35 million television sets in the U.S. In England, the number surpasses 4 million. In France, we have around

200,000. Some consider 200,000 to be a small portion, relative to our population of 43 million inhabitants, and so they see television as only a pastime for the wealthy. Things are not so simple. A survey concerning radio and television carried out in 1954 by an official weekly publication showed that more than 50 percent of television owners are skilled workers, foremen, employees, or craftsmen. Or take another example, which represents only one specific case, but a significant one: in a mining town near Lens, comprising 1,000 households, I counted more than 200 television sets—which means that, at this point, the phenomenon of television has a working-class [*populaire*] dimension.

We should not draw mistaken conclusions from the statistic of 200,000. The growth curve of this phenomenon presents the same characteristics nearly everywhere. There is an initial phase in which the buyer hesitates. Then comes the moment when the newly affluent middle classes are the ones buying the sets. Finally, in the third phase, sales rates increase abruptly and reach working-class locales. Thus the phenomenon extends to all sectors of the nation. There is only one category that continues to put up resistance—always the last holdouts—namely, the intellectuals. They had the same attitude with regard to radio and cinema.

To support Joffre Dumazedier's claims, and in light of developments since April 1954 (we now have around 280,000 sets in France), here are some recent statistics from the RTF:

Who Is Buying Television Sets?

Employees and officials: 29%

Specialized workers: 28%

Subtotal: 57%

Shopkeepers and manufacturers: 11%

Executives: 11%

Professionals: 7%

Female professions: 7%

Other: 7%

Total: 100%

NOTES

From "La Télévision: Moyen de culture," *France-Observateur* 297 (19 January 1956), and "Sociologie de la télévision," *France-Observateur* 298 (26 January 1956).

1. Jean Painlevé (1902–1989), son of the famed mathematician and French prime minister, grew up in an anarchist milieu and was close to surrealism in its first years. Studying biology, he made some two hundred films from 1927 on, many of them on underwater fauna. Entertaining and pedagogical, they impressed Bazin, who wrote an essay on Painlevé. Painlevé began experiments using television after the war.

2. Bazin will retract the word "belied" in "The Sociology of Television," below.

3. Joffre Dumazedier (1915–2002) was a French sociologist of strong Marxist leanings who founded Peuple et Culture in 1945. Bazin worked through that organization and certainly knew him well. In 1954 Dumazedier founded an international group for the study of leisure. In 1955 he co-authored *Télévision et éducation populaire,* as well as a UNESCO book in English on TV and rural education. Many other books would follow, especially *Vers une civilization du loisir?* (Editions de Seuil, 1962).

24

Do We Really Need Those Serials?

It seems that TV cannot do without the serial. All the opinion polls and all the fan mail from viewers prove this. But must the public be obeyed on this matter? What good does it do for the state to refuse to authorize private networks if its own channel proposes the same programming?

You will doubtless ask, by what right do I presume to appoint myself censor of the majority and criticize the appetite for daily serials that a huge number of TV viewers share? I have no such right, I admit—except that of a certain good sense. Everybody knows that the popularity of the serial is based on how it intoxicates the imagination. It does so by creating a need that arises from frustration: the interrupted story. Of course this method turned out well for Scheherazade, thanks to whom we have *One Thousand and One Nights*. So it is not the method itself that is condemnable: [to see the problem] you have to bring in genre and subject matter.

While I agree that the serial can serve literature (Balzac himself...), it poses an additional danger on TV. Do we not reproach the small screen for its power to fascinate? The psychological problem, then, is not so much to attract spectators by automatizing their daily habits, but rather to liberate them from their fixations so as to turn them into receptive and lucid viewers, people who choose the programs they watch at convenient times. Must we add the risks of habit and reflex to the enslavement already inherent with TV? The smoker's tobacco already makes him a slave of pleasure; must we blend it with some opiate that turns him into an addict who, at set hours, feels an uncontrollable need for his drug?

These are awfully big words for a small vice, you will say. Do the dreadful Westerns that are sliced up at the hands of French TV deserve to be compared to narcotics of the mind? I would acknowledge that this comparison would work in their favor if their targeted victims weren't children. You can quarrel with my earlier argument, but only insofar as it doesn't concern children. Everyone is in agreement that in their case, TV poses a problem of household psychology, indeed of psychology period. Most serious is not so much the serial in itself as the fact that it is addressed foremost to children, just by the choice of films shown.

But here again the vice might be balanced by the quality of the show. And since we're dealing with habits, so much the better if the habits in question are good ones! God knows that I have nothing against the Western and even less against animals! But *Brave Eagle* and *Rin-Tin-Tin* truly represent the worst types of the genres they "illustrate."[1] The silly and jingoist moralism of these wretched Z-series productions brings no naïve charm in compensation. This category of American films possesses all the defects of Hollywood without any of its better qualities. They confuse the spirit of childhood with sociological cretinism.

I might forgive TV for complicating my family life by magnetizing my son's powers of attention at set hours, if I weren't ashamed of the thing that holds the attention it has so violently conscripted. Do we really need serials? I would say not, even were I to go against Gallup himself. But if they are forced on us, then let's pray they do not contribute to the moronic state of our offspring.

NOTES

From "Faut-il des feuilletons à la T.V.? Intoxication et crétinisme," *Radio-Cinéma-Télévision* 430 (13 April 1958).

1. *Brave Eagle* was a CBS series that aired in 1955 and 1956 and featured a Native American protagonist. *The Adventures of Rin-Tin-Tin* was an ABC serial of over 150 episodes broadcast from 1954 to 1959.

25

A Superb Clown Made Incoherent by TV

On Sunday evening, July 29, the RTF presented the most absurd program imaginable—absurd not in its subject, but in its treatment. This was a reportage about an extraordinary and extravagant individual: Professor Cincinnatus Malladoli, resident of St-Pierre-la-Garenne, in the department of the Eure. An heir to Baron Münchausen and Paul Léautaud, this incredible eighty-seven-year-old character owns a castle yet lives in a trailer.[1] The castle in fact is occupied by his animals (horses, deer, and llamas), whose training is the principle occupation of this curious man. He has furnished his home à la Pitilliatas: that is, with rod puppets whose invention and circulation date back, if I understand correctly, to the period of his childhood.[2] Moreover, the professor makes categorical judgments about his fellow clowns that he keeps perfectly up to date in a card file; he characterizes these individuals as "hot air stoves"[les fourneaux]. In the universe of Cincinnatus Malladoli, "hot air stoves" are the equivalent of Jean-Paul Sartre's "bastards." They are characterized by idiocy as well as bad faith in business. The professor's destiny thus depends on his vigilant and fastidious monitoring of these "hot air stoves," in order to keep them out of his commerce, in both senses of that word.

And finally, Cincinnatus Malladoli is an ingenious inventor. Notably, he engineered a hippomobile, which is a kind of truck where the horse, positioned *inside* on an inclined plane, sets the wheels of the vehicle in motion, like a hamster in the cage it turns. The obvious advantage of this machine is that it goes faster the heavier its load of "live weight." Professor Malladoli presents such creations in a travelling circus that gives only charity performances.

I must now confess that I owe my knowledge of Professor Malladoli more to the excellent presentation of the weekly news bulletin [intended for the press] than to François Gir's show, whose aim seems to be to sidestep its subject.[3] Without such extra information I doubt the average TV viewer could have understood what the program was about. This was, first, because the host, Claude Darget, outdid himself in offhand insolence, usually talking while saying nothing, at the expense of the program's hero, who was treated with the same superficial impertinence Darget gives zoology in *La Vie des animaux*. Let me add that as a spectator, nothing has been more annoying to me than forcibly being made complicit with Claude Darget's heavy irony, for which the unfortunate old man unknowingly paid the price. But in any case, I don't believe that another host could have salvaged this report, whose two main handicaps lay in its brevity and its live transmission.

A half hour would have been plenty to present the subject if it had involved lots of prerecorded material from an extensive film shoot, where editing would make it possible to select the most significant shots and turn them into a logical, workable presentation. But inherent difficulties in live broadcasting entail inevitable waste in the most favorable cases; so we can imagine that a thirty-minute program on the small screen might contain scarcely fifteen useable minutes. And in reality, I think we were left with no more than ten. If they really are unable to give an hour to François Gir, or assign him a commentator tasked with explaining the image instead of diverting us, why don't they proceed with a filmed reportage, or at the very least with a combination of live and recorded footage? *Ciné-Panorama,* for example, has demonstrated that a pre-filmed report can be just as vibrant as live shooting, and I do not see what the latter adds to the subject here. We have seen, alas! what it takes away, which is to say: precision, time, and intelligibility.

Too bad! I would have very much liked to know Professor Cincinnatus Malladoli.

NOTES

Originally published as "Le Professeur Cincinnatus Malladoli ... dont la T.V. a fait un clown incompréhensible," *Radio-Cinéma-Télévision* 34 (12 August 1956).

1. Baron Münchhausen was an eighteenth-century figure so notorious for fabricating extravagant tales that his name is synonymous with the outrageous. Paul Léautaud was a well known and acerbic French theater critic who died the year Bazin's article appeared.

2. Chapiteau Pitilliata was a popular circus from the first half of the twentieth century.

3. François Gir (1920–2003) was Sacha Guitry's principle assistant director after World War II. He also worked on and acted in Jean-Pierre Melville's *Bob le flambeur* (1956). From 1954 on, he directed many television shows.

26

TV Can Popularize without Boredom or Betrayal

I have always believed that television's wonderful technology should leave no viewer cold, and that a series initiating the viewer into the mysteries of the medium would be riveting. Now it's true that raising technological issues involving television might appear to be almost insurmountably difficult; on the other hand, nothing of value can be achieved by attempting to sidestep them. So we must pay homage right away to the creators of the show *Toute la télévision* [All of television] for having had the courage to grapple with such problems honestly. The results thus far have been uneven though convincing. We can draw some useful lessons from this program about what the popularization of television could be like.

Let me start by hailing the dazzling success of the second program in the series, where Etienne Lalou and Catherine explained how a television show is produced in all its aspects from A to Z.[1] The mise-en-scène was especially effective and intelligently planned, allowing us to see the entire arrangement with perfect clarity. Moreover, this mise-en-scène was strikingly idiosyncratic since it had no object other than … itself. Igor Bar-rère staged the analysis of his own mise-en-scène, cameras were aimed at one another, and the technicians responded to Etienne Lalou's questions while carrying out the work that illustrated their responses. All this was utterly fascinating; what could be more dramatic than the live broadcast of a live broadcast, a kind of game of mirrors—a single one of which, if broken, would have virtually shattered all the others!

On the other hand, the first episode, dedicated to electronics and camerawork, was a failure—especially, in my opinion, because they were afraid to really analyze the question. This was a mistake. First of all, the miracle of broadcasting and of the genesis of the TV image seems fascinating a priori. It's true that it would be impossible to account for these miracles without dis-cussing their technology. But if they were afraid to do so, what was the point of making such a program at all? Their mistake lay in the belief that sheepish and incomprehensible explana-tions are less boring than more complete ones that dare to con-front complexity.

The last installment—devoted to the system of transmission and the European network—was, by contrast, meticulously complete. All the major problems were addressed seriously and with clarity. It was interesting, yet dull. Something was missing.

THE DIRECTOR'S TASK: "RETHINKING" HIS PROGRAM

Using the example of this one success bookended by two half failures, I think we can take away the following lesson: intelli-gent popularization is possible on television as it is elsewhere. The true path lies in a pedagogy of the visual, which knows how to simplify problems without distorting them and which displays them in a lively, unexpected, and dramatic way. This doesn't happen when one limits oneself to interviewing the various section heads about their specific departments. The task of the director is to rethink the subject of his program from top to bottom and to deliver it organized in a psychological hierarchy. It has to surprise, interest, and hold the attention of the spectator. These simple truths are applicable to all so-called "serious" programs that offer to popularize a specialized field of art or technology.

NOTES

From "Toute la télévision: Vulgariser sans ennuyer, ni trahir," *Radio-Cinéma-Télévision* 214 (21 February 1954).

1. Catherine Langeais was one of the principle *speakerines* in early French television, discussed by Bazin in chap. 18. See the appendix for Etienne Lalou and Igor Barrère.

PART FOUR

Television and Cinema

27

Television and the Revival of Cinema

Reflections on telecinema really should be subdivided into many series of problems, certain of which have in common only the use of actual celluloid.[1] That's why I will immediately eliminate the category of the televised newsreel, which I treated in my article on reportage, since I consider it an asymptote of live coverage.[2] On the other hand, the use of pre-filmed sequences within live dramatic programs already poses an aesthetic problem. If my hypothesis about tele-theater was right, this new hybrid form just mentioned seems closer to theater than to cinema.[3] The feeling of "liveness," equivalent to that of "presence," risks being compromised by the intrusion of film. I have neither the ambition nor the time to supply a proper response to this question. I will only say that the interpolation of filmed sequences is certainly legitimate, but that there are, if not formal proscriptions, at least certain counter-indications as well as certain optimal indications for its use.

I have been able to note in the course of watching quite a few dramatic programs that doubts dealing with recorded material create a particular unease when the filmed sequence is there to exteriorize the action—let's say, when the director uses the cinema to transport his characters into an exterior décor or somewhere incompatible with the TV studio. Here the filmed portion (telecinema) feels like a kind of trick or special effect that the director uses to avoid the conditions of tele-theater.

Still, this process troubles me less when the filmed natural décor is at least contiguous to what's happening live. For example, in the midst of a detective play, whose title unfortunately escapes me, Marcel Cravenne allowed his characters to move from the interior of a wharf-side bar to a barge fifty meters away. Their movement to and fro on a real barge on a canal had certainly been filmed earlier, but beyond the fact that this was merely a transition, the dramatic space, far from being destroyed, was actually rendered clearer and more coherent—even more lifelike—by such a cinematic hyphen. This effect would have been very different and less felicitous if the action had been divided further into a third dramatic space, for example the inspector's office at the PJ.[4]

Another especially apt use of telecinema consists in employing it for action sequences, whether these are meant to take place in the past or in the imagination. The ontological unhinging (if I can use the term) of the live-image and the image-image is implied in the very nature of the one and the other. So far we've only addressed a secondary use of cinema as an accessory. Let's look now at how it is used for itself.

Right away we naturally have the pure and simple retransmission of feature films that were not produced for television. You might think that the problem here is identical to that of broadcasting music from records on the radio, where a work is not appreciably modified by being technologically disseminated. Let me note, however, that the quality of the small electronic image in relation to the large cinematographic one is far from having attained the technical fidelity that phonographic microgrooves give to sound. What's more, these very technological limitations of TV are the basis of Hollywood's counteroffensive: CinemaScope.

Despite such drawbacks, the popularity of programs that retransmit films is immense, and it is useless to hide the fact that only economic disputes between television and film distributors have kept this from becoming a norm. What's the reason? Probably the fact that no matter how mediocre from an artistic perspective, a film in a movie theater constitutes a spectacle that is technologically far more elaborate and consistent than what can be staged on TV because of the latter's much lower budgets. This consistency at the material level corresponds to a mental reality.

A film is an oneiric system, an imaginary microcosm, whose force of gravitation—which I keep repeating, is independent of its artistic quality—works more powerfully on the imagination than pure television. To television's capacity of distraction, any movie shown on TV adds cinema's capacity for escapism. This capacity, though reduced on a small screen, is brought into the home. And is it reduced? Yes, in general, but I have said that some films benefit, if not from simply being viewed on TV, then from being re-viewed. I must not try to explain why today, but it's a fact I've verified many times over. You should add to the pluses of rebroadcasting films the following fortuitous but real advantage (at least to all cinephiles): thanks as much to the reluctance of distributors as to the scale of its viewership, television is obliged to rummage through stocks of old movies that have hardly any commercial value. While these films are often quite bad, you can find among them a few masterpieces as well as some quite interesting movies that have become practically invisible in the commercial circuit. I would call TV an "unwitting cinematheque." Actually not as unwitting as all that, not since Frederic Rossif has been responsible for programming. Unfortunately these old assets are beginning to be exhausted, and evidently we have gone through the best films first.

FILMS PLAY ON AMERICAN TELEVISION

All the same, we know that the commercial battle between television and cinema is starting to become outdated, at least in America, but since the United States is a leader on this issue, we must plan in accordance with what happens there, where this conflict has been most acute. Today we are no longer in a cooling off period but in one of collaboration. The problem of the retransmission of commercial films is certainly not going to be completely resolved despite the sale of RKO's collection by Howard Hughes. There will be a solution only if, in one manner or another, costs are paid, film by film, at the point of reception. Although we shouldn't dismiss this solution outright (in fact everyone is talking about it again just now), this isn't the direction that has been adopted; moreover, it would stand opposed to Hollywood's artistic politics, which wants to impose color and widescreen.

On the other hand, in America television is just now offering a second chance to the film industry by ordering up a huge quantity of movies thirty to ninety minutes long that are being shot by a number of Hollywood directors and with current or former stars. Robert Florey's quite interesting study goes into detail about this new situation created by television for Hollywood technicians who are often threatened with unemployment or underemployment.[5] A good many films have already been made for the television networks by directors like Hitchcock, John Ford, Capra, Leo McCarey, and so on.

Of course Robert Florey realizes that many of these films are not expensive (dear) in both senses of that word [*cher*]. But he lets us understand that thanks to their meager budgets and the rapidity of production, these films let those who love their craft rediscover the freedom of inspiration that characterized Hollywood's earlier heroic era. A thirty-minute film made under these conditions (two or three days of preparation, then the same number of days for shooting) costs only $25,000. A ninety-minute film, then, would probably come in for less than $100,000. Converted to francs and taking account of the cost differences between France and the United States, you could estimate these TV features at something under twenty million francs, which is five to six times less costly than the cheapest French commercial film.

Unfortunately we're unable to see any of the TV films Robert Florey writes about. For my part, about two years ago I was able to see some short police procedurals commissioned by American TV but shot here in France. The limitations that the scenarios and the technology placed on the directors (men of some genuine talent, whose names I'm withholding) must have been the cause of their mediocrity. However, to read Robert Florey is to believe that the situation has changed.

OUR BEST DIRECTORS COULD USE TELEVISION

In France two or three years ago we glimpsed some encouraging possibilities that move in the direction of Robert Florey's account—specifically, in a children's TV series made by Serge Grave in 16 mm.[6] Their inspiration, truth be told, is quickly used up, and you can reproach Serge Grave for returning to the police suspense genre. But, all things considered, you can find in these films something of the charm of Feuillade.[7] It would be perfectly legitimate for this genre, based on a wealth of improvisation, and on the speed of shooting, to recover its youth via television.

In any case, the least one can say is that the attempt has yet to be made under optimal conditions. It is certainly not by, say, handing over the direction of *Madame Bovary* to Jacques Chabannes that one will open new pathways. But why don't our major directors, so often underemployed, accept the chance, if it is offered, to "amuse themselves" like Hitchcock or King Vidor by making (in eight days and in the spirit of 16mm) one of the many scenarios that might please them and that they'd never get a chance to make for a large commercial project. They would need, it's true, a certain kind of courage and youthful spirit, which I don't want to believe our directors have less of than their American counterparts. In any case, they haven't been tested. What is holding things up? The artistic future not only of television, but also perhaps of cinema now has a chance to rediscover some new sap and vitality through grafting a wilder, younger bough onto a venerable stump.

It would indeed be naïve and not dialectical to believe that the influence plays only one way … Television has launched cinema in its widescreen venture, but at the same time, TV rehabituates film audiences to stripped-down spectacles without any elaborate technique, whose attraction comes only from the interest of its subject matter and the intelligence of the auteur.

This can certainly produce disappointing results, as with *Marty,* but also better ones, like *Blackboard Jungle.* And why not even attribute, for example, the relative box office failure of Rossellini's recent films to their being ahead of their time? As Jacques Rivette said so well, in the swift precision of Rossellini's style, one finds something that belongs to television. Yes, the little screen proposes to revive the cinema.[8]

NOTES

From "La Télévision et la relance du cinéma," *France-Observateur* 311 (26 April 1956).

1. The portmanteau term "telecinema" is more frequent in French than English. The first paragraph of this essay delimits what Bazin includes in the category. In its first few years the journal he founded, *Cahiers du Cinéma,* carried the following on its yellow cover each month: "Revue du cinéma et du télécinéma."

2. See chap. 3.

3. Bazin's ideas about dramas enacted on TV can be found, for example, in chap. 13.

4. PJ is an acronym for the *police judiciaire,* charged with interrogating subjects accused of crimes.

5. Robert Florey (1900–1979) began working in films with Louis Feuillade as a teenager in France before moving to the United States in 1921, where he assisted Josef von Sternberg, among others. He became a sure-handed director of low-budget horror features, many quite good and well known. He also wrote about cinema for periodicals and kept the French up to date with the latest happenings in Hollywood.

6. Serge Grave (1919–1995) was a child actor who starred in Sacha Guitry's *Roman d'un tricheur,* among many other films. His adult career sputtered around 1950; perhaps this is when he began making his 16 mm films for children.

7. Louis Feuillade (1873–1925) directed hundreds of films for Gaumont, including a number of world-renowned serials, beginning with

Fantomas, Les Vampires, and *Judex.* He is seen as the great director of narrative film in its age of innocence.

8. In fact, Rivette's important proclamation "There is a television aesthetic" he claims to have learned from Bazin. See his "Letter on Rossellini," in Jim Hillier, ed., *Cahiers du Cinéma: The 1950s* (Cambridge, MA: Harvard University Press, 1985), 197–198.

28

Television and Cinema

In my last article on television and cinema, I put aside for the moment the case of certain shows made up of cinematic montages, as these pose several distinctive problems.[1] I made reference to several TV series that differ greatly in terms of quality and in the way each of them deploys cinematic material. It seems to me, however, that they have enough features in common, at least in their basic principles, to be studied together. They include, in particular, Frédéric Rossif's *La Vie des animaux, Editions spéciales* by Rossif and François Chalais, Marcel L'Herbier's *Du côté des grands hommes* [Among the great men], and even, in a pinch, *La Séquence du spectateur* [The spectator's sequence] and *A vous de juger* [You be the judge].

Their common denominator lies, first and foremost, in the fact that these programs are made up of fragments from preexisting films, selected and organized to the director's liking. The latter might make his selections and edit them according to some documentary theme, as in *La Vie des animaux;* a documentary argument, as in the installment of *Editions spéciales* on the atomic era or alcoholism; or without any preconceived idea and somewhat at the mercy of circumstance, in the case of *La Séquence du spectateur* and *A vous de juger.* In any case, the films from which the programs are composed are treated as raw material in the service of television.

There is no reason to hide the fact that creation of these montage-based programs is entirely the result of practical contingencies. First, there is the difficulty of acquiring relatively recent commercial films to be broadcast in their entirety on television. In addition to the reservations of many distributors, under pressure from exhibitors, the rental fees charged tend to be very costly. I have noted before that in America a modus vivendi seems to have been found, but only because the private networks are in a position to offer outlandish sums of money thanks to their advertising contracts (General Motors recently paid $500,000 for a sneak-preview broadcast of Laurence Olivier's *Richard III*).

Receipts of that order effectively represent the equivalent of a theatrical run lasting several months. In any case, television's need is so great that the usable stock of cinematic material might exhaust itself too quickly. Needless to say, programs comprised of film clips open up prospects of combinations that are theoretically inexhaustible. For these two main reasons—the one economic, the other practical—ideas for programs built on the use of film clips should of course be given top priority, with those in charge of programming favoring them. We shouldn't regret this even if we must nonetheless express some reservations.

The compilation film is an entirely legitimate genre when it makes use of what is essentially raw documentation—footage of current events, for example. But once the montage is completed, the result is no longer "raw." It has acquired a logical, rhetorical, and aesthetic unity that if broken does damage to the whole. Take, for example, Capra's famous series, *Why We Fight*. Each of these seven films is a work made up of raw footage, but can we imagine the existence of an eighth film that would be a montage in the second degree, made up of clips from each of the original seven? You see how absurd and contradictory this suggestion is. So what are we to think, then, when faced with fiction films where each shot, completely constructed, is tightly connected to all the others purely by virtue of its very nature as an imaginary creation?

A GOOD CINEMATIC ANTHOLOGY

Of course, in literature we recognize and readily accept the practice of "selected fragments" and of citation, but not of something that would involve producing a novel out of a skillfully composed mosaic of pages, paragraphs, or sentences, for instance, from Stendhal, from Balzac, from Flaubert, from Zola, from Eugène Fromentin, from Colette, and so on.

Having identified the dangers and limitations of the process, I would say that its justification in practice comes down to moderation, skill, tact, and also intellectual loyalty. Certain of these programs, taking all kinds of liberties with regard to subject matter, have demonstrated a sense of cinematic quality that largely makes up for their authors' sloppiness. I am thinking in particular of the *Editions spéciales* by Rossif and Chalais. In addition to the educational value with regard to the chosen subjects (the denunciation of alcoholism, for example), it constitutes a brilliant cinematic anthology, and we congratulate its authors for having known how to assembled it. On the other hand, I confess that I was rather bothered by Rossif's ingenious series *La Vie des animaux,* constructed out of numerous documentaries that treat this theme; it is true that Claude Darget's exasperating and incompetent voice-over didn't help matters. But the formula has revealed itself to be virtually inexhaustible.

It would of course be ridiculous to overdramatize the matter. Practiced with skill by people who know and love the cinema, the method can avoid degenerating into scandalous thievery, even when the works being plundered are of minor quality. Nevertheless, it seems to me that a certain critical vigilance is required if we do not want to see this second-degree cinema turn to tinkering, pure and simple! Beyond these transitional formulas, the solution for the future will always rest in the production of films specifically made for television.

NOTES

From "Télévision et cinéma," *France-Observateur* 316 (31 May 1956).
1. See chap. 27.

29

Is Television a Degradation for Filmmakers?

I recently read a blurb in the press that Claude Barma is shooting *Casino de Paris* in Germany. It even adds that "he is the first director to abandon TV for genuine cinema." Then I heard that Stellio Lorenzi has projects under way along the same lines. Meanwhile I learned that French TV is in talks to broadcast the films that Alfred Hitchcock has directed for American TV. Is not the coming together of these news items significant? Indeed, everyone knows that American TV is hiring the biggest names in Hollywood. Hitchcock already noted, but also Capra, John Ford, Mack Sennett, Leo McCarey, King Vidor, and others. Furthermore, this has come about largely due to the modus vivendi that has established itself between cinema and television.

In France, it has been completely different, and remains so. The techniques of directing for TV have been gradually developed by young men who no doubt had a bit of experience (often as assistants) in theater or cinema, but whose principal asset lay in the talent and the budgets they were given. They have learned their new craft practically by inventing it. Perish the thought of criticizing this method, the advantages of which are quite evident. I only want to note that in France, moving up in the directorial craft seems to go from TV to cinema. A young man would assuredly prefer to direct for TV rather than being first or second assistant in cinema, but a film remains more or less his ideal. The mirror image of this situation is clearly seen in the fact that not a single great film director has made anything at all for TV. If things were the same in France as in America, we would be watching TV programs directed by Jacques Becker, Marcel Carné, Robert Bresson, Jacques Tati, René Clément, René Clair. (Yes, there's Marcel L'Herbier, but he's the exception that proves the rule.)[1]

There's surely no need to hide the obvious material reason for this state of affairs. In Europe, cinema pays much better, while in America, the financial standing of a director goes up when TV offers him a contract. While this may be the main reason, it is perhaps not the profoundest. Some established film director might well find himself getting interested in TV for the fun of it or to gain additional experience, if he didn't have the more or less conscious impression of declining or of wasting his time.

Is there a basis for this prejudice? The American experience seems to prove the opposite. The speed of execution of these TV films and their reduced budgets do not have to be negative constraints. On the contrary, the director can paradoxically use these to rediscover a greater freedom of working methods and a rekindling of inspiration that too often is lost in "genuine cinema."

NOTES

From "La Télévision est-elle une déchéance pour les cinéastes?" *Radio-Cinéma-Télévision* 387 (16 June 1957).

1. Of these seven film directors, all of them highly prominent in the history of French cinema, only Marcel L'Herbier turned to television, and he did so decisively in 1953, working only in that medium thereafter.

30

Some Films Are Better on the Small Screen Than the Large

It will take a few days to draw a conclusion from the experiments that comprise the current form of telecinema. I was thinking about this the other night while watching *La Petite Marchande d'allumettes* [*The Little Match Girl*] for the first time on the small screen. I had already seen this film, directed by Jean Renoir in 1927, three or four times, but I discovered that on TV it came off very successfully.

I think I can understand at least one of the reasons for this. Some feelings do not resonate well with the vague publicity of the darkened theater, nor with the superhuman dimensions of the movie screen, and we'll come back to this. But in the specific case of *La Petite Marchande d'allumettes,* in reducing the image to the scale of the small easel painting, television restores its true proportions—that of the canvas of Auguste Renoir—and at the same time reveals the purely pictorial balance of Renoir's direction. The dissonance between the story's sentiments and the symbolism of the objects, like that between Catherine Hessling's acting and the expressionism of the special effects, fades and disappears: form and inspiration are perfectly merged. I cried at the death of Hans Christian Andersen's little heroine.

This particular success of telecinema reminds me of another instance: the broadcast of *Les Parents terribles* by Jean Cocteau.[1] This time, by a strange paradox, and thanks to a double refraction through the cinema *and* through television, the original play finds itself restored to its hideous intimacy. While the phenomenon was not so much a sensory experience as a psychological one, the technical effects of the direction were never hurt by the smallness of the screen; on the contrary, the restricted screen reinforced instead the casual familiarity yet implacable perceptiveness of the camera with the characters. This is because in cinema, proximity is felt via the enormity of the faces or objects, while television restores it nearly to its actual dimensions.

But the fact is that some films "gain" from telecinema while others (alas, more numerous!) lose nearly everything; this ought to concern film directors, who tomorrow may perhaps start working either specifically, or *also,* for television. This would free us of the prejudiced stupidity by which a film for TV is simply more elementary in subject and framed in such a way that the faces remain in the central zone of the screen and never beyond the American shot. But before reaching this point, French television must first accept telefilms seriously from the straightforward angle of broadcasting. The image is almost always of an insufficient crispness, and in very poor contrast. As for 16mm, it's usually a catastrophe. I admit that the visual tone of the copies isn't always ideal, which is yet another reason you need to monitor the contrast during the course of broadcasts, and to rectify this each time there is a need. Just setting the contrast once and for all at the beginning of the film is insufficient.

But I have also heard talk from various sides that the equipment used for telecinema is outdated and ready for retirement. Is it true, for example, that the current lenses are not even tinted blue?[2] And yet it is precisely because telecinema constitutes a significant economic portion of programming that we need to give it special care, renovating the equipment and entrusting it to competent personnel. This way, we might envisage recorded programs taking the place of live broadcast without feeling a sense of horror.

NOTES

From "Certains films sont meilleurs au técinéma qu'au cinéma," *Radio-Cinéma-Télévision* 218 (21 March 1954).

1. Cocteau adapted his fabulously successful 1937 play into a film in 1948, which Bazin found very important. See his "Theater and Cinema" in *What Is Cinema?* (Berkeley: University of California Press, 2004 [1968]).

2. Applying a thin blue coat to a lens reduces the amount of light that the glass tends to reflect back toward its source. This also reduces potential flaring. Invented during World War II, this process became standard by the 1950s.

31

Should Television Be Allowed to Chop Films to Pieces?

Television seems to be making increasingly frequent use of selected cinematic fragments, and for a variety of purposes. You can already list three regular programs: *Au Royaume des images* [In the realm of images], *A vous de juger*, and *La Séquence du spectateur* (which was just given two program slots), not to mention miniseries like the three programs that Frédéric Rossif recently devoted to the work of Marcel Pagnol. Such proliferation is beginning to pose problems that perhaps deserve mention.

The use of film fragments offers television several obvious benefits. First, it makes it possible to put together a cinematic display when the entire film would be inaccessible. This is the case with *A vous de juger*, the excellent weekly current affairs program in which Jean L'Hôte presents clips from new films that are just coming out in Paris. After initially sinning through excessive ambition, this program now makes the best of its limited resources thanks to the witty commentary of F. Chalais.

Exploiting the same practice, and drawing on a stock of films amassed over fifty years, original broadcasts can be organized whose thrust is different from that of any of the works involved. Frédéric Rossif nearly went too far along these lines with his montages for *La Vie des animaux*. He borrowed clips from a variety of major documentaries but neglected to cite his sources, at least on the first installment. Accompanied by a carefully scripted narration, the compilation was presented as a totally new film. Here we reach the limits of what this practice should permit. Relations between cinema and television are already complicated enough without aggravating them with ruses that come close to aesthetic fraud.

In the ciné-clubs we have always dreamed, usually in vain, of being able to put on an evening of fragments of films where the logical connection between analogous subjects or styles would illuminate some aspect of the works or some artistic problem of the cinema in general. In fact, this effort is virtually forbidden to ciné-clubs because of the prohibitive costs that it entails. These same costs are, however, relatively minimal for television. In this spirit, Frédéric Rossif was quite successful with a montage on *La Musique de film* that had an excellent voice-over commentary. On the other hand, recently he entirely missed the mark with his series on Marcel Pagnol. The reasons for this failure are clear and instructive. First, he should be reproached for relying far too much and offensively on brief fragments where much longer clips, in the absence of the entire work, were called for. Breaking down Pagnol's films into three centers of interest (Giono, Raimu, and "the World of Marcel Pagnol") seems a bit arbitrary, especially inasmuch as the commentary made no effort to justify these categories.[1] Then there was a certain sadism in showing a tiny fragment of the same film in each of the episodes instead of a single clip, three times as long, in one of them. All the same, we should never lose sight of the fact that the practice of making an anthology from fragments is an unnatural mutilation and demands serious justification. We would have learned more about Pagnol through the unabridged projection of three or four of his films. Bringing these fragments together does not give rise to any new critical idea that could not be deduced from the entire body of work.

Dedicated as it is to the history of cinema, *Au Royaume des images,* in contrast, constitutes the type of show where fragments are essential. Why did it have to happen that René Jeanne and Charles Ford made such poor use of them?[2] It is shocking that these expert film historians invariably selected extremely dubious samples whose banality rivals their inadequacy. I realize that the choices are limited and depend on which films are available outside the Cinémathèque. But then why not at least have attempted to fill in the gaps with photographic documents, or straighten out the confusing perspectives with the narration? Here again, the fragmentation of artworks is more or less useless if their juxtaposition may give rise not just to irritation but to error.

Obviously, film fragments constitute cinema only in an incomplete state, and so they call for supplementary information. It is shocking that these shows, which specifically purport to be didactic, fail to provide it. In its modest way *La Séquence du spectateur* offers a lesson for everyone. Viewers write in to request this or that sequence that they would like to see again. Although this method may be highly unreliable, the show so far has managed to avoid most pitfalls. The kind of voyage through cinematic time and space that Claude Mionnet offers us each week is not unpleasant. He has the good sense to work up an introduction and simple summary for each film, and he takes particular care to edit his sequences so that they conclude, every time, on a natural dramatic moment. This way he usually avoids the frustration we can feel when fragments are edited with neither care nor taste.

A few elementary rules are already emerging thanks to these different programs: to only use fragments that do justice to the films they come from; to resort to this only in cases of material necessity, or when putting well-chosen clips together casts each one of them in a new light; and finally, in all cases, to try to reduce the drawbacks of the practice to a minimum through careful editing and narration.

NOTES

From "A-t-on le droit à la télévision de couper les film en morceaux?" *Radio-Cinéma-Télévision* 208 (10 January 1954).

1. Jean Giono, the famous novelist, known for his return-to-the-earth and pacifist views, scripted a number of Pagnol's greatest films (*Joffroi, Angèle, Regain, La Femme du Boulanger*); Raimu ranked among France's, indeed the world's, most famous actors in the early years of sound, thanks largely to his starring roles in Pagnol's *Marius* trilogy, as well as in *La Femme du Boulanger* and *La Fille de puisatier.*

2. René Jeanne (1887–1969) and Charles Ford (d. 1989) were film historians who frequently worked in collaboration.

32

From Small Screen to Widescreen

Now that *A King in New York* has evidently marked the end of a series of important releases, we will no doubt go through a period of relative calm until the end-of-the-year holidays, allowing me to return to some films that I have regretfully neglected—two American productions, *The Bachelor Party* and *12 Angry Men*.[1] Both their content and their form justify putting these films side by side. Both illustrate in a particularly significant way the current renaissance of social realism in American cinema. More precisely, a renewed critical realism shines a cruel, sometimes implacable light upon the lifestyle of that country and upon the implicit morality that subtends it.

It is remarkable that most films with social themes belong to the same type of production. Shot in black and white and relatively cheaply, they are hardly spectacular. To draw an audience they count instead on the interest of their topics and on the truth of their sociological material. Technically, they could have just as well been filmed not only before CinemaScope, but in 1937.

In fact, they illustrate a curious phenomenon: the backdraft of television upon cinema. When Hollywood first had to confront massive competition from the small screen, producers thought they could do so by increasing spectacle, and thus leave television far behind. From this came experiments with 3D, with various large-screen formats, and with the ubiquitous use of color. Then, once the crisis had passed, a modus vivendi was instantiated between the small and large screen, and TV little by little came to appear not as cinema's number one enemy, but on the one hand as a kind of cheap outlet where young artists could experiment with their ideas and their skills, and on the other as a major modifier of public taste. It was certainly correct to presume that a public bored with too much TV would love to find, in contrast, a luxurious image at movie theaters, immense, clear, and colorful. Yet it was also true that having gotten used to seeing black and white programs every day at home—programs that, despite a cruder look, nevertheless treated immediate and familiar topics—this public should find it quite natural to look for such topics in movies without a lavish veneer, carried out in the spirit of television, yet with greater care. This assessment of television thus carries two contrary consequences for cinema. On the one hand, we have found a major rise in spectacular productions, but on the other, we've seen a genre of film that disdains visual luxury and elaborate mise-en-scène in favor of its subject matter, and above all, its value as social testimony.

Hence, we have *The Bachelor Party* and *12 Angry Men*. The first is directed by Delbert Mann and written by Paddy Chayefsky, already famous for *Marty,* which was another of his successes on TV before it triumphed as a film.[2] To my tastes, this new, second work is better than the first. *Marty* was perhaps more adroit, but also more sentimental and a trifle melodramatic. Its story, you will recall, concerns the problem of marriage between two timid and quite plain young people. *The Bachelor Party* takes up the same question "a posteriori," if I dare say so, revealing the financial and psychological worries of the middle-class American household. The least one can say is that conjugality hardly seems to be paradise. But I haven't space to analyze the multiple sociological lessons of this extremely rich film, brilliantly directed in a deceptively neutral manner.

Even more brilliant, as well as less spectacular, is the directorial accomplishment of another young transplant from TV, Sidney Lumet, and on a film produced by and starring Henry Fonda, *12 Angry Men*. The story is challenging since it takes place entirely in the confined space of a deliberation room of an American court. Twelve jurors are there to decide the fate of a young defendant whose guilt no one questions—no one except a single juror who enters "not guilty" in the initial round of voting. Everybody knows that the American judicial system requires unanimity. So the next ninety or one hundred minutes of the film will be dedicated to showing us, without ever leaving these few square meters, just how Henry Fonda, though alone at the start against the conviction of the rest, comes to shake the certitude of each juror and ultimately obtain twelve ballots exculpating the accused. You can imagine the resources of dramatic imagination and of psychological realism that went into keeping this film exciting from start to finish while never departing from its subject. Sidney Lumet brilliantly carries the day, and *12 Angry Men* deservedly won the Grand Prix at the Berlin Film Festival.

NOTES

From "Du Petit au grand écran," *Education nationale* 33 (28 November 1957).

1. *A King in New York*, directed by Charlie Chaplin, was released in Europe in the fall of 1957 but not in the United States until fifteen years later. *The Bachelor Party* (1957) was written by Paddy Chayevsky and directed by Delbert Man in a 1.85:1 format.

2. *Marty*, written by Paddy Chayevsky, directed by Delbert Man and starring Ernest Borgnine, took four Oscars in 1955.

33

Sacha Guitry Is Confident about TV, Just as He Was about Cinema in 1914

The last of Frédéric Rossif's three programs devoted to Sacha Guitry's films was one of the most fascinating he has ever mounted for the television screen; moreover, it constitutes a model of the combinations possible between television and cinema.[1] No doubt its interest comes first from the value of the documents presented. We know that Sacha Guitry, who by 1914 was already a pioneer of the "portrait films" that have been proliferating in recent years, had the brilliant idea of documenting some of his most glorious aging contemporaries: Rodin, Auguste Renoir, Edmond Rostand, Claude Monet, Saint-Saëns, Sarah Bernhardt. Today we recognize that these two or three hundred meters of film are priceless, that they constitute a kind of collector's item, of which only an attentive and exceptional use should be made. No doubt we could "duplicate" them, as Nicole Védrès did for several clips of her *Paris 1900*, but the photographic quality here is noticeably diminished, to say nothing of the emotion, the charm always associated with anything original.[2] Finally, these crude documents ought to be narrated, and who better for that than Sacha Guitry himself? In short, we see all that is unique in such a notion. Only television could bring this off, since it is assured of an audience (let's not say a "public") of 200,000 or 300,000 viewers, a number that would not justify the production of a film for commercial distribution, but that is appropriate to the scale of a more intimate, more "live" [*direct*] event like this, as a kind of illustrated conversation with viewers.

Sacha Guitry, obviously, took it no less seriously than did Frédéric Rossif. This grand man of the theater, who believed in the cinema in 1914, today puts his faith in television. Let us salute him! His abundant, polished commentary, perfectly in tune with the images and with the breaks between them, was evidence of that. With great intelligence, Sacha Guitry spoke from his "study," or rather from a set re-created in the studio with some original pieces that had adorned his actual workplace. Thus a certain intimacy was preserved that is one of the psychological fundaments of television.

And yet I will surprise many viewers when I say that the program was entirely prerecorded. From this I draw two conclusions.

1. That it is possible on television, as on the radio, for certain types of prerecorded programs to retain the characteristics of live shooting while eliminating its disadvantages. This depends on one condition that has not yet been perfectly achieved: that the image recorded on film not be noticeably inferior to the broadcast of a live image. On the radio the recorded voice is absolutely identical to the voice in a live broadcast.

2. Made by television and for television, this program, with only the slightest modifications, would constitute an excellent cinematic spectacle, and one can only eagerly hope that it will soon find a cinematic audience, once the original documents are reproduced. This wish does not contradict the beginning of my article,

for no doubt the success of the enterprise would require the opportunity and conditions afforded by television. With its clear success, the program now represents a well-developed sketch of a film, perhaps strange and unusual, but perfectly composed. The same phenomenon arose with Stellio Lorenzi's program about the Musée Rodin.[3] Television reminds cinema of something it has long forgotten: the advantages of semi-improvisation, of working off the cuff. Between television and cinema there can be more than mere collaboration; there can be genuine symbiosis. In not selfishly trying to take from cinema any more than may be useful to it, television could inject new lifeblood back into cinema.

NOTES

Originally published as "Sacha Guitry a fait confiance à la télévision comme il avait fait confiance au cinéma en 1914!" *Radio-Cinéma-Télévision* 156 (11 January 1953).

1. Sacha Guitry (1885–1957) was one of the most successful actor-playwrights in the history of French cinema and certainly of French television. Having written a couple of plays at a young age, he took up the camera and created in 1915 (not 1913, as Bazin would have it) *Ceux de chez nous* (Those who are ours), filmed portraits of a number of the most famous Frenchmen of the time. He would return to the cinema only after sound arrived, permitting his inimitable voice to dominate the many scripts he wrote and directed. He was a favorite of François Truffaut and other New Wave critics.

2. Bazin wrote an important article on *Paris 1900* (N. Védrès, 1947) that is available in the first volume of *Qu'est-ce que le cinéma?* (Paris: Editions du Cerf, 1959). *Paris 1900* is a compilation of film documents from the first decade of cinema.

3. See chap. 17.

34

Jean Gabin Gets TV's "Sour Lemon" Prize

For one in his series of roaming broadcasts, Stellio Lorenzi took us to visit the film studios at Boulogne-Billancourt last Saturday afternoon.[1] This was an excellent idea from the outset, enticing almost all viewers, since everyone in the world is curious about the backstage of the movies. Now for those a bit familiar with the actual work in a studio, this did not promise to be so simple an undertaking. There's a paradox (that would take too long to develop here) by which the universe of cinema is actually the least photogenic in the world. This is perhaps because the realism evident in a film requires an immense complexity of processes whose synthesis comes together only at the end, on screen. Whatever the case, Stellio Lorenzi seems to have anticipated the problems that would arise should the TV camera really try to meddle in the shooting of a film. So he very wisely hung around the antechambers, with the stage management, the workshop for the sets, and above all the dubbing auditorium, about which we TV viewers were treated to the most sensational reportage conceivable. Since the Orthicon camera is capable of capturing a scene even if it is in half-light, and since it can reproduce an image projected directly on a screen, we were able to be present—and without any special effect—during the dubbing of a musical scene in an American movie.

But ultimately we want to visit a film studio in order to watch something actually being shot, so Pierre Tchernia was obliged at last to decide to take us onto a sound stage. There he met Jean Gabin and Madeleine Robinson resting between two shots of a film by Georges Lacombe.[2] The few questions he tried to ask were met with incredible boorishness by Gabin, who, after feigning not to hear them, finally responded with insolence and ill will. I should say that Pierre Tchernia's submissive humility really pained me. A television reporter oughtn't feel like he's in the way when he is the delegate of 300,000 viewers; after all, it is his job to treat M. Gabin the way he deserves to be treated, that is, as someone whose occupation is to be appealing, and who shouldn't forget that he is paid exactly for that. If his annoyed insolence only proves that Gabin's intelligence isn't at the same level as his talent, this incident might pass as insignificant, but it stands as a symbol for the kind of welcome cinema seems ready to extend when television comes visiting.

NOTES

Originally published as "A Jean Gabin, le prix Citron de la Télévision," *Radio-Cinéma-Télévision* 160 (8 February 1953).

1. Many of France's and the world's most important films were made at the Boulogne-Billancourt studios, beginning with Gance's *Napoléon* and Dreyer's *La Passion de Jeanne d'Arc* and including Renoir's *La Grande Illusion* and Carné's *Hôtel du Nord*. Tati's *Les Vacances de Monsieur Hulot*

would have been in production there at the time Bazin wrote about this televised visit to the famed cinema site.

2. The film in question is *Leur Dernière nuit* (Their last night), which premiered in October 1953 starring Gabin and Robinson and directed by veteran Georges Lacombe.

35

"The Glass Eye" Will Reveal a New Hitchcock

Like several other seasoned Hollywood directors, for a few years Hitchcock has been doing more work for TV than for cinema. He has already produced several dozen short films for General Motors (each about a half hour long), for which he always selects the subject and supervises the mise-en-scène, sometimes personally serving as director. But even when he's not near the camera, these TV films definitely carry his mark, the famous "Hitchcock touch," which he knows perfectly well how to inject even though he is monitoring things from afar (as I noticed, for instance, when at the end of the production of *To Catch a Thief* the director—back in Hollywood—sent amazingly precise orders via telegram to the technicians in the south of France who were completing the shoot).

Whatever the case, we will have the chance to pass judgment with "The Glass Eye," a supernatural story in the vein of the ventriloquist sketch in *Dead of Night*.[1] The reader will forgive me for not disclosing anything more about the plot, so as not to spoil enjoyment of the film.

Although we're lagging behind other European networks, this programming of Hitchcock's TV-films gives us a chance to bring up or remind the reader of the important revolution taking place in America, where the production of films for TV has greatly surpassed the production of movies for the big screen. In Hollywood several studios owe their continued ability to pay expenses entirely to the TV productions that are being shot on their stages. Many of the larger studios from Hollywood's classical era have practically gone under or are on the road to complete conversion in partnership with TV firms. The trend of the public deserting movie theaters may have been momentarily stalled by Operation 3D, but it has begun again and is worse now than before. Theaters by the thousands have been transformed into bowling alleys, supermarkets, and parking garages.

Must we be alarmed by this evolution, covering our heads with ashes while we mourn the impending death of cinema? Nothing could be less certain. Surely we are witnessing a radical evolution of American cinema, at least as we have been accustomed to think of it for the last thirty years; but already, with films like *12 Angry Men* or *The Bachelor Party,* we have been able to observe that the backflow from TV to cinema has not been completely devastating or sterilizing. Of course, there will inevitably be a huge number of idiotic works among those films produced for TV, but wasn't this the case in the early years of cinema? On the other hand, the rapidity of TV production and the relative paucity of its resources actually guarantee a certain freedom in working method, encouraging creative resourcefulness, something that Hollywood relinquished long ago, at least according to the fine reports received from directors like Robert Florey.[2] With TV, cinema can be rejuvenated.

NOTES

From "*L'Oeil de verre* va nous révéler un nouvel Hitchcock," *Radio-Cinéma-Télévision* 426 (16 March 1958). "The Glass Eye" was the first episode in the third season of Hitchcock's TV series *Alfred Hitchcock Presents*. It aired October 6, 1957. The story, written by Stirling Silliphant, was directed by Robert Stephens.

1. *Dead of Night* was a 1946 British film directed by Alberto Cavalcanti composed of several eerie sketches.

2. Robert Florey (1900–1979) moved from his native France to Hollywood in the late 1920s and became a solid director of mid-level films, as well as an expert on special effects. He embraced television and from 1953 on he directed episodes of *The Loretta Young Show*, *Hitchcock Presents*, *The Outer Limits*, and other series.

36

Hitchcock on TV

We have of course been awaiting with great curiosity this series of films directed by Alfred Hitchcock for American TV. It is perhaps a little early to judge them, though it is probable, and even expected, that some will prove more or less successful. Here the screenplay must play a larger role than it does in the cinema, in proportion to the corresponding economy of the mise-en-scène. It seems that the series consists of short detective stories based on a type of denouement that is sufficient to justify a short story format but that would obviously not support the dramatic and psychological development required by a standard-length film. From this angle, we can think of telecinema as the opportune complement of classical cinema. The latter, with its ninety-minute format and its expensive mise-en-scène, is obliged to reject a host of minor screenplays that would naturally find their expression in a shorter and less costly style. It's this virtually nonexistent part of traditional film production that, in a way, television has been recently developing. We shouldn't expect only marvels from it. In fact, the amount of rubbish will have to be proportionally greater than in commercial cinema, but the sheer quantity of production ought to allow for a good number of successes. What would be really desirable is for our TV to have the funding to afford offering just, and only, the cream of the abundant Anglo-Saxon telecinema.

Returning to Hitchcock's first two installments, we were a bit disappointed in not being able to see them alongside American TV films of the same genre. But any comparison to Hitchcock's cinema is unfair! Nevertheless, we have enjoyed rediscovering here on TV the "touch" of this successful auteur in the dark humor of the final images, as well as in the prologues and epilogues that feature Hitchcock himself.

NOTE

From "Hitchcock à la T.V.," *Radio-Cinéma-Télévision* 430 (13 April 1958).

37

Renoir and Rossellini: Two Top Recruits for Television

While certain young directors of French television, like Claude Barma, Marcel Bluwal, or Maurice Cazeneuve, seem on their way to working at least part time in cinema, this year two great film directors, Jean Renoir and Roberto Rossellini, are offering the small screen their prestigious collaboration.[1] The first has just finished his shooting script for *Dr. Jekyll and Mr. Hyde,* which he expects to film during November.[2] It's an updated version of Robert Louis Stevenson's novel, starring Paul Meurisse. While this production will be made as a film, it will be done in the spirit of television, that is, in a style as close as possible to live TV [*en direct*]. The exteriors, to be shot around Versailles, will be done on the sly, with many cameras cranking simultaneously and without the awareness of people passing by.

As for Rossellini, his intentions are very different. He is finishing the montage and narration of one part of a number of filmed reports that he gathered in India. This will result in a series of ten programs focusing on aspects of a whole suite of specific problems that India faces and to which the filmmaker brings his observations and his viewpoint.

There's no doubt that, independent of their own interests, these two experiments bring something brand new to our television. Remember that in America a good number of Hollywood's most seasoned and recognized directors regularly collaborate with television. True, the economic conditions are different there, but in France don't we find that "established" cineastes distrust, out of hand, the idea of working for the small screen? Meanwhile those in charge of television don't try hard enough to appease them, instead exuding—at least until now—their own skepticism about the abilities of important film directors to adapt to the small budgets and the rapid tempo of work in television.

Let's hope that the results of this first encounter may ease the worries of both sides and open a fertile era of collaboration, from which, for its part, the cinema has a lot to gain, as has been demonstrated in America by films like *Marty* and *The Bachelor Party*.

NOTES

From "Deux Recrues de choix pour la télévision: Renoir et Rossellini," *Le Parisien Libéré* 4388 (21 October 1958).

1. Bazin was right that all three of these TV directors tried their hand in cinema at the end of the 1950s and the beginning of the 1960s, but in fact, all three remained stalwart TV directors for their entire careers.

2. Though shot for television and in a new TV style, Renoir's *Le Testament du Docteur Cordelier* (officially known in English as *Experiment in Evil*) was first shown at the Venice Film Festival in September 1959. Its official release on both TV and in the Paris theaters, however, wasn't until November 16, 1961. It actually starred Jean-Louis Barrault, who replaced Paul Meurisse.

38

Renoir and Rossellini Debut on TV

In its programming lineup for the coming winter, RTF is offering us the television debuts of two great film directors, Jean Renoir and Roberto Rossellini. On various occasions in these pages, I have often bemoaned the French bias that has kept our filmmakers at a distance from the small screen, something that doesn't happen in America. These prejudices have been more or less reciprocal, with television's policymakers seemingly skeptical about the ability of notable cineastes to adapt to the technical and economic constraints of TV. Nevertheless, while of course recognizing the financial impact of America's private system, I do not think that these material questions are a priori insurmountable; the problem, rather, is psychological and aesthetic.

Renoir's upcoming experience will doubtless immediately demonstrate just this. But to launch this enterprise, in addition to his enthusiastic spirit, the director of *La Grande Illusion* will need certain virtues that you find all throughout his work as a filmmaker—the penchant for revitalization and experimentation that has always pushed him to take new risks in relation both to his subjects and to his technique. Still more important, perhaps, is the deep humility this artist exhibits before his art, which means he never overlooks any opportunity to work on whatever he takes a fancy to, without worrying about compromising his "standing" as an established director. Renoir is hurling himself toward TV without worrying about the meager budget that will be offered him, just as he did, in another era, when he agreed to film *Tire au flanc* or *On purge bébé.*[1]

Now, at issue here is a modernized version of *Dr. Jekyll and Mr. Hyde,* in which the dual role will be taken up by Paul Meurisse.[2] For various economic and technical reasons, it will be entirely prerecorded on film. Still, Renoir plans to direct it in the spirit of a "live" show, limiting himself as far as possible to one take per shot, so as to keep the actor within the ambience of tension and risk that belongs to live recording. What's more, the shooting conditions will often impose this constraint, since there will be important exteriors (in particular, the streets of Versailles) that Renoir plans to film surreptitiously with several hidden cameras (as he did at the beginning of *Boudu sauvé des eaux,* on the banks of the Seine). The expected duration of the shoot, at around ten days, means that this will be work done in the heat of the moment [*travail à chaud*], the profound motivation of which definitely resides in the overall style deployed across this telefilm, rather than in being finicky with plastic or technical details.

If there exists anywhere in the postwar cinema a man who would be comparable to Renoir in his spirit of initiative and adventure and in his professional nonconformism, it is definitely Rossellini. And there's a lesson in this coincidence. But the auteur of *Païsa* has moved in another direction. The series of ten programs that he's nearly finished editing will draw on the

enormous documentation he recorded in India, mainly in 16 mm. Organized around a variety of themes, these films, narrated by the filmmaker, will be brief chapters, as it were, of *India 58*, bringing us Rossellini's account of contemporary India in documentary form but fundamentally in the same spirit of human understanding as *Germany Year Zero*.[3]

NOTES

From "Deux Grands Cinéastes vont faire leurs débuts à la télévision," *Radio-Cinéma-Télévision* 458 (26 October 1958).

1. These two films were both shoestring productions, the second a 1930 exercise to test the technical and economic viability of sound. It turned out to be an unexpected hit, opening the door for Renoir's ambitious sound films, beginning with *La Chienne* (1931).

2. *Le Testament du Docteur Cordelier* would come out simultaneously on television and in theaters in November 1961, after a premiere at the 1959 Venice Film Festival. Between the time Bazin wrote this article and the actual production, Jean-Louis Barrault had replaced Paul Meurisse.

3. *India vista da Rossellini* appeared in installments on Italian television beginning in January 1959. Its running length is 251 minutes. In 1958 Rossellini prepared a ninety-minute theatrical film comprising four episodes called *India Matri Bhumi* (India motherland) but at the time known as *India 58*. Although its first public screening seems to have been at Cannes in 1959, Bazin evidently saw a working version of it shortly before he died.

39

Cinema and Television: An Interview with Jean Renoir and Roberto Rossellini

In a few weeks French Television will broadcast two major programs whose credits include the names of two of the most important film directors: Jean Renoir and Roberto Rossellini. In the United States, film auteurs like Welles and Hitchcock have already grappled with the problems posed by the "small screen." In France, however, this is the first initiative of this kind, and on the eve of these two shows airing, we felt it would be interesting to publish the testimony of the two filmmakers.

RENOIR: I am preparing a film version of Stevenson's *Dr. Jekyll and Mr. Hyde* for television. I've transferred the story to the present day, and to Paris and its suburbs, for I felt that certain suburbs at night were more striking than the streets of Paris. Actually, my adaptation is still faithful to the original. The names are French, and I'm going to introduce the program with a little talk, as if it had to do with something uncanny that really happened a short time ago on a street in Paris.

ROSSELLINI: My first program for French television will be about India. I made ten short films while I was there, with television in mind, and it is these films that I am going to show. I'm doing the commentary myself, as well as providing the necessary linking passages.

BAZIN: When you're making a television film, M. Renoir—shooting more or less off the cuff with one or several cameras—do you manage to keep a sense of actuality in the direction itself?

RENOIR: I would like to make this film—and this is where television gives me something valuable—in the spirit of *live* television. Of course this would not be a live show, since it would be recorded in advance on film, but I'd like to make the film as though it were a live broadcast, shooting each scene only once, with the actors imagining that the public is directly receiving their words and gestures. Both the actors and the technicians should know that there will be no retakes, and that, whether they succeed or not, they can't begin again.

In any case, we can only shoot once, since some parts of this film are being shot out in the streets and we can't afford to let the passersby realize that we're filming. Because of this, if I need to reshoot a scene, everything will fall apart. And so the actors and technicians must feel that every movement is final and irrevocable. I'd like to break with cinema technique, and very patiently build a large wall with little stones.

BAZIN: Obviously this kind of film can be made much more quickly than an ordinary cinema production.

RENOIR: I've just done a shooting script, and the result works out to a little under 400 shots. I believe these will be more or less the number of shots that will appear in the film. For some reason, I've discovered by experience that my shots usually average about five or six meters each (16–20 feet), though I know it sounds a bit ridiculous to gauge things this way—I have a hard time believing it, but it's a fact. If, for example, I have a hundred shots in a movie, I end up with between 500 and 600 meters (1,600–2,000 feet) of film. Anyhow, I imagine that 400 shots will give me a film of about 2,000 meters—in other words, of average length.

BAZIN: Are you thinking of showing the film in the commercial cinema as well as on TV?

RENOIR: I don't know yet. I'll probably try it out with an ordinary cinema audience. I think that television now has sufficient importance for the public to accept film "presented" in a different way. I mean that the effects achieved are no longer entirely dependent on the will of the director and the cameraman—the camera can produce effects almost by chance, as sometimes happens when you get a wonderful newsreel shot.

BAZIN: But doesn't television present a classic problem in technique—that of the quality and small size of the image? For the mass-produced films of American cinema, the directors seem to lay down certain rules in shooting, the main actors have to remain inside a sort of square in order to keep the action always in the picture.... Do all these restrictions of the medium frighten you at all?

RENOIR: No, because the method I'd like to adopt will be something between the American and the French approach. I believe that if one follows the American TV technique, one risks making a film that will be difficult for audiences to accept on the screen. But by adapting these techniques, one should be able to arrive at a new cinematographic style that could be extremely interesting. It all depends, I think, on the starting point, the conception.

I believe Roberto would agree with me that in the cinema at present the camera has become a sort of god. You have a camera fixed on its tripod or crane, which is just like a heathen altar;

about it are the high priests—the director, cameraman, assistants—who bring victims before the camera, like burnt offerings, and cast them into the flames. And the camera is there, immobile—or almost so—and when it does move it follows patterns ordained by the high priests, not by the victims.

Now, I am trying to extend my old ideas, and to establish that the camera finally has only one right—that of recording what happens. That's all. Of course, this task requires several cameras, because the camera cannot be everywhere at once. I don't want the movements of the actors to be determined by the camera, but the movements of the camera to be determined by the actor. This means working rather like a newsreel cameraman. When a newsreel cameraman films a politician's speech or a sporting event, for instance, he doesn't ask the runners to start from the exact spot that suits him. He has to manage things so that he can film the race wherever it happens. Or take an accident: to present a catastrophe in a truly admirable way—say, a fire, with people rushing about, firemen—the cameramen must situate themselves so as to give us an impressive spectacle, since this spectacle will not be repeated for the benefit of the camera. The camera must be operated in accordance with the imposing spectacle—and it is this, more or less, that I would like to do.

ROSSELLINI: I think what Renoir has just said brings out the real problem of film and television. In practice, there are, strictly speaking, hardly any really creative artists in the cinema; there has been a variety of artists who come together, pool their ideas, then translate and record them on film. And the actual filming itself is very often secondary. The real creative artist in the cinema is someone who can get the most out of everything he sees—even if he sometimes does this by accident—and it is this that makes his work truly great.

RENOIR: That's the point. The creator of a film isn't at all an organizer; he isn't like a man who decides, for instance, how a funeral should be conducted. He is rather the man who finds himself watching a funeral he never expected to see, and sees the corpse, instead of lying in its coffin, getting up to dance, sees all the relatives, instead of weeping, running about all over the place. It's up to him, and his colleagues, to capture this and then, in the cutting room, to make a work of art out of it.

ROSSELLINI: Not only in the cutting room. Because I don't know whether, today, montage is so essential. I believe we should begin to look at the cinema in a new way, and start by abandoning all the old taboos. The cinema at first was a technological discovery; and everything, even editing, was subordinated to that. Then, in the silent cinema, montage had a precise meaning, because it represented language. From the silent cinema we have inherited this myth of montage, though it has lost most of its meaning. Consequently, it is in the shots themselves that the creative artist can really bring his own observation to bear, his own moral view, his particular vision.

RENOIR: You are right: when I spoke of editing I was using a convenient phrase. I should instead have talked of choice, rather like Cartier-Bresson choosing three pictures out of the hundred he's taken of some incident, and those three are the best.

BAZIN: Television is still rather frowned on—particularly by the intellectuals. How did you come to it?

RENOIR: Through being immensely bored by a great number of contemporary films, and being less bored by certain television programs. I ought to say that the television shows I've found most exciting have been certain interviews on American TV. I feel that the interview gives the television close-up a meaning that is rarely achieved in the cinema. The close-up in the cinema is essentially a reconstruction, something prefabricated, carefully worked up—and, of course, this has yielded some great moments in the cinema. In practice, you take an actress, you stick her in a certain atmosphere—she is very worked up, and the director is worked up too. You push her more, more, more, until she is in a position to make an admirable expression. This is just the kind of artificial expression that has resulted in the most beautiful moments in cinema.

When I say "artificial," I don't mean it as a criticism, since we know that, after all, whatever is artistic is artificial. Art is necessarily artificial. This said, I believe that in thirty years we have rather used up this type of cinema and that we should perhaps move on to something else. In America I've seen some exceptional television shows. American television, in my opinion, is worthy of admiration, extremely rich. Not because it is better, or because the people working there have more talent than in France or anywhere else, but simply because, in a town like Los Angeles, there are ten channels operating constantly, at every hour of the day and night. In these circumstances, obviously, one has the chance of finding remarkable things, even if the selection overall is not good.

I remember, for instance, certain interviews in connection with some political hearing, with parliamentarians interrogating people, and these people answering. Then, suddenly, we had a huge close-up, taken with a telephoto lens, a picture of a human being in his entirety. One man was afraid, afraid of the legislator, and all his fear showed; another was insolent, insulted the questioner; another was ironical; another took it all very lightly. In two minutes we could read the faces of the people, televised via telephoto lens with their heads taking up the whole screen: we knew them, we knew who they were. I found this tremendously exciting; I also found it somehow an indecent spectacle to watch, an indiscretion. Yet this indecency came nearer the knowledge of man than many films.

ROSSELLINI: Let me make an observation on that note. In modern society, men have an enormous need to know each other. Modern society and modern art have been destructive of man: man no longer exists—but television is an aid to his rediscovery. Television, an art without traditions, dares to go out to look for man.

BAZIN: There was a stage when the cinema appeared to be doing the same—particularly at the time of the great documentaries of Flaherty.

ROSSELLINI: Very few people were looking for man, and a great many were doing everything necessary for him to be forgotten. Inevitably, the public was instructed to forget man. But today the problem of man is profoundly, dramatically at stake in the modern world. So we should benefit from the immense new freedom television gives us. The television audience is quite different from that of the cinema. At the cinema, you have an audience with the psychology of the crowd. In television you're talking not to the mass public but to ten million individuals, and the discussion becomes much more intimate, more persuasive. You know how many setbacks I've had in my cinema career. Well, I realized that the films which were the most complete failures with the public were exactly those that, in a little projection theater before a dozen people, people liked the most. It was a complete reversal. Something that you see in a projection room with an audience of fifteen people has an entirely different meaning than when you see it in a movie theater with two thousand people.

RENOIR: I can confirm that. I have had the same experience myself. If we were to have a competition of failures, I'm not sure which of us would win.

ROSSELLINI: I'd win, I'd beat you by a long way ...

RENOIR: I'm not sure. I have the advantage of age ... so I could beat you. Be that as it may, take the example of my film *The Diary of a Chambermaid* [1946]. It was very badly received by the American public, for one simple reason: because it is a drama, with the title *The Diary of a Chambermaid*. People expected to laugh their heads off at a film with Paulette Goddard called *The Diary of a Chambermaid;* they didn't, and they were dissatisfied. In the early days of television a TV company bought this film and it is still watched with admiration by enthusiasts. Thanks to television I've made a great deal of money out of it. So, this proves that I was wrong. I thought that I'd made a cinema film; and in fact, without realizing it, I'd made one for television.

ROSSELLINI: I had an interesting experience with *La Voix humaine.*[1] I wanted to establish the film's capacity to penetrate to the very roots of a character. Now, with television, one rediscovers these feelings.

BAZIN: What's more, it's very clear, though less in France than in America, that television gives something back to the spectacle of cinema, whether in black and white or in color. If audiences used to look to films for something bigger and richer than what television could give them, perhaps now, accustomed to the constraints of television, they may be ready to accept a restrained cinema and look for something simpler again. This might mean a reconsideration of the conditions of film production.

RENOIR: At present, if a film wants a chance to be profitable in the French market, it has to be a co-production, unless there is some certainty that it can be sold for enough on the French market. Now, in order to sell abroad, you have to consider the tastes of different audiences, and one ends up making films that lose all their national character. But the curious thing is that national character is what attracts international audiences. So the cinema is in danger of losing both its individuality (due to the demands of co-productions) *and* its market.

BAZIN: So the answer, as you see it, is that films should be able to recover their costs in the home market, and should in consequence be made more cheaply?

RENOIR: Exactly. For instance, I hawked the script of *La Grande Illusion* around all the film companies for three years and no one would touch it, all the studios insisting that the film wouldn't make any money. But at that time they did not have the excuse of not wanting to take risks, since films were paying their way. *La Grande Illusion,* for instance, had already recovered its costs after its run at the Marivaux Cinema in Paris. Money was easier to come by and one could afford to experiment. You could even afford to fail, since one good undertaking allowed the financing of other failures. The trouble about the present cost of films is that you either have a sensational success or you lose a lot of money. As a result producers play it safe, and when one plays it safe, art is no longer possible.

ROSSELLINI: I think the mistake of European producers is in trying to follow the American pattern without realizing that the whole basis of American production is completely different from our own. In America, the basis of the industry and of the cinema itself is in the manufacture of the actual equipment. In the United States, in the early days of cinema, once all this machinery had been built, there was a corresponding need to produce films for it. Thus, from the point of view of films themselves, producers could operate in an uneconomical way so long as it allowed them to maintain a monopoly over the market. European producers, instead of working toward a European cinema, with its own set of particular demands and possibilities, followed in the path of the Americans, which brought about the great crises of the cinema.

But there may be other reasons of a moral, or even a strictly political, nature—not only in Europe, but around the world. It's a fact. All the mass culture media have had enormous success. At the beginning, the masses were starved for culture; and, profiting from this public appetite, the people feeding it have supplied a false culture, simply in order to condition the masses in the way that best suits certain great powers.

RENOIR: I'm not so sure of that. I have a sort of faith in the immense stupidity of the men who run gigantic enterprises. I believe that they are always naïve children, rushing headlong toward what looks as though it ought to bring them money. I believe the phrase "make money" haunts them, even if they fail to make any. Provided they bring out a product that is theoretically commercial, they are quite happy, even if they lose money on it. In the cinema, the word "commercial" means a film that has no daring, that corresponds to certain preconceived ideas that are accepted by the market. A commercial film isn't necessarily one that makes money, not at all. The term has become a sort of shorthand category [*définition*].

ROSSELLINI: You once said to me that the commercial label went to the film whose aesthetic ideal was what was wanted by the producer.

RENOIR: Exactly: and this ideal, desired by the producers, doesn't, I think, derive from views as thoughtful as the ones you express. I don't think it derives from anything more than the practice of a naïve, incomprehensible religion—one that works against their own interests. I don't believe that producers are powerful enough, or cunning enough, to be Talleyrands trying to reshape the world in their own image. I get the impression that the cinema, in any given country, puts out products that undermine the ideal on which the religion, so to speak, of these producers ought to rest.

For instance, for film production to continue as at present, it needs a well-organized, stable society. And right now we are fast approaching the point of producing films that undermine all the classic wisdom that society has passed down. It seems to me that it is in the interests of the producers to maintain a certain standard of morality, since if they don't do this, immoral films won't sell. If there are no morals, why would you expect immoral films to be appealing? If you like to see Mme. Brigitte Bardot making love simultaneously with her lover and her maid, it's because you think this is prohibited. But too many films like this will make people think this is moral, and people will stop going to see them, since they will seem normal. Well, these producers are going to ruin themselves.

ROSSELLINI: Yes, the producers have ended up creating ersatz substitutes for human emotions. Love, passion, tragedy—all emotions are deformed.

RENOIR: These people are destroying themselves, since, in order to sustain their little business, they require a stable society, and yet they are now going about destroying that society. During the hundred years of romanticism, it was possible to score a great theatrical success by relying on the fact that the daughter of a workman couldn't marry the son of a duke. And this was because people believed in social differences. Society, by maintaining its faith in social divisions, also maintained the conditions in which such drama could succeed ... Each work of art contains in fact a morsel of protest. But if this protest turns into destruction, if the system blows up, the possibility of such drama at once vanishes. This is what is happening now. We have reached the stage in eroticism of the little ménage à trois I mentioned. Next time, I suppose, daddy will be one of the three, daddy making love with the girl. That's nice, isn't it? Then it will be mama. And what comes after that? We'll reach a point when there will be nothing new they can show, since no one will know how to outbid the last player.

In short, they are in the process of killing the goose that lays the golden eggs.

I am sure that the great quality of the American films from fifteen or twenty years ago sprang from an American Puritanism that put up barriers to American passions. Those early American films thrilled us all, we adored them. When we saw Lillian Gish, who was probably going to be assaulted by the villain, we trembled, because the fact of being raped meant something. Today, what can you do with the rape of a girl who has already made love to the entire town, to the valet, to father, mother, and the maid? It is no longer interesting—she can be raped and no one will give a damn.

ROSSELLINI: In the last analysis, people instinctively construct the society they desire.

RENOIR: Absolutely. Certain material restrictions are extremely useful for artistic expression. Obviously, the fact that Muslims cannot reproduce the human figure is what allowed them to produce Bukhara rugs, Persian art, and so on.

We can only hope that people will reconstruct the barriers that make artistic expression possible, and restore the necessary constraints. Absolute freedom, because it allows anyone to do exactly what he wants, does not allow complete artistic expression. This sounds like a paradox, but it's true. Probably men who are extremely wise, extremely clever and adaptable, will rediscover the necessary constraints, as they did for instance in painting. Cubism, after all, was nothing but a deliberate constraint adopted after the exaggerated and destructive freedoms of post-impressionism.

ROSSELLINI: Yes, but the constraints arise immediately from the fact that man has an ideal. Your own ideal, that's already a constraint.

RENOIR: But I don't believe that constraints arise out of man's ideals. I think they emerge almost physically. I think it's just like when you cut yourself and it becomes a bit infected. You have white blood cells that flow to the cut and cause it to heal. Speaking of which, Nature, who works marvelously, has been able to slow down cars that can travel at a hundred miles an hour to just three miles an hour in the streets of Paris ... because balance is the law of Nature.

BAZIN: You both seem to approach television in different ways. You, M. Renoir, are again looking for that commedia dell'arte spirit, which always attracts you; and you, M. Rossellini, seem to be returning to the interests that made you the originator of Italian neorealism.

ROSSELLINI: Someone—I've forgotten who—said something that really struck me: that we are living in an era of barbarian invasions. We're also living at a time when man's knowledge is becoming ever deeper, but when every man is a specialist on a single subject and ignorant of everything else. This disturbs me, and I'm returning to documentary because I want to hold people up to people. I would like to escape from this rigid specialization and return to the broader knowledge that makes it possible to achieve a synthesis, because that, after all, is what matters.

BAZIN: You made *India 58* and the documentaries for television simultaneously. Do you think the documentaries influenced the other film?

ROSSELLINI: When I shot the film, I had less fun. In the documentaries I was exploring a precise world, and in the film I tried to summarize my experience of it. The two things complement each other.

RENOIR: I can summarize Roberto's position and my own: Roberto is continuing the pure French tradition—of delving into humanity: whereas I try to be Italian and rediscover the commedia dell'arte.

ROSSELLINI: I'm striving to set a variety of enterprises in motion, not just a single film; if you produce a range of work, you can, in a way, help toward forming public taste. You help the public to understand certain things. It's very difficult for me to find a screen subject at present; I don't know what subject to take on, there are no more heroes in life, only miniature heroisms, and I don't know where to look for a story. We lack that extraordinary and exciting élan that drives a man to throw himself into an adventure. But perhaps it exists somewhere in the world. What I am trying to do is a piece of research, a kind of documentation on the state of man today all over the world. And if I find dramatic subjects, exalting heroes, I may move toward a fiction film.

But the first stage is research, the observation of man, establishing a sort of index, and this has got to be systematic. Think of everything there is in the world—all the folk music to be recorded—and think of the needs of radio and of the record industry. They are huge. When you go to Peru, Mexico, Haiti, you can find heaps of things that will pay for the enterprise without tying you up in big capital expenditure.

RENOIR: I think there is another reason for our interest in television, Roberto. It may be because the importance of technique in the cinema has vanished during the last few years. When I began in films, you had to know your trade thoroughly, to have all your technical skill at your fingertips. We didn't know, for instance, how to make a dissolve in the laboratory, and because you had to do it in the camera you had to be absolutely clear in your own mind about when you wanted the scene to end, since the moment at which you placed the dissolve at the end of the scene could not be changed. Nowadays the technology is such that, in practice, a director would waste time on the set if he concerned himself with technical problems. He becomes now something much closer to a playwright or novelist [*un auteur de théâtre ou un auteur littéraire*].

The Bayeux Tapestry is more beautiful than the modern Gobelins tapestry. Why? Because Queen Mathilda had to say to herself: "I haven't any red, I'll have to use brown; I haven't any blue, I must use some color like blue." Obliged to make use of crude contrasts, of violent oppositions, she was forced to struggle constantly against imperfections, and her technical difficulties helped her create great art. If the job is technically easy, real art is rare, since the spur to creation does not exist; yet at the same time, the artist today who is no longer limited by technical difficulty is free to apply his invention to different forms. Today, in fact, if I conceive a story for the cinema, that story would do just as well for the stage, or for a book, or for television; creativity itself becomes a specialization, whereas in the past, material specialization was the specialty. And I think that makes for a major change.

All the arts, or all the industrial arts (and after all, the cinema is simply an industrial art), were noble at the beginning and have been debased as they perfected themselves. I mentioned the tapestries, but it's the same thing, for instance, in pottery. I did some work in ceramics myself, trying to rediscover the technical simplicity of the early days. I rediscovered it, but artificially, and this is what led me to plunge into a genuinely primitive trade: the cinema. With ceramics, the best I could manage was a false "primitivism," since I deliberately rejected all the developments of the potter's technique and limited myself, voluntarily, to simpler formulas. This was hardly authentic; it was a mere concoction of the mind. However, the case of pottery is really remarkable. Take, for example, the earliest works from Urbino, in Italy, all of which are masterpieces; despite this, you could not say that all of Urbino's potters were great artists. So how is it that every vase, plate, and saucer to come out of Urbino was a masterpiece? Simply because each potter encountered certain technical difficulties, and these aroused his imagination. And so it is that, today, we are left with the rubbish from Sèvres. Forgive me, but my father, who worked in pottery, explained to me that technique has developed to the point of painting on a vase with colors that cover the full spectrum, as one paints on canvas or paper. Ceramics as such are gone, finished. As an art, ceramics existed only when there were only five or six colors available, when the ceramicist had only a limited palette and difficult techniques.

But the cinema is moving the same way. The people who made those fine early American or German or Swedish films weren't all great artists—some were quite indifferent ones—but all their pictures were beautiful. Why? Because the technique was difficult, that's all. In France, after the splendid first period, after Méliès and Max Linder, films became worthless. Why? Because we were intellectuals trying to make "art" films, to produce masterpieces. In fact, the moment one allows oneself to become an intellectual instead of an artisan, one is falling into danger. And if you and I, Roberto, are turning toward television, it is because television is in a technically primitive state that may restore to artists that fighting spirit of the early cinema, when everything that was made was good.

NOTES

Originally published as "Cinéma et télévision: Entretien avec Jean Renoir et Roberto Rossellini," *France-Observateur* 442 (23 October 1958). Interviewer: André Bazin. Original French text edited by Bazin, Jean Herman, and Claude Choublier. A good portion of this interview appeared in English in *Sight and Sound* 28 (1959). I have amended and filled out that translation to present a complete version here.

1. *La Voix humaine* is the French title of Rossellini's *La voce umana* (The human voice), released in Italy in 1948 as the first episode in a three-part film called *Amore*. Anna Magnani starred in this one-person adaptation of Jean Cocteau's play.

40

About Television: A Discussion with Marcel Moussy and André Bazin

A.B.: How is it that you, a novelist and dramatist, were first driven to turn to television, and then to adopt your precise technique within television? You began not with *Si c'était vous* [the TV series, If it were you] but with theatrical adaptations?

M.M.: Yes, I started with a commissioned adaptation of Ben Jonson's *The Alchemist*. This gave me the opportunity to recognize certain limits and certain possibilities of television. This play—a great satirical farce that I believe had a tremendous influence on theater—was a partial failure on television, and I wondered why. The blame fell neither on the acting nor on Jean Prat's direction, but rather, I think, on a few distinguishing features of Elizabethan plays: a certain tone, a certain vitality. The dominant tone of this work is one of diatribe and argument, something that absolutely does not carry over to television. Conversely, the few scenes where the relationship between the two characters became more intimate stood out— and did so in proportions that were way out of tune with the whole. From this I concluded that there really does exist a certain mode of theatrical expression that loses all of its power on television.

That was, so to speak, my first negative observation. I met with Marcel Bluwal about all this; he already had some very clear ideas about the assets of television and about what he wanted to do with them. He had ideas concerning contemporary topics. We argued about these, and it was from this first confrontation that the series *Si c'était vous* was born: contemporary themes treated in a new way, at least in relation to what had been done in France until that point.

A.B.: Were you influenced by American films in the style of *Marty* and by whatever texts by Chayefsky you were familiar with?

M.M.: Yes. Exactly at that moment I became acquainted with some of Chayefsky's plays (although I never saw the film *Marty*). There was in them an example of a kind of expression that was perfectly adapted to the medium of television, with all the traits of this writer and of American TV.

ESCAPISM FOR TODAY

A.B.: In what way do contemporary social themes seem to you to be better suited to television than the themes of Elizabethan theater, for example? What is it about the "timeliness" of these subjects that you feel has a particular affinity with television?

M.M.: I think one of these characteristics is the way people *receive* the televised spectacle. When they go to the theater, the framework of the stage is enough to isolate the spectator from what he is going to see, and to allow him, for example, to envision the possibility of taking a step back in time. You are ready for all of this when you go to the theater. You are much less ready for it when watching the show in your own home.

A.B.: And in relation to the cinema? Is there a contrast to make here as well?

M.M.: In cinema, as in the theater, one easily accepts temporal shifts, but here it is in the hope of seeing something bustling on a more or less epic scale, a saga, something that the size of cinema permits.

A.B.: So one expects from the cinema an escape that you don't think is generally expected of television?

M.M.: Television offers plenty of other kinds of escape on a daily basis, but it is a *contemporary* escape: all the variety shows, for example, present forms of escape. But it is dangerous to pass judgment on the basis of just two years' experience. It is very possible that others may find a style of dream, of dramatic fantasy. If Bluwal and I did not go in this direction, it was first of all because of our particular temperament, but it was not off limits. Many authors who feel they have an aptitude in that area would be discouraged by a decree like the one I believe De Sica pronounced recently, that "television must be neo-realist." It may have been this way so far, but that doesn't prohibit other possibilities. Perhaps later I will make ... problem plays! [*des pièces à thèse*].

DRAMA AND THE PROBLEM PLAY

A.B.: One of the surprises for me of your shows and their particular quality, in fact, was that a priori they exhibited all of the disadvantages of the problem play. If one were tasked with assessing them on the basis of a synopsis a few pages long, one would have every reason to be wary of the entire undertaking, because in each you deal, in a rather didactic way, with a contemporary social scenario that expects the spectator to take a moral position in relation to the problem raised. And all this does not bode well. Still, the result is excellent.

M.M.: When faced with a problem, with some particular case, the dramatist is not easily enticed, because the problem assumes the existence of a solution, and the solution, if it is already foreseen at the outset, will drag the problem play down. At that point, we clearly get the sense that the dramatic work will be reduced to orienting the characters in a certain direction, hampering their freedom, just to arrive at the solution that was established at the start. This was not the case for us, because we don't have this hidebound attitude, or else because, vaguely sensing the danger of the problem play, each time we had to define the relationship between two characters, our only recourse was to deepen that relationship, so that we truly forgot the point of departure. It is always irritating when an author seems to situate himself in front of his characters and say that he is listening to them, that he is letting them live. We end up with something à la Pirandello, but all the same there is some truth to this notion. A deep sympathy for the characters makes it possible for one to momentarily forget oneself through them, so that their freedom endows the dramatic structure with an impression of premeditated lack of direction.

A.B.: Your response is valid for all works of art, not just for television. If your plays ring true, it is because their characters have autonomy, plus moral and psychological truth of their own: yet what strikes me is that throughout each play, you never lose the thread that makes it a demonstration, or at least an exposition, of different aspects of some problem, whether it concerns the housing crisis, juvenile delinquency, adolescent education . . .

You offer, if not the development of a thesis, at least the presentation of a variety of hypotheses on the subject; yet, despite this, your play retains a kind of dramatic value, on the one hand, and a human, psychological, and moral value on the other hand, which gives it its significance.

M.M.: What I am about to tell you nearly contradicts what I said earlier. On any given problem—divorce, for example—all the possible positions have been upheld by characters who are in fact human beings. Indeed, I believe that by distributing among a certain number of characters the different positions to be upheld, one automatically ends up making a kind of panoramic tour of the question: within a single family, for example, the clash of positions in relation to the generations is a priori dramatic in itself.

THERE IS A JUST MEASURE TO INTIMACY

A.B.: Now let's approach the problem in a more formal way. As a novelist and, at the same time, a dramatist, what is it about the resources proper to television that struck you as a fresh and interesting strength?

M.M.: When one is curious about technology and the various means of expression, any change is welcome. I did nothing but theater for the initial five years of my writing career. When I first tackled the novel, I felt some uncertainty that originated, I think, from the simple fact of making the change. Television gave me the same feeling, as it would to any person involved in a transition. However, this isn't the case for everybody: I know novelists who cannot conceive of changing their mode of expression, because they rank the novel far above everything else.

What is it that I believe to be specific to television? In theater I was accused of resorting to a series of tableaux, of changing the setting frequently. I felt I was emulating the Elizabethan theater's quick scene changes, something that has always appealed to me. I realized that on television this was the most normal thing, and that one had at one's disposal an extraordinary mobility in comparison with the theater. On the other hand, television, more than any other medium, allows one to render a certain intimacy that would be intolerable in the theater; the cinema has sometimes been able to bring this across, though, curiously, there it takes on an almost monstrous aspect. There is a kind of proper measure when it comes to staging intimacy, and it is specific to television.

A.B.: Cinematic intimacy is founded more on the close-up than on the nature of cinema itself. For by its nature, cinema is not intimate at all, since it addresses a group of spectators, even if this group remains individualized and doesn't create a community as happens in theater. Cinematic intimacy, as you say, is a monstrous effect, because it is almost "spatial."

M.M.: That's it. If you suddenly introduce a close-up [in a film] in order to render a moment of intimacy, the impression of such a visual shock is very distracting in relation to what will follow. We are brutally pulled closer, whereas television constantly maintains a close distance between spectacle and spectator.

A.B.: Your shows were broadcast live, with one part prerecorded. Bluwal succeeded in rendering the articulation of these two components absolutely invisible. The whole thing had the suppleness of a film and yet, in fact, it was live. Do you feel that this issue of the live broadcast is essential? If the whole show had been recorded in advance, do you think its quality would have been the same?

M.M.: I believe in the virtues of live shooting for the simple reason that it allows one to "stage" a show, that is, to give the actors the feeling that they belong to a sort of dramatic line that is lost when one shoots in bits and pieces. What's more, this is what Chayefsky told me when I met him in Paris: he badly regretted the gradual disappearance of the live broadcast.

On the other hand, in our experience, Bluwal and I had every advantage, for, out of every hour or hour and a quarter of live performance, we used ten to fifteen minutes of filmed material. This allowed us to "aerate" the piece considerably, to make use of exterior cutaways that served not merely to establish atmosphere, but also to advance the action. This was the first time that we could allow ourselves such a thing, and it is something the Americans have never been able to do. In New York studios, they only have the right to use stock footage from film archives for the exterior, atmospheric scenes.

AMERICAN TABOOS

A.B.: This comparison leads us to another, this time between the conditions of work as Chayefsky describes them and the conditions you had at Télévision Française. Did the latter provide you with all the necessary means to fulfill your aims and the style of your play?

M.M.: Yes, absolutely. No limitations. I was able to have a set design that entailed up to twelve or fifteen pieces of scenery. I don't believe that one could hope for more, given the size of a studio.

A.B.: According to what you have read of Chayefsky, does it seem to you that American writers have more resources or fewer at their disposal?

M.M.: I have the impression, at least from the prefaces, that their resources are much more limited. It must be mentioned, though, that these texts were written four years ago, and are all related to work done for studios in New York. The new tendency is to relocate to Hollywood and to shoot film, but the conditions in which the plays are filmed are even more limiting, given that shooting is done, I believe, in three days.

A.B.: As for "fundamentals" [underlying American TV], Chayefsky makes mention of numerous taboos.

M.M.: Which are imposed by a sort of commercial censorship. Television is first and foremost an advertising medium. At least that's the feeling of the people who sponsor it, who pay for it. Among its taboos: adultery, abortion, social values, adult reality, pessimistic drama. This is virtually a summary of the themes that we have addressed or tried to address, with the exception of political controversies.

A.B.: It must be noted that these taboo topics are nonetheless evoked in the Chayefsky plays we have seen in the cinema. But, apart from these constraints specific to American overall mores, he alludes to a problem of duration: the obligation to accommodate ads that appear two or three times over the course of the show, and so cut his plays into acts. Such slavery to structure is rather astonishing, when you realize that, ultimately, Chayefsky has built an entire dramaturgy on it.

M.M.: We have seen other types of constraints.

A.B.: But these are entirely external.

M.M.: Aristotle, too, weighed dramatists down, but for a more noble servitude. On the other hand, this obligation to cut shows into three acts keeps American televised plays oriented toward the theater. For, as Chayefsky says, he must come up with two "dramatic twists." For our part, we have always been spared this obligation, so that we can achieve a much more cinematic shape.

A.B.: Another constraint, of a far more material order, still has to be mentioned, insofar as it has a direct bearing on creation. Chayefsky gives us rather precise statistics on matters concerning American writers. He finds that they are badly paid, but the amounts mentioned are extravagant in comparison with French figures. This isn't meant to be a complaint, but an equal effort [for a teleplay] deserves to be remunerated at the same level as a theatrical piece or a scenario for a film.

M.M.: On television, an author should be able to put together a dramatic series in a year and air it the following year. This is out of the question with current costs: producers must move from one play to the next immediately. And it is very difficult to keep up the pace.

NOTE

From "Propos sur la télévision," *Cahiers du Cinéma* 90 (December 1958). This interview was conducted just as François Truffaut was making final adjustments to the dialogue Marcel Moussy had written for *Les 400 Coups*. The interview appeared three weeks after Bazin's death.

PART FIVE

Cinerama and 3D

41

New Screen Technologies

Up to now people have discussed new technologies in the absolute, in relation to films in themselves, as if these were independent of how they are exploited in theaters. But let me make the point that everything in cinema begins with exhibition. "People" didn't create CinemaScope because "people" felt some aesthetic or psycho-visual need for a larger screen; instead it was cinema's need to win out in a competition against television, one of whose weak spots lies precisely in the restricted size of its image.

Moreover, we shouldn't have to imagine that cinema's dependence on its commercial exploitation is a consequence of the capitalist economic regime, thinking we need only liberate cinema from capitalism so as to transform it. Look at the Soviet cinema, which apparently hasn't shown any greater revolutionary taste in technological matters: 3D has remained at the stage of the prototype there; you see nothing in the Soviet Union that is comparable, for example, to Abel Gance's experiments. From the perspective that concerns us, the fact is that the relation between exploitation and production is not uniquely nor even principally based on profit. It's based more on technological and psychological grounds.

Technology? Let's take the example of 35mm film, which was by happenstance the measure established by Edison. The absurdity of this single standard was obvious long ago in relation to the requirements of certain essential technological advances (notably for the format of the image on screen). But all attempts to establish a larger gauge for celluloid have regularly failed because this would mandate an overhaul of projection equipment. Another example: the failure of color processes similar to Rouxcolor, which have an enormous economic advantage but require such special care in projection that theater owners have been reluctant to complicate their lives by adopting it.[1] In fact it will always be more expedient to invest tens of millions in the research and development of chemical processes—including the building of labs—if these allow the distribution of color copies on sturdy stock that are simple to deal with, as opposed to spending just tens of thousands for an optical process that requires just a little more attention and skill from the projectionist, no matter how perfect it may otherwise be.

As for the psychological dimension of the problem, I can quickly pull out an example: the failure of 3D. We can call this a failure from here on out, since films recently made via this process are being shown in their flat versions not just in France but also in America. However, if you ask the managers of theaters (those who still have a choice between the two versions) about the reason for their decision, they tell you that the need to interrupt the projection twice and bring up the lights while reloading the projectors turns the public off.[2] This inconvenience is surely more crucial to the public than wearing glasses or even suffering migraines. Hence it is likely that, in the end, the future of 3D was tied to the fact that most theaters run with but a single set of projectors, and those upsetting reminders of reality, twice per film, alienated the audience. And don't forget the crucial importance of selling candy during the intermissions; in the main this is what mandates the timing of interruptions in the overall program.

Let me say in conclusion that the cinema presents itself in unstable equilibrium rather like an upside-down pyramid, with its head pointed down. At the summit (i.e., the point touching the earth) would be the production side, while the base—that which weighs down on it—would be the exhibition sector. No matter the cost, everything operates so that this narrow pressure point remains exactly beneath the center of gravity. But if the created products that climb from the zone of production up toward the zone of commercial exhibition don't quickly spread out in uniform fashion across the entire width of this heavy base, the pyramid topples over, which is the same as saying that the initiative is immediately abandoned. Under these conditions, you can see how vain it is to discuss the future of various technologies strictly with regard to their artistic advantages.

I am not preaching pessimism here, only the historical realism to which my profession as critic renders me particularly sensitive. Let me say that, given that the major developments in the technological evolution of cinema are outside the reach of our initiative or at least of our control, it is more fertile and interesting to consider them a priori as progress rather than take them a priori for degenerations in the name of purely aesthetic criticism. It was this kind of criticism that almost unanimously condemned the talking cinema at its birth. Such curses did nothing to cinema, one way or the other. I am the first to recognize the real inconvenience of CinemaScope in its current state, and personally I would even say that perhaps it has brought me more nuisance than pleasure, but that's not for me to decide. If CinemaScope survives its early experimental stage, it's because it deserves to survive, and if it does survive, then this is due to the cinema and not to my critical imagination. CinemaScope seems interesting not so much for landscapes as for the way it renews the value of the close-up. As for montage, apart from the fact that it has not at all been proven that we haven't attained a renewal of cinematic grammar in the CinemaScope frame (look at films like *Written on the Wind* or *River of No Return*), I don't for a minute acknowledge that montage is required for cinema or is even the essential factor of its aesthetic; it might be healthy for it if we go back to a mise-en-scène based on the organization of space around the actor and in relation to him.

NOTES

From "Techniques nouvelles," *Arts* 518 (1 June 1955). This article is a transcript of Bazin's lecture at the International Congress of Filmology that took place at the Sorbonne in Paris in April 1955.

1. Rouxcolor was a French additive process that placed a lens divided into four quadrants in front of the main film lens. Each quadrant was filtered for a different color, producing four small images on each frame of 35mm black and white film. As with CinemaScope, a similar lens was then placed in front of the projector lens to reconstitute the colors that had been filtered initially. Marcel Pagnol's *La Belle Meunière* (*The Pretty Miller Girl*, 1948) was the only film made in this short-lived process. Bazin patriotically holds up the possible future that Rouxcolor deserves if only a larger gauge film like 70mm could be used for more surface area, and if only projectionists would agree to be especially vigilant, since fuzziness occurs readily when four images converge on a huge screen far away.

2. The more opulent theaters did not require interruptions because they had two pairs of projectors and could switch from one to the next at each reel change. But smaller local cinemas operated with just two projectors, both of which were required to view a 3D film and both of which had to be reloaded each time the reels ran out.

42

Cinerama: A Bit Late

It will probably take two years for this invention (which has shaken the columns of the cinematographic temple and challenged CinemaScope) to slip from the core of our curiosity. Cinerama is now inside our walls and I have not yet heard a conversation beginning with "Have you seen Cinerama?" On the contrary, I see how easily we are resigned to put off the discovery for a few more weeks or months.

This remark only means that the situation is not commercially viable. It is quite possible that during this period the Empire—whose curse as a theater is notorious—may actually find the two and a half million spectators filing into it that it evidently needs to amortize the operation.[1] But this will happen in the way a big spectacle succeeds at the Folies-Bergères or at the Châtelet, that is, thanks to people coming in from the provinces. The fact is that Cinerama is scarcely more than a spectacle attraction with its quota of surprises, of novelty, and of physical splendors that justify the price of the tickets. From the strictly cinematographic perspective, however, I think that its interest has become limited. Limited, yet still unquestionable; and this is what I want to address all the same.

I should quickly bring up the essential technical weak spot of the process, recognized even by its producers: the near impossibility of achieving an invisible match among the three side-by-side projectors. This was already a problem for the triple screen of Abel Gance, but for the creator of *Napoléon*, this problem became less significant since he so frequently projected three separate images. This matching problem did not come into play any more if the screen's totality was used for just exceptional moments that he chose so that the sutures could scarcely be felt. Abel Gance's Polyvision has only aesthetic justification; its alibi lies in the technology itself. Far from voiding the ideas of the prophet of the triple screen, Cinerama only confirms his ideas to be well-founded.

But I don't want to return to the problem of Polyvision, about which Abel Gance has already told us a good deal in these pages, and so let me limit myself to a critique of Cinerama in relation to what is a truly important historical phenomenon, the enlarging of the screen.[2]

Without doubt, CinemaScope diminished the shock that Cinerama should have provided. In a certain sense the latter is only a screen that is noticeably larger than those we are used to. And certainly Cinerama's spectacle sequences give us nothing more than the impression of being shot in Super-CinemaScope, as for example in the sequence showing the staging of *Aida* at La Scala in Milan. Its hideous décor and costumes, as well as its choreography, easily bear comparison with almost any Judeo-Egyptian epic in CinemaScope.[3] Only the perfection of stereo sound gives some momentary interest to the film, during the sequence of the young Viennese choir. But it would be bad faith to argue against the fact that certain other sequences amount to far more than the multiplication by a certain coefficient of our already familiar screen size. I am particularly alluding to the flight above the United States. In this case the emotion is powerful and unprecedented.

A first observation demands to be made: the impression of depth definitely exists (at least when there is some displacement along the axis of the camera's angle). But it is certain that this impression is not at all a factor of realism; it is, rather, much more its consequence. It was only a commercial swindle when the publicity campaign of the new projection technologies stood under the sign of 3D (because CinemaScope doesn't really render things in depth); this was principally a psychological mistake, since it takes the effect for the cause. What is so pleasing about Cinerama is the realism of its spectacle, realism so great that it sometimes edges into depth [*relief*]. But depth cannot very well reinstate realism, just as we have seen happen in the stereo-optical 3D films that the public has shown it doesn't want.

What now? Can we say what realism is? I would define it essentially not by the rendering of depth but rather of space. For the first time, or nearly so (I'll speak in a minute about some rare CinemaScope images), I became aware of the limits of all the images available up to the present, finding them all unable to render space because they restrict themselves to translating it through the geometrical symbolism of perspective. I don't have the room here, nor the competence, to analyze the reasons behind this discovery of space, but surely one cause relates to the size of the angle of vision. That angle in Cinerama is 146 degrees, thus roughly equal to that of natural vision. And in the same way as in natural vision, you are in effect physiologically unable to completely synthesize all the elements of the image;

you have to let your gaze wander not only by moving your eyes but by turning your head.

Earlier I mentioned a hesitation. In effect I had had an analogous impression, but to a lesser degree, in watching three CinemaScope films at Cannes, *La Pêche au thon* (USA), *Ile de feu* (Italy), and *Continent perdu*.[4] Compared to its powerful utilization in these three films, the CinemaScope we have seen up to now in story films has been practically nonexistent. It is significant that what's at issue in all these cases, including Cinerama, concerns documentary spectacle.

Let me then extrapolate from these experiences, which seem to permit a sketch of a theory of widescreen. Misunderstandings concerning it proceed from the confusion between the two aesthetic natures of the screen. In effect, the difference is between considering it as if it were a hole versus if it were a frame. When you say, for example, that the screen is a "keyhole" (Cocteau), or a "window opening on the world," you affirm its capacity to deliver something to see. But when you speak of an image being well constructed, a shot being balanced, you compare the screen to a painting where the proportions of the frame matter. But it is true and proper to affirm that a larger hole is, well, a hole that is larger. From this perspective the superiority of CinemaScope is thus self-evident [*lapalissade*]. On the other hand, it is absurd to pretend that the "marine" format is superior to the square format because its value is patently relative to the subject inscribed within it.[5] This banal observation delivers a decisive critical notion. It permits us to define a priori the only genre where the enlargement of the screen must, in essence, be considered genuine progress: the documentary. Adjustments to this principle apply only to certain details. It is clear, for example, that if the object of the documentary is small and circumscribed by nature, the size of the screen is a matter of indifference or even, at the limit, an encumbrance. But the general advantages are considerable in the pure documentary, where plastic composition is a parasitical preoccupation. On the other hand, you can dream about what Flaherty would have been able to do with CinemaScope or Cinerama, since for him the spatial relations between man and nature constitute the infrastructure of his mise-en-scène.

From this one can deduce the superiority of widescreen in the mise-en-scène of "fiction films," either when the story is supported by documentary subject matter or when the mise-en-scène is based precisely on spatial relations. For such films, widescreen allows for more free play beyond montage. But in general, except for these two important exceptions, the enlarging of the screen brings with it no a priori aesthetic superiority other than one of a psychological order.

Since the cinematographic spectacle is never defined only in itself but rather also in relation to the public, everything that contributes to the active participation of the spectator is progress. We have seen that opening the angle of vision contributes to this—the opening relative to the size of the screen. But this angle can be just the same for two screens of different proportions. We know theaters that have been equipped for Cinema-Scope by cutting the height of the old screen in half, resulting in a painfully constricted spectacle that is hardly as satisfying for the eye as the old screen of traditional proportions. The real problem is thus never one of format, but one of surface. What will probably constitute a genuinely positive acquisition in our current technological commotion is the viewer's habituation to large images and to the demands these make on our eyes. It will be a matter of covering huge surfaces in a technically satisfying fashion. Until all the results have come in and been tried out, VistaVision constitutes the most promising process along these lines. I am speaking of true VistaVision, with the film unrolling lengthwise and so permitting, as it already does in New York, a projection on a screen that is as wide as that of Cinerama ... "but much higher"![6]

NOTES

From "Un peu tard ...," *Cahiers du Cinéma* 48 (June 1953). This article is a review of *Place au Cinérama* (*This Is Cinerama*), which included an introductory presentation by Lowell Thomas and Merian Cooper followed by a dozen discrete sections like "Temple Dance," "Niagara Falls," "Bullfight in Madrid," and "America the Beautiful." On May 16, 1955, it came to Paris's Empire Theater, which had been redesigned for it, and played continuously until the beginning of 1957, when *Cinerama Holiday* replaced it.

1. The Empire was born as one of the world's great music halls. The notorious swindler Alexandre Stavisky made it his headquarters. After he was killed early in 1934, it was transformed into a first-run film theater. The Nazis then turned it into the largest "soldiers' cinema" in the world. This dark past haunted its postwar resurrection as a legitimate theater, then again as a flagship movie theater for Pathé. Cinerama gave it yet another life.

2. Gance had discussed all this six months earlier in *Cahiers du Cinéma* 41 (December 1954).

3. Bazin is undoubtedly reminding his readers that the first CinemaScope film to be distributed was the biblical epic *The Robe,* which premiered in the United States in September 1953 and in France three months later.

4. Although he indicates that the first title comes from the United States, perhaps Bazin is speaking of *Tempo di tonni,* a 1955 Italian documentary on tuna fishing. All three of these CinemaScope documentaries would then hail from Italy, since that is also the provenance of *Isole di fuoco* (a short by Vittorio De Seta) and *Continente perduto.*

5. "Marine" format refers to the very wide framing used in horizontal sea paintings.

6. VistaVision was Paramount's contribution to the various widescreen options. Instead of squeezing the image anamorphically onto the 35mm gauge like CinemaScope, it flipped the 35mm celluloid in the camera so it ran horizontally, producing a wide image without distortion. This process lasted about a half dozen years but is considered the forerunner of 70mm.

43

Cinerama, a Disappointment

And so, nearly three years after it appeared in New York, and lagging behind its arrival in Canada, England, Japan, and Italy, Cinerama has at last come to Paris. We no longer need to rely on accounts from travelers but are in a position to judge for ourselves this spectacle that has turned cinema upside down. Don't forget that Cinerama is at the origin of a partial revolution in production, since Hollywood felt that enlarging the image was the way to counter the competition from television, by renewing a hunger for spectacle. Then, just in the way that Professor Chrétien, impressed by Abel Gance's triple screen, imagined that one could compress any image via anamorphosis, and avoid the complications of triple projection and shooting with three cameras, so Hollywood recognized in CinemaScope the possibility of efficiently commercializing widescreen and stereo sound.[1]

Also, don't forget that technological conditions effectively doom Cinerama a priori to a limited release in a few theaters worldwide—the most optimistic estimate would be perhaps two or three theaters in a country like France. The production-exhibition relationship is thus radically different than it was in classical cinema. From this perspective, CinemaScope looks like an adaptation of Cinerama's innovations to the conditions of traditional exhibition.

This is also why in 1955 Cinerama cannot produce for us the effect of surprise and shock whose echo we hear in the accounts of spectators from 1952. We can maintain our critical stance while understanding that this earlier public must have been overwhelmed. In a sense, then, we are better off when it comes to assessing the impact and future prospects of Cinerama, but we shouldn't remain aloof or be insensitive to the strikingly new emotions that Cinerama has to offer.

· · ·

There can be little doubt that Cinerama will usher in a new stage in cinematic realism. The impression of depth (nearly absent in CinemaScope) that used to be emphasized in its marketing does indeed exist, but it is not the most significant phenomenon, because here, depth is merely the by-product of realism. This is also the reason for the disappointment felt by those who had hoped to compete with Cinerama by using stereoscopic 3D, a still more effective technique. In practice, the third dimension does not produce the feel of reality: it is a consequence of that feel, which is irrefutably restored to us here in a way that moreover feels novel, and with surprising efficacy.

Certainly, some sequences of the Cinerama spectacle give us the impression of discovering something for which all images previously known, including those of cinema, were only a rough approximation. I find myself hesitating to use the word "image" in reference to Cinerama and so, in order to avoid it, I have replaced it with "sequence." This is because, if we are still dealing with a reproduction of reality, this reproduction is so physically effective, at least at certain moments, that it no longer corresponds to our traditional concept of the image. It's true that this impression was likewise felt by the first spectators of cinema, and so it will likely become similarly dulled for us as we get used to it, especially given that the Cinerama image is unfortunately not perfect, since, distressingly, it calls attention to its own artificial nature.

In spite of improvements to the Cinerama screen (which provide exceptional luminosity and allow for the perfect rectification of the image despite a pronounced curvature), the original shortcomings of *Napoléon*'s triple screen remain virtually unchanged after twenty-five years. Indeed, the synchronicity of the three projectors and the perfect alignment of perspectives during shooting are not sufficient to guarantee the flawless joining of the three images. This would require the most exact registration during the film's development in the lab, and above all the perfect calibration of color—ideal conditions that are unlikely to be fully maintained. In any case, at the present moment, the three vertical seams remain clearly visible and often prevent the mental synthesis of the three images into a single unified whole, even when frequent transversal movements are designed to visibly refute those seams.[2]

In my view, this flaw—which will no doubt be lessened, but which will almost certainly persist—confirms the wisdom of Abel Gance, who made use of panoramic views only in exceptional moments. Generally he preserved the individuality of each of the three screens to perform a kind of spatial montage, playing with the plastic relationships, both affective and intellectual, between the three images. Of course, it is difficult to know whether this "Polyvision" has a future. One wishes that Abel Gance had found the means to demonstrate it, since only in this vein could one really believe in the existence of a Cinerama aesthetic except for one precise but limited domain. So I want to talk about the documentary.

.   .   .

To my mind, out of the entire, artistically uneven jumble of short sequences that makes up the spectacle *This Is Cinerama*, the only incontestable successes have been the great documentary passages—and especially, in spite of its length, the segment filmed from a plane flying over the United States.[3] Here the need for realism is doubled: in the object itself and in its reproduction. If the artistic composition of fiction films, which always imply choice, might stand to lose more than it gains from the uniform enlargement of the screen, surely from the moment when documentary value takes precedence over artifice, any added realism in the image is beneficial. This was definitely the lesson to be learned at the most recent Cannes festival. At last, and for the first time, we seemed to discover a reality that eluded earlier photographic methods—that is to say, the reality of space. We already have color film. Cinerama, and CinemaScope to a certain degree, open the era of a cinema of space.

Here we have the only specific aesthetic advancement that Cinerama and CinemaScope have to offer: anytime that space constitutes a dramatic component of the event being filmed, anytime recourse to a wider field is a decisive gain for the mise-en-scène. Unfortunately, the debilitating spectacle of the trumpets from *Aida* at La Scala in Milan gives us reason to fear that Cinerama is committing the same error as CinemaScope: confusing spectacle with space and sheer quantity with weight-bearing surface! The few seconds of Cinerama that gave me a glimpse of what a dramaturgy of space might be occurred during a brief piece of footage on the running of the bulls—an immense stationary shot encompassing both the bleachers and the arena. Yet here, for the first time, I could precisely locate the rapport between beast and man!

NOTES

From "Le Cinérama," *France-Observateur* 263 (26 May 1955).

1. Henri Chrétien invented his "Hypergonar" anamorphic lens in 1928, just after Abel Gance's *Napoléon* made a splash using three screens. Chrétien's device is placed on the camera to squeeze a wide view onto a normal 35mm film strip, which, after development, is unsqueezed by a similar lens in front of the projector. A wider screen, of course, needs to be installed to hold this 2.35:1 image. Despite its convenience, it was never exploited until Hollywood studios turned to it as an inexpensive way to approach the width of Cinerama, which had premiered in September 1952 but which was very clumsy.

2. Bazin errs here. There are only two vertical seams where three screens meet.

3. *This Is Cinerama* (produced by Merian Cooper with Lowell Thomas, 1952) was a compilation of twelve episodes, the climax being "America the Beautiful."

44

Cinema in 3D and Color: Amazing!

As of last night, Parisians can now see the 3D films that were one of the big attractions at the recent Festival of Britain.[1] Films in 3D and in color, let me add, for while the system still entails wearing special glasses, those glasses are no longer red and green, as they were before. They are exactly like sunglasses, made from a lightly tinted glass that does not distort colors. This technique for stereoscopic filming and projection was developed by Raymond Spottiswoode. As with the old method that used anaglyphs, as well as Louis Lumière's more recent version using polarized glass, the new system involves two distinct images of the same object projected on the screen, with a certain spatial discrepancy between them. Thanks to the glasses, each of the two images is perceived separately by one and only one eye. Each eye thus sees a different image, as occurs in reality, and the viewer's mind reconstitutes three dimensions out of these two distinct perceptions. Incidentally, this same venerable principle of stereoscopic photography was practiced by our grandfathers.

But its application to cinema poses numerous optical problems that until now had not been satisfactorily resolved. Mr. Spottiswoode deserves credit for having determined with precision the importance of the various technical factors in play. Thanks to his calculations, the filmmaker is the master of his world in three dimensions: he can accentuate them, situating his shots in space, in relation to the viewer, or to better serve the interests of the scene.

The most sensational use that has been made of this process can be credited to a young Canadian animator who remains in the vanguard of experimental cinema: Mac Laren.[2] His two animations *Now Is the Time* and *Around Is Around* literally juggle space. With a few colored lines and dots, he constructs a prodigious abstract ballet in space, as dazzling as a fireworks display above the heads of the spectators.

These two films "drawn in 3D" are accompanied by three documentary shorts whose appeal is less consistent. A filmed ballet, *Le Cygne noir* [The black swan], provides a sense of what 3D could bring to dance films. However, it is in black and white, whereas 3D undoubtedly makes the absence of color more noticeable. We will of course always prefer a long walk on the banks of the Thames when the riches of Technicolor are added to the surprising effects of stereoscopic vision. Fortunately the program was filled out first by an old Mack Sennett piece with his irresistibly madcap humor, and then, above all, by a prodigious animation from Tex Avery that far surpasses Walt Disney's best work of the last few years.

NOTES

From "Le Cinéma en relief et en couleurs: Surprenant!," *Le Parisien Libéré* 2432 (9 July 1952).

1. The Festival of Britain was a large-scale exposition held throughout the summer of 1951 on the south bank of the Thames. It was a celebration of the new decade, now comfortably beyond the postwar rebuilding stage. Technology was featured and, in cinema, 3D was first demonstrated in a new theater designed for the festival, which is currently the National Film Theatre. A half million people attended the 3D screenings, which were among the top attractions of the entire festival.

2. Bazin of course is referring to Norman McLaren (1914–1987), whose name he gets wrong and who was not really so young, being 38 at the time, four years older than Bazin. The two would become friends.

45

A New Stage in the Process: Math Equations for 3D

Georges Sadoul, in the first volume of his monumental *Histoire du cinéma,* advanced the quite likely hypothesis that the inspiration for cinema was 3D photography.[1] An earlier historian, Potonniée, made the same claim: "It was not the discovery of photography but rather the stereoscope that opened the inventors' eyes. By capturing figures frozen in space, photographers realized that their images lacked the movement necessary to make their images of life a true copy of nature" (*L'Invention du cinéma,* p. 29). Stereoscopy is nearly as old as photography. A half century ago, amateur photographers commonly used double-lens stereoscopic cameras. If someone in your family was an amateur photographer, you will probably still find stashed somewhere in the corner of the attic some stereographic plates holding two seemingly identical negatives. When positive photographs are made from these, they are viewed through the two eyepieces of a special box built in such a way that each eye sees only one of the image pair. The impression of three dimensions was quite pronounced [in this system], although the different planes appeared rather flat, as in a diorama.

EVERY EYE FOR ITSELF

As we all know, the stereoscopic effect is based on the synthesis of binocular vision, which is how we perceive three dimensions in the real world. Each eye perceives the same object from a slightly different angle. Our brain receives two images that are not identical and it must synthesize them into a single 3D image. Quite probably, binocular vision alone does not account for our perception of space; several other factors are at play: light, movement, perspective, and so on. All these help one-eyed viewers to appreciate depth too. Still, binocular vision remains the essential factor.

Yet standard photography, as in the movies, cancels out binocular vision. Basically, as the image obtained is a projection of three-dimensional reality on a two-dimensional plane, each eye sees exactly the same image (see opposite page). From whichever angle the spectator views the screen, he sees the object as if with *a single eye*—the viewfinder of the camera. The challenge is thus to find a way to present each eye with its own image corresponding to the normal angle of vision in the real world.

The first solution hit upon was the anaglyph. It works by simultaneously projecting on a single screen two images taken by a stereoscopic camera, with one image tinted red and the other green. The spectator wears glasses with the lenses tinted, respectively, red and green. The eye with the red glass perceives only the red image, and the other eye sees only the green one. The brain synthesizes these two distinct images with an undeniably striking 3D effect.

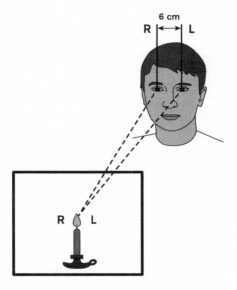

But anaglyphs had several drawbacks. In particular, they fatigue the eyes and reduce total brightness. Around 1935, Louis Lumière brought out a more elegant solution to the problem, polarized lenses. Again, two images are projected, but this time under normal white light, polarized in converse senses. Glasses fitted with special (though colorless) lenses separate the images in the same manner as colored glasses do.

THE 3D FORMULA

This same technology is behind the latest 3D films now playing in Paris after being featured at the Festival of Britain. These new films, however, have made several advances on their predecessors. First of all, the awkwardness of the glasses has been minimized: today's glasses have the same style and weight as ordinary sunglasses; their lenses are very light and slightly shaded and do not affect color. They work equally well for color films and for black and white. Of the five films screened in this initial program, three are in color.

But the real breakthrough is more technical, and spectators will appreciate the effect without grasping the cause. The stereoscopic reproduction of a three-dimensional scene onto a flat screen poses deeply complex problems. To understand them it's enough to realize that in reality our eyes never stop working. In reality we never perceive the ensemble of spatial planes in one single glance. Our gaze "wanders" from one plane to another. At this moment, while I am writing, my eyes *converge* on the tip of my pen while the lens of each eye *focuses* about 30 cm in front of me. Each eye is really a miniature instant camera whose framing and focus keeps changing at the dashing speed of my attention. Despite its shallow depth of field, the mobility of my gaze creates the illusion of seeing all at once a reality that I'm actually constantly dissecting.

However, stereoscopic film images cannot have such flexibility; they are recorded in blocks by two lenses whose axis of convergence, focal point, and focal length must stay fixed for the duration of the shot and be identical for every spatial plane. A young English scholar, Raymond Spottiswoode has expressed this complicated problem in mathematics.[2] Thanks to his formulations, we now know not only what the convergence of the lenses and the focal plane should be for any given scene's depth, but we also know the rather ample limits within which this 3D effect can be modulated. In other words, the filmmaker now has just as much creative control over the third dimension as his various lenses give him over framing and visual style.

The following sketches explain the key principle behind these complex equations. Given that our eyes are separated by a dis-

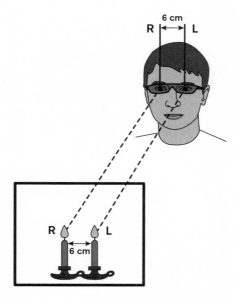

tance of 63mm on average, a point at infinity translates onscreen as two points separated by the same 63mm, with the axes of our two eyes in parallel. Notice that the image seen by the left eye is on the left, and that of the right eye on the right (see above). But if I want to move that same point into the space *in front of the screen,* halfway to the viewer, I have to flip the two images, so they remain separated by 63mm onscreen, but the left image is now on the right side and vice versa (see next page). You readers skilled in geometry can follow this reasoning through to understand that the relative position onscreen of the two images varies according to the position in space of the object closest to the spectator.* Modifying the axis of convergence of the camera lenses places the spectator nearer or further from the action.

---

* The main drawback to the stereoscopic process, which initially upset certain viewers, depending on their sensitivity (to the point of causing

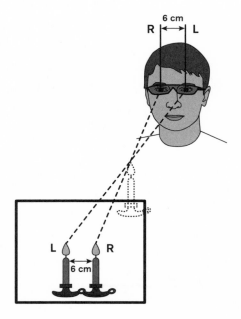

MCLAREN AND SYNTHESIZED 3D

The mastery of these stereoscopic formulae allowed Norman McLaren to create *animations in synthetic 3D*. By using only one standard camera and calculating the precise separation and axis of convergence for each part of the image, McLaren freely moves lines, points, and surfaces within space. The result is dif-

---

headaches), comes from forcing the eyes to *converge* on an imaginary image (see above) while each eye's lens remains *focused* on the real image onscreen—otherwise one sees only confusion. In the real world, convergence and focus are linked—the more steeply my eyes converge, the nearer their focus becomes. When I look at the end of my nose, I go cross-eyed and work hard to see clearly. But at the cinema, I dissociate these two physiological actions. With enough time anyone can do it, and while this generally takes only a few minutes, some people need more time and must find it tiresome.

ficult to describe to anyone who has yet to see some of the "flat" animations of this prodigious film artisan; from his small Canadian laboratory, he is revolutionizing the field of animation with his brilliance and poetic sensibility. I hardly get at this last aspect of his experiments by describing them as *abstract painting in motion and in 3D.* Years ago, Fernand Léger made *Ballet mécanique* by transposing his painting practice into black and white photography of real objects. Today, 3D color cinema would give him a means that is purely painterly although unimaginable outside of 3D cinema: the painter can now create moving forms in space. If one day 3D cinema evolves beyond a trivial scientific curiosity, as it will likely do, directing the garden hose to spray the audience will not be enough to astonish us.[3] The distant future of 3D cinema will see a leap as great as the one from *L'Arrivée d'un train en gare de La Ciotat* to the train engine sequence in *La Bête humaine.*[4] The labor of Mr. Spottiswoode and its still-experimental application in the films at the Festival of Britain already prove that 3D affords the same interpretations, with a function as orchestrated and utterly *artistic,* as "flat" cinema. Let us nimbly take this new and decisive step toward total cinema.

NOTES

From "Un Nouveau Stade du cinéma en relief: Le relief en équations," *Radio-Cinéma-Télévision* 131 (20 July 1952). Grant Wiedenfeld produced the first draft of this translation.

1. Bazin's famous essay "The Myth of Total Cinema" was in fact written as a review of Sadoul's book, *L'Invention du cinéma* (Paris: Denoël, 1946).

2. Raymond Spottiswoode (1913–1970) was a director and producer of war effort shorts during World War II for the Canadian Film Board. The University of California Press published his excellent *Grammar of the Film:*

An Analysis of Film Technique in 1950. It was a staple in film education for two decades, in part because of the precision of its explanations.

3. A reference to the early Lumière film *L'Arroseur arrosé* (*Tables Turned on the Gardener*).

4. Both of these films feature onrushing trains. The first, by the Lumière Brothers, was shown in their initial 1895 program, while the second is Jean Renoir's 1938 masterpiece. Bazin chooses this pair because spectators are on record claiming to have been frightened by the Lumière film, which they described as three dimensional, while Renoir was widely praised for "penetrating" real space in his long opening sequence of the train rushing through the countryside, the camera aboard.

46

Will a War in Three Dimensions Take Place?

You will say that the passage from silent to sound cinema proves that a revolution is possible even when this involves a technological overhaul for distribution. This may be true, but at what price? When in 1927 Warner Brothers risked all they had on the attractiveness of sound, what they needed was nothing less than the energy that despair musters; their company was about to go bankrupt. You may also think that, with the economic crisis just around the corner, the exploitation of this new technology during the years 1928–1930 helped cinema through a very difficult moment that it had to undergo like all other industries. And so the sound cinema was able to supplant the silent, but only thanks to a certain number of conditions that came together in a conjunction powerful enough to conquer the inertia of distribution. Technologically, in fact, cinema had been quite ready to speak much earlier. If a desperate Warner Brothers had not agreed to buy the Western Electric patent that had been refused by other major studios, perhaps cinema would not have spoken for another decade. At the base of this technological disruption, there had to be an economic fear vital enough to drive a producer to take major risks to exploit it.

Such fear exists again today, given falling attendance in all the world's markets, first and foremost in the United States. Of course there isn't panic yet, but the persistent indication of all the statistics doesn't leave much doubt, and the American studios can see far enough ahead not to wait until they are forced by the specter of bankruptcy before reestablishing some equilibrium between expenses and receipts. A poor national cinema like our French one, working within a limited market that can hardly expand, has no other options except to make films more cheaply. But a production house with sufficient capital might prefer the strategy of huge moneymaking investments capable of profoundly and permanently modifying the conditions of the market.

It is often said that television is one of the factors that has alienated the public from cinema. Actually, this isn't at all certain, at least not in some direct and simple way. In America, the only country where television has sufficiently taken hold so as to make statistics meaningful, it appears that the drop in film attendance is just as great in regions that aren't yet reached by broadcasts. Inversely, in zones with the highest density of receivers, the point of saturation seems already to have been reached. Rather than a worsening situation so unfavorable to cinema, one could expect a certain form of weariness vis-à-vis television, against which cinema maintains a few advantages, mainly color, at least for the time being. In any case, it isn't television that should be held responsible for the loss of fifty million viewers in France since the war.[1] The most one can accuse it of is contributing to the general hemorrhage, whose cause is certainly less direct and much deeper.

.   .   .

Anyway, what is at stake is bringing the lost public back to the theaters and, with this goal, Hollywood, having seen the attraction of cinema succeed at the local level, thinks it can perhaps arouse the appetites of blasé spectators by renewing the basic aspect of the cinematographic image itself. They don't have to invent anything to accomplish this, only to release or re-release onto the market certain old technological processes that up to now, because of a lack of sufficient economic pressure, have never been able to overcome the inertia of the distributors.

The success or failure of the enterprise clearly may depend on the funds expended for advertising, and on the number and importance of the pilot theaters where the experiment is to be tried out ... all this to help prime a siphon that should get the public flowing back from the street into the hall. The effort to supply all this is so great and the risks so considerable that there must be, as we said, a supremely overriding reason. But whatever the energy and capital expended, it will not be enough if in the commercial launch it doesn't find a favorable response with the public. And nothing is less certain than the public. It is hardly clear that the interest aroused will go beyond the stage of curiosity; the siphon can definitely and quickly be broken, neutralized. In any case, there will likely be a choice made between binocular stereovision and the widescreen; it would be truly shocking if these two processes could maintain themselves simultaneously.

You might even confidently predict the failure of both enterprises with more or less long odds, if they aren't able to quickly pass beyond the stage of being a mere attraction so as to justify themselves on the artistic plane. Let's not forget that the cinema itself nearly remained stuck at the level of scientific curiosity and fairground attraction. Its first crisis arose in 1897. It didn't take the public more than eighteen months to let it become just another spectacle, demoted quickly from café concerts to fairground tents. The cinema as we know it resulted from a second birth, that of the cinema spectacle, with Méliès its principle artisan. The public's already sated curiosity required something of more durable interest to follow, and it got it in works composed and constructed for the imagination. So it could be that 3D with glasses has failed thus far because the films made for it have been of the documentary type.

Insofar as prognostics can express an idea in an area where the favor of the public comes into play, for my part I would gladly put more trust in widescreen than in 3D, precisely because it seems to me that its aesthetic resources are superior. Our current postcard style screen has become more and more a technological constraint against nature. The evolution of cinema since sound, overall and in particular during the past decade, leans to a negation of montage and of plastic aesthetics, at least the sort of pictorial plastics based on the existence and proportions of the frame. In *La Règle du jeu* [*The Rules of the Game*], for example, Renoir no longer used the screen as a place of his mise-en-scène; rather, it served him as a way to hide his characters behind its black borders. Montage itself relies indirectly on the dimensions of the screen, to the extent to which the close-up is conceivable only in a tight frame. Widescreen, on the other hand, bases *découpage* fundamentally on the long shot. In Abel Gance's triple screen, just as in Cinerama, the three juxtaposed screens can be dissociated at will. So montage remains possible and can even be multiplied by a spatial montage of three simultaneous images. But CinemaScope carries only one image and on a single screen. Should we then imagine a truly expandable screen that would bring us back around to the use of the iris to concentrate attention on a single point of the scene, something that was the equivalent of a close-up in films just before montage? These are so many hypotheses, the choice among which is worth leaving to the impending history of cinema. It won't be much longer.

NOTES

From "La Guerre de trois dimensions, aura-t-elle lieu?," *L'Observateur politique, économique et littéraire* 153 (16 April 1953). The title is a pun on Jean Giraudoux's famous 1935 play *La Guerre de Troyes n'aura pas lieu* (*The Trojan War Will Not Take Place*). Bazin, writing during the Cold War, adds the connotation of World War III.

1. Bazin here calculates the annual drop in attendance, and he could have made things look a bit worse. According to Françis Courtade in *Les Maledictions du cinéma français* (Paris: Alain Moreau, 1978, p. 235), the number of tickets sold in France dropped from a high of 424 million in 1947 to 356 million in 1952. That's a loss of 68 million, or sixteen percent.

47

The Return of *Metroscopix*

A recent first-run release gives me the chance to add a postscript to a more general inquiry. It concerns a highly publicized spectacle presented as the first part on a program with an American comedy. Now, this program precedes the upcoming distribution of *Bwana Devil,* the warhorse of United Artists, a film in 3D and color; so the current release might appear to the layman as the avant-garde of Operation 3D.

You are allowed to be stunned when a serious American company, which has no need to behave like some Persian rug seller, dares to put back on the market, as if it were brand new, a piece of merchandise that is twenty years old, and to blanket this with a massive and grossly ambiguous advertising campaign. For the famous film, *Metroscopix* ("So real that it leaps from the screen"), is actually an attraction that came out in 1933 or 1934. It is nothing more than a series of special-effect turns (a fireman's hose aimed into the theater, a baseball thrown so it will strike the viewer in the face, etc.), shot with a two-strip stereo camera using the century-old anaglyph process. This means that depth is obtained through the simultaneous projection of two images, one red, the other green, watched by spectators wearing a pair of glasses furnished with filters of these same colors.

Unless I'm mistaken, this short must have been the very first commercial 3D product ever released, and some of my readers will certainly remember having seen it several years before the war. Well, here it is, so they can see it again today, retrieved from the firm's storage blockhouse. In any case it is accompanied by a short subject, *A Murder in 3D,* a naïve and inoffensive parody of a Grand Guignol skit, which didn't figure on the 1933 program. I doubt, however, that it was shot more recently, since the style of the mise-en-scène and the décor clearly come from the same epoch.

This said, these little films, which are quite adroitly directed by the way, work well enough, their depth effects often intense and irresistible. However, they reestablish, as if that were needed, the crippling inconveniences associated with the ana-glyph process: the imperfect sharpness of the two slightly sepa-rated images, the tremendous absorption of light, and above all, the intense ocular and nervous fatigue.

On the other hand, the program of 3D films presented eight months ago at the Broadway, following the Festival of Britain, displayed definite progress over this barbarous, archaic form. The sharpness of images (all in color) was handled via Polaroid glasses, which are large and comfortable, reducing to a mini-mum one's visual fatigue. Beyond that, the camerawork, with Spottiswoode in charge of focus, took account of the physiology of sight, so that the spectator's eyes were never forced to con-verge abnormally. Besides, it is thanks to the majority of these improvements that the Technicolor feature *Bwana Devil* was made, as it is obvious that any 3D process requiring glasses of inferior quality would be destined to fail. Even with the inconvenience now greatly limited, wearing these is still a handicap large enough to put the commercial success of the enterprise in doubt.

NOTE

From "Métroscopix," *L'Observateur politique, économique et littéraire* 154 (23 April 1953).

48

The House of Wax:
Scare Me . . . in Depth!

Here at last is a film in full stereoscope relief which for the first time makes the ultimate worth of the third dimension perceptible. We're not talking about a revolutionary masterwork; this is far from that, but simply a film rather adroitly made and in a manner different from how it would have been made in the standard flat format.

Naturally the intellectual and artistic level is not very high, but neither were the first films of Lumière and Méliès. The script, which limits itself to taking up a theme already treated twice in the cinema, once in a silent version, once in sound, doesn't pretend to be anything more than a fairly naïve horror tale of the Grand Guignol variety: a sculptor who has gone mad and is the proprietor of a type of Musée Grévin murders the models he is attracted to so as to preserve them in wax.[1] You can guess that verisimilitude is not the strength of this story, which unrolls as a simple succession of scenes of terror without genuine danger; this scarcely matters to the spectator, who has really come only to experience a delicious but inoffensive dread. What counts more for us is the realization that generally, without this illusion of depth, the scenes would lose most of their emotional value. All it takes to convince the spectator of this is to close one eye behind the glasses: the action falls flat, literally and figuratively.

The fact is that fear, surely more than all other feelings, is linked to the perception of space, from fear of a void, which we call vertigo, to fear of the night, in which all perils emerge. When the first film audiences ran from the train entering the station at La Ciotat, it was due to the fact that in its absolute novelty, the reproduction of movement on a flat screen provided the illusion of depth. Habit has made us lose this feeling, but it has started to return thanks to the extra large screens of Cinerama and CinemaScope that renew our vision. We will get used to these in turn.

In *House of Wax*'s favor, let's note that its director knew how to choose a subject made for the new technology. And this time the image seems nearly sharp enough. The Warner Color may not be in perfect taste, but it looks satisfactory and agreeable. As for those glasses, while they may bother certain people for specific physiological reasons, to me they seemed quite tolerable (different from my impression while watching *Bwana Devil*). Must we expect that *House of Wax* sounds the death knell of flat cinema the way *The Jazz Singer* did for silent movies? Nothing is less certain. It doesn't appear that 3D will renew the realism of the screen nearly so radically as did sound or even color. Outside of certain specific themes (like horror, precisely) the third dimension adds nothing essential to the action of flat cinema, and it brings with it in return some real inconveniences: in addition to the need to wear Polaroid glasses, you have the annoying impression that the characters have shrunk, appearing at certain moments like Lilliputians. For these and other reasons, I can easily imagine that in the future we will have certain films made in 3D—just as certain films are already made in color—but without the third dimension becoming an absolute or habitual norm.

There's still the large screen, but that's another story.

NOTES

From "*L'Homme au masque de cire:* Fais-moi peur . . . en relief!," *Le Parisien Liberé* 2733 (27 June 1953).

1. Founded in 1882, the Musée Grévin was (and remains) Paris's home for wax figures and associated spectacles.

49

The Real Crime on *La Rue Morgue*: They Assassinated a Dimension!

In his recently published and excellent book *Le Cinéma,* Henri Agel recruits Doniol-Valcroze for the following opinion: "If CinemaScope had been exploited as it could have been, today, fifteen years later, the director would be able to choose the proportion of his images the way a painter can decide the format of his canvas."[1] Yes, a variable screen certainly is the ideal solution to the problem of screen dimension, and it is technically possible too, without a doubt. Despite this, I still harbor great skepticism regarding the future of the variable screen and continue to oppose it to CinemaScope because I believe neither in its practicability nor in the probability of its general commercialization. This is because the technological progress of cinema is not brought about by the logical demands of art, or even by the economic conditions of *production,* but rather everything happens from the standpoint of *exploitation.*

The case of Rouxcolor and similar processes is highly typical.[2] The principle of Rouxcolor, in fact, is by far the most economical, simple, and rational in the realm of color film, because

it completely eliminates the enormous dependence on the laboratory by reducing color breakdown and synthesis into a simple
optical operation during shooting and projection. But Rouxcolor was doomed to failure from the start, for the sole reason
that it complicates the projection of the film, that is to say, it
complicates exhibition. Cinema can be visualized as a pyramid
whose tip is the filmmaker and whose base comprises thousands
of screening rooms where the public and proprietors make the
rules without really knowing to what extent the projection is a
faithful rendition of the original. In any case, it is always more
expedient to invest thousands at the level of production than to
cause the usherettes to lose fifty francs in concession sales.
Which Gallup poll is going to tell us whether the audience
would ultimately rather do without a documentary than without
Eskimo Pies?[3]

HITCHCOCK: A VICTIM OF THE FAILURE OF 3D

These reflections came to me this past week, while watching
Phantom of the Rue Morgue, which four Parisian theaters are running in its flat version, imitating American theater managers in
conceding the complete failure of stereoscopic relief. Alerted to
the fact that the version in three dimensions (3D, as we say) was
not doing as well as the 2D version, the American distributors
decided, pure and simple, to send out separately the two copies
necessary for stereoscopic projection, so the films produced
for 3D last year were nearly all projected in their flat versions.
If you go to see *Phantom of the Rue Morgue* you will easily discern
the moments in the direction that were intended for three
dimensions, and their presence appears absurd after you realize
this.

Many of these 3D productions were small films without great aesthetic pretensions, whose only appeal resides in a few entertaining effects. There simply is not much left of them now. But this problem is somewhat more serious when a film by Alfred Hitchcock is at stake, like *Dial M for Murder*, which very probably will be released here in two dimensions, as was the case in America.

LUCKILY, THERE ARE SOME CONSCIENTIOUS EXHIBITORS

It's my duty to point out, at least for the benefit of the Parisian public, that one conscientious and intelligent manager of a network of theaters is attempting to show 3D films systematically in their original version during their "second run." This way, an excellent Western like *Hondo*, projected flat but at full price in "exclusivity," can be seen in 3D, and at reduced price, in certain Parisian neighborhoods.[4] This manager deserves a great deal of credit, since he does this while correctly understanding that the public does not respond very well to the constraints of the process. They don't like wearing glasses and they protest the two interruptions necessary to reload the projectors that run simultaneously. Now, the more savvy spectators of the "exclusive" theaters never worry about these annoyances, something that incidentally cancels out one of their excuses. This manager alone risks facing such drawbacks. He also accepts the slight complication of his job that goes with distributing glasses, and his projectionists deal with a few more issues than their colleagues in order to assure a noticeably proper projection. But alas, a swallow does not bring about spring, and cinema will continue to depend on the vendors of ice-cold Eskimo Pies.

NOTES

From "La Véritable Crime de la rue Morgue: On a assassiné une dimension," *Radio-Cinéma-Télévision* 263 (30 January 1955). The title refers to *Phantom of the Rue Morgue*, a 1954 3D production directed by Roy Del Ruth and starring Karl Malden. It opened in Paris in January 1955.

1. Henri Agel, *Le Cinéma* (Paris: Casterman, 1954). Jacques Doniol-Valcroze (1920–1989) was at the outset the most active of the three founding editors of *Cahiers du Cinéma*, since Bazin was ill during this period and Lo Duca was there mainly for his connections and his name. Doniol-Valcroze shared a column with Bazin in *L'Observateur.* He wound up participating in the New Wave, making a number of feature films from 1961 to 1964.

2. Rouxcolor was a French additive color process that used a complex lens attached to both camera and projector. It ultimately failed to take hold. See note 1 in chap. 41.

3. Bazin is satirizing the indifference of theater owners to the quality of projection, as opposed to their effort to promote concessions. They would be ready to sacrifice the documentary short subjects, required by law at the time, if they could sell more food. The Eskimo Pie was the first ice-cream bar distributed internationally.

4. *Hondo*, directed by John Farrow and starring John Wayne, was shot with a dual-strip 3D method but released almost exclusively in its flat version. It premiered in late 1953 in Houston and was first screened in Paris in December 1954.

50

The 3D Revolution Did Not Take Place

When you let your memory take you back to the ambiance that reigned over the cinematographic world barely three years ago and then consider the current state of cinema, it seems that you first must declare that the "War of 3D" did not take place.[1] Let's remember that the launch of new technological formats almost always occurs under the advertising slogan of "depth" (i.e., three dimensions). Perhaps genuine 3D cinema would create a real revolution, comparable to what occurred with sound. In fact, today nobody even remembers sitting before a CinemaScope film and having believed for a moment that it had anything to do with a third dimension. As for the only commercial process that actually restores a true impression of volume, that which requires anaglyph processes and has improved with Polaroid glasses, we know that its failure has been swift and decisive, and that films shot in this process are more often than not exhibited flat. The only important, incontestable technical transformations to emerge after these three years of gestation are those that affect the dimensions of the screen, or, more precisely, its proportions. Let's scan the situation.

CINERAMA AT AN IMPASSE

Recall first of all that this development stems from an impressive "invention," the rediscovery of Abel Gance's triple screen under the name Cinerama. You hardly need to play the prophet to pronounce that Cinerama will surely go down in cinema as just what the Châtelet or, better, the Folies-Bergère has become to theater, that is, nothing more than a few specially furbished movie theaters around the world, holding the same program for a full year as they struggle to pay off enormous costs.[2] The reason for this stagnation is deep and crippling: while impressive and convincing within the domains of spectacle and documentary, Cinerama is visibly impotent in pulling off a dramatic story. Despite all its technological attractions, cinema is decidedly and primarily an art born from theater and the novel, an art of man and his destiny. If the triple screen were to have an aesthetic future, it will assuredly not be via the exclusively spectacular use of Cinerama, but thanks to the intellectual dimension that gave birth to Polyvision.[3]

Be that as it may, and while it is still in operation, Cinerama has had no other notable consequences than to resuscitate an entire gamut of "widescreens," of which two formats have lasted, CinemaScope and VistaVision. But before getting to these two major processes, an important issue already puts them in arrears. Under the influence of fashion, and wanting to adapt to the latest cinematographic look, most theater owners have thought it necessary to equip their halls with one of the so-called "panoramic" screens, whose arbitrary proportions seem generally determined mainly by the architecture of the room itself. Despite financing via the Aide Law [Fonds d'Aide au Cinéma], these hasty and badly planned installations have for the most part had the consequence of introducing blur into the projection. Such "modernization," worthy of Père Ubu, also boasts the advantage of requiring us to see films shot in traditional format that have been amputated by a third or a quarter of the height of their image.[4] That anyone could have conceived such an operation—and, against all reason, that they thought it wouldn't empty the theaters, but on the contrary, would bring some spectators back—this is something that opens up vertiginous perspectives into the psycho-sociological abysses of the cinematographic fact. Unless we should simply view this as a contemporary confirmation of Florian's tale,[5] in which the Publicity Monkey easily convinces the spectator at his magic lantern show that an image cut off by a third is actually twice as large.*

ILLUSION OF SPACE ON SCREEN AND IN THE THEATER

But let's return to CinemaScope (and other similar processes). Its success from here on out is incontestable, since 32,000 theaters around the world are already equipped to render it, thus assuring a very large distribution for anamorphic films. This success came about despite certain faults in the process: principally, deformation and blur. Noticeable progress has been made on the problem of blur (especially as far as the lateral zones of the screen are concerned), but an ugly squashing of faces still remains, at least in certain shots. We also have to note that image quality depends on the specific theater and is very unequal.

* It is true that there is also another conclusion to draw that I hardly dare formulate: it is that the framing, the famous sacrosanct framing, hasn't nearly the importance that the aestheticians of cinema have believed.

A dedicated study ought to be undertaken to ascertain the impression of space provided by the CinemaScope screens. A superficial and purely geometrical logic would have it that this impression flows exclusively from the angle formed by the eye of the spectator related to the two extremities of the screen. Unfortunately geometry is not the decisive factor here; I personally hold that the effect of space is the complex result not only of the relation of the spectator to the screen, but of this screen itself to certain privileged dimensions of the theater, and principally to those of the face of the wall holding the screen. Certainly, very large theaters with giant screens generally obtain a better result than the smaller ones, where the 1:2.55 screen tries to inscribe itself as a ridiculously tight band in place of the old 1:1.33 screen that was twice as tall. This doesn't keep the best CinemaScope theater in Paris from also being the smallest one: a private room on the Champs-Elysées, where the projection occupies the entirety of a back wall, from floor to ceiling. The impression of space here is really optimal.

As to the problem of blurring, it has also greatly evaporated since the foggy *Robe,* yet it still remains a weak spot of Cinema-Scope, which it seems could be fixed by using a 55mm negative, which would reduce the grain of the positive image over that of 35mm. In any case, an analogous principle is the basis of VistaVision, which I won't go into since its characteristics have been laid out previously for you.[6] In addition to the great clarity of the image, which becomes absolutely sensational when the projection is equally horizontal, VistaVision's real interest lies in its 1:1.85 screen ratio, a ratio that definitely seems the most fortuitous and pleasing of all that have been tried out until now, since it is spectacular enough to satisfy the eye, yet still rational enough to satisfy the mind.

A SUM-UP OF WIDESCREENS

So even provisionally, what conclusion can be drawn from this examination of the situation? Technologically, the balance sheet of the entire "3D" operation is largely negative because the quality of the projection, if not of the image, is often inferior to what was available long ago with old equipment and films. Still, the inherent weaknesses of shooting in a new format and projecting in standard format shall soon be no more than a memory. But we have to fear that the results of "modernization" will remain with certain theaters for a much longer period. One practical conclusion: a conscientious and organized spectator should always choose his films; now he will equally need to choose his theater. Don't use your good money to encourage exhibitors who screen traditionally shot films as if they were panoramic. From the artistic point of view, a first obvious consequence will be to hasten the evolution of color, though for all that, we shouldn't say that black and white productions are then doomed. I have already pointed out that on the margins of spectacle cinema we have the assertion of another type of production, "social" and "psychological" films like *Marty* and *Blackboard Jungle*.

But from a more general viewpoint, the overall outlook for new technologies in cinema seems quite positive, without being revolutionary. Positive, first of all, because on the whole you will appreciate that the fact of having tried to substitute three or four different formats for the old screen with its immutable proportions has broken worn-out habits and awakened the formal imaginations of filmmakers to rethink their mise-en-scène (look at *Lola Montès*).[7] Reciprocally, the level of curiosity aroused by all this commotion can only help stimulate the spectator's attention. But positive, above all, because it's no longer debatable that

CinemaScope offers intelligent, gifted directors new resources of mise-en-scène while, as we've already stated, the widescreen isn't always obligated to subjects that feature "grand mise-en-scène." It can accommodate psychological dramas just as well, if not better, than it does Westerns (look at *East of Eden*).[8]

However, it would be without question regrettable to see CinemaScope universally supplant films made in the smaller format. The plurality resulting from the current competition of processes is ultimately our guarantee of variety and liberty, at least while we await the highly problematic variable screen discussed in this journal in February. This theoretically ideal solution runs into several commercial and psychological objections that may prove exceedingly difficult to overcome.

Whatever comes about, even our great confidence about CinemaScope shouldn't allow anyone to see in this a genuine artistic revolution, like the radical renewal of cinema that we saw four years ago. The cinematographic spectacle hasn't really changed its nature, its topics remain roughly the same, and even montage, which so many intelligent people thought was on the verge of disappearing, has simply been adapted to new visual circumstances, without breaking with the fundamental laws coming down from our inheritance from Griffith.

NOTES

From "La Révolution par le relief n'a pas eu lieu," *Radio-Cinéma-Télévision* 324 (1 April 1956).

    1. Here, as in chap. 46, Bazin puns on the title of Jean Giraudoux's play *La Guerre de Troyes n'aura pas lieu* (*The Trojan War Will Not Take Place*).

    2. Both these theaters feature grand spectacles for tourists and seldom change their programs.

3. Polyvision is the name Abel Gance gave to his triple screen process, which he deployed far more as a means for spatial montage—different images on different screens at the same time—than for the "surround" effect of a single image stretched across three screens. Thus montage relates, in Bazin's mind, more to intelligence than spectacle.

4. Bazin refers here to Alfred Jarry's scatological play *Ubu Roi,* a hallmark of Dada. Père Ubu is sometimes rendered in English as "Old Turd."

5. Jean-Pierre Claris de Florian (1755–1794) is considered second only to La Fontaine as an author of French fables, of which he composed more than a hundred. Arrested during the French Revolution for some of his writings and for his noble birth, he died of tuberculosis after his imprisonment.

6. Evidently the VistaVision formula had been explained in an early issue of *Radio-Cinéma-Télévision.* This process, developed by Paramount in 1954, runs 35mm film laterally in the camera, making much more of the negative's surface available for registration, and doing so without anamorphosis. Bazin was correct that this format proved both sharper in focus and simpler to use than most; it lasted less than a decade but was a kind of trial run for 70 mm.

7. Max Ophüls's lush *Lola Montès,* considered a triumph of widescreen filmmaking, had come out at Christmas 1955, just four months before Bazin wrote this essay.

8. Elia Kazan's CinemaScope production of the highly dramatic *East of Eden* was screened in Paris in October 1955, six months before this essay appeared.

PART SIX

CinemaScope

51

Will CinemaScope Save the Cinema?

Everyone, even among the mass audience, now recognizes that Hollywood is working to resolve one of the most severe economic crises in its history. And it is doing so through two military operations; on the one hand there is 3D (this avant-garde stereoscopy is already visible on French screens), and on the other hand there is the war machine in CinemaScope, *The Robe,* which has already been seen on Broadway and will soon take up its position in Europe.

Everybody also recognizes that acute competition from television is forcing Hollywood into a corner where it has to accept the risks of a maneuver that disrupts the technological norms not just of production, but also of exhibition. Or at least, everybody thinks he knows this, for the particulars of the problem are not so simple. Hence my purpose here is precisely to try to put some order into all this.

Let's begin with some clarifications of a very general nature. First, we can note that this time the crisis is not turning into hysteria or panic. Certainly tremendous confusion still reigns,

and we are seeing the "major studios" make the most contradictory of decisions; each one has its own strategy (or claims it has,
since often the same strategy is merely re-baptized), and while
some of the larger companies have almost completely suspended
production for several months now, one can see a minor studio
like Monogram double its annual roll-out of B movies destined
for standard-size screens. But, again, this confusion has not—or
at least not so far—turned to hysteria and incoherence. Hollywood's early golden age is over. So when it throws everything
into CinemaScope, Fox is not really repeating the high-stakes
poker game of Warner Brothers and the talkies. In spite of a crisis at the box office that has become more pronounced over the
last five years, none of the American companies is yet close to
bankruptcy. They are probably in a position to ride out a long
Malthusian scenario without putting themselves in danger of
extinction. In other words, this technological experiment is relatively controlled, and once the wind of public sentiment has
clearly turned one way or another, Hollywood will no doubt be
able to draw the proper conclusions.

The situation will surely be far graver for unemployed technicians and actors in America. But for a few months at least, the
outlook is not really so alarming, since television is consuming a
great quantity of inexpensive and quickly made films that
employ lots of personnel. Certain stars are also moving over to
television, while others take advantage of their forced vacations
to come to Europe to shoot co-productions. Just remaining here
for eighteen months allows them to avoid paying income tax
(which is well worth the corresponding loss of salary). In short,
the situation could become very worrying five or six months
from now, but by then things will no doubt be clearer and work
will be able to resume, though at a different pace.

These remarks are not intended to minimize the significance of the crisis—on the contrary, since it would be impossible to do so in the face of statistics I'll cite later—but merely to define its climate and above all to underline the fact that Hollywood remains in control. It is important to know this if you believe, naïvely, in some momentous collapse, in the complete disappearance of Hollywood into some economic morass from which European cinema would benefit. Hollywood won't cast its "three dice" like a desperate gambler.[1] Rather, it will develop its current campaign with caution and resolution, supported by massive advertising; it will overcome the reservations of theater owners through short-term financial perks that encourage the conversion of their movie screens, and so on—in short, it will play all the trump cards that a powerful, conscious, and organized capitalism possesses. This is not to say that all the obstacles—and they are numerous, as we shall see—must be eliminated. But they will at least be tackled with the utmost efficiency, in Europe as well as in America; and I hardly see how this American experiment could be derailed by the old continent's resistance. The film revolution will be universal or it won't take place at all. Whether we like it or not, Hollywood remains the magnetic pole of the cinema, at least in the domain of technology. We can see this clearly today: Cinerama, which is nothing but Abel Gance's triple screen, and CinemaScope, which was invented twenty-five years ago by Professor Chrétien, suddenly have a chance at a future, solely because of the interest that America, anxious about business losses, has taken in them.

At first glance this observation might seem to convey a pessimistic reflection on the notion of progress in cinema. I will certainly need to elucidate this viewpoint, but only after having attempted to analyze its sociological and aesthetic aspects. Let's

stick to economics for the moment, and briefly recall the causes
and scale of a crisis whose seriousness cannot be debated.

. . .

The spread of television stands as the immediate cause for the
drop in attendance. In five or six years the American cinema has
lost about half of its domestic patrons, which has meant the clo-
sure of 5,000 movie theaters (France doesn't even have that
many) and will, sooner or later, mean the bankruptcy of several
thousand others. The concurrence of the swelling of this crisis
and the rise of television obviously does not leave any room to
doubt that the latter was the principal factor in the former.
Unfortunately we can't assume it is the only factor. Various indi-
cators suggest that today's 20 million American television sets
have only served to crystallize and hasten a tendency that was
already under way among the wider public. Indeed, once it
began, this trend could be felt even in regions where television
had not yet been introduced, and it has continued to intensify in
areas saturated with TV sets. Furthermore, we know that in
various European countries, and particularly in France, though
the number of television sets here is still insignificant, a troubling drop in film attendance has been recorded for several years
running. Thus everything is unfolding rather as if the American
public's deep and general lassitude had seized upon television as
an opportunity to express itself. The significance of the statistics is thus all the more alarming, and the hemorrhage cannot be
stopped merely by cauterizing the wound inflicted on the cinema by television.

By sheer instinct—an instinct that is long established and
that, as we will see, is not without value even from an aesthetic
perspective—Hollywood understood that its defensive reaction

against television would need to be of a *spectacular* order. Let us not forget that the recent evolution of cinema, even in America, has been toward the interiorization of mise-en-scène at the expense of *spectacle*. Moreover, this process has been dictated as much by market conditions as by the laws of aesthetic evolution. Some new *Birth of a Nation* produced with all of today's technological advances is unthinkable, because such a film would no longer be able to amortize its production costs (the case of *Gone with the Wind* is so miraculous that Hollywood is wary of imitating it). The recent biblical epics of Cecil B. DeMille are pathetically cheap compared to his productions of thirty years ago. Now we have to look to Russia (and possibly to India) to find films with huge casts of extras, made without regard to costs. Clearly, however, cinema's lasting superiority over television lies precisely in its spectacular resources, and in these alone. I say lasting because the TV image will in all likelihood remain restricted to America's standard of 625 lines (just as cinema's celluloid strip is locked in at 35mm, a size arbitrarily chosen by Edison).[2] No matter what TV's other technical qualities may be (even color and 3D may arrive someday), the legibility of its image will remain quite mediocre. And TV will continue to be an essentially family-oriented medium, shot for the small screen. In any case, big screens designed for collective viewing are of interest only for broadcasting live news shows. As for something like telecinema, the image quality will continue to be quite inferior to that of cinema. So it's logical that any cinematographic counteroffensive would develop on the chosen terrain of film's unique superiority, by reverting to its potential to deliver spectacle.

In truth Hollywood did not proceed by deduction. This paradigm arose from a simple New York attraction whose success has reached colossal and undreamed-of proportions: Cinerama. After two years of continuous exhibition, seats still must be reserved six months in advance. We know what Cinerama is: three screens positioned one beside the next along the circumference of an arc, on which three synchronized filmstrips are projected to form a single view. Abel Gance had done as much twenty-five years earlier in *Napoléon,* where, moreover, he ran through all the permutations that three screens make possible, creating sensational effects of spatial montage. This process has also been behind panoramic photography.[3] So whatever value Cinerama may have doesn't derive from its technological originality, even if everyone who has seen it comes away realizing how truly impressive it is.

Still, the widespread deployment of Cinerama raises problems of exhibition that are nearly insurmountable. Cinerama requires a theater of the appropriate size and shape; three separate projectors, each with its own booth; and above all a very delicate synchronization of the three film strips, the result of which is not always perfect even in the ideal conditions established for the prototype that is being exhibited right now. As far as the film industry goes, the fundamental question remains: what complications will there be for exhibition? This is why, for example, a process as simple and astoundingly inexpensive as Rouxcolor doesn't stand a chance to develop, for the simple reason that it complicates the projection of the film; it will always be more expedient to invest tens of millions in labs for the chemical processing of prints than to ship exhibitors certain prints that are non-standard.[4]

Hence the enormous superiority of CinemaScope over Cinerama. Thanks to the anamorphic lens invented by Professor Chrétien, the triple image of Cinerama can be squeezed onto a film strip of normal proportions. A corresponding lens then unsqueezes it during projection. In actual fact, the resulting width of the image is only two and a half times that of the normal screen, but experience shows that this is entirely sufficient to achieve maximal effect.

Certainly CinemaScope will still upset exhibition, and in a serious way. You can quickly see that theaters must have the proper architecture. Those originally constructed with narrow proportions, especially so-called tunnel theaters, don't have a rear wall large enough to hold a CinemaScope screen. In France, for example, it is estimated that fewer than 20 percent of theaters are currently ready and do not require some sort of transformation. In addition, CinemaScope equipment, completely monopolized by Fox, is quite expensive. A special screen of extra brilliance is required, one whose luminosity is uniform when viewed from any angle.

These many complications, serious though perhaps not insurmountable, have been the pretext for the appearance of an ersatz CinemaScope that tries rather crudely to solve them by covering them over. Indeed, right now in Paris, as in other major cities, you can find "panoramic screens" that are absolute frauds. These promise two advantages: first, their variable proportions permit them to be adapted to most standard screens; second (and crucially), they immediately transform any standard movie into a wide-format film. It's worthwhile explaining how such amazing geometrical prestidigitation works; actually it's a simple exercise in ratios. Most films come in a 4:3 proportion, while a CinemaScope image is double the width (I'm rounding things off for simplicity's sake), thus 8:3. But we learned in school that you can multiply a fraction by dividing its denominator, which is just to say that in place of doubling the length of the image, you can simply and casually *slice it in half lengthwise.* After all, $\frac{8}{3} = \frac{4}{1.5}$. This half image, when projected with the appropriate lens, covers a screen surface precisely identical to that of genuine CinemaScope—that's how the trick is turned. This might sound like a joke, but the terribly official, terribly serious, and terribly wise "Technical Commission of French Cinema" now recommends that henceforth all producers prepare every film for such panoramic projection, by concentrating the "useful" portion of the image in the central half of the frame. The projector of each theater will be equipped with a masking plate cut to the panoramic proportion of the screen in order to conceal the "useless" part of the image. As things stand at the moment, with films not having been shot with this surgical operation in view, the framing is at the discretion of the projectionist, whose job is to decide whether to decapitate the characters or cut off their legs, following his own idiosyncratic inclination. But already the most serious directors are composing their shots in such a way that without too much damage their images can undergo this excision, lopped off by a sixth at top and a sixth at bottom. Stupider even than the catoblepas, cinema is eating its own feet because it thinks this will make it grow.[5]

So what's the difference, you might ask, between a large screen and one that has been cut down? Isn't the spectator's angle of view the same? Yes, no doubt, but here we should clarify exactly what CinemaScope is.

Cinema's current optical specifications aren't solely defined by the proportions of the image, but also by what can be introduced into the frame. Different from the human eye with its single lens, the camera has at its disposal a full range of lenses of varying angles of openness. The use of short focal lengths positioned at great angularity can compensate for cinema's narrow screen. Yet some serious drawbacks accompany this, since the further a lens differs from the eye's characteristics, the more noticeable will be the deformations of perspective. The tremendous advantage of Professor Chrétien's Hypergonar is to multiply by two the angle of the lens while not altering any other of its optical characteristics. When projected on widescreen, the result is not simply to enlarge the spectator's angle of vision—the angle that depends on where his seat is relative to the rest of the theater—but to genuinely increase the field of what he can see of the photographed reality. If you want a comparison, just cut a wide rectangular window in a piece of cardboard, then attach a photograph to the cardboard behind the window. The angle formed by my eye in relation to the lateral edges of the image varies with my distance from the cardboard, but the image itself doesn't change at all, since this has been forever determined by the angle of the lens from which it was shot. Now take away the photograph and treat as the "image" what you can see through the cut out masking. This time it really matters how far you move toward or away from the cardboard, since the angle of vision actually increases according to the size of the triangle whose summit is my eye and whose base is the width of the cutout. This is the genuine angle of view that counts, more than the angle that is formed by my seat in relation to the screen. The "panoramic screen," this ersatz CinemaScope, increases only this less crucial second angle, meanwhile actually shrinking the height of the image. So the true content of the image is divided by half, relative to the standard 4:3 screen, or divided by four with CinemaScope in mind.

·   ·   ·

This sorry example of the "panoramic screen" demonstrates the extent to which the evolution of cinema is subject to accidents of an entirely commercial origin. And this leads me to ponder what really counts as a notion of progress in film. Certainly, progress in all the arts depends upon technology. We know what the evolution of painting owes on one side to the general implementation of perspective, and on the other to the discovery of new siccatives, or drying agents. However, we oughtn't say that the history of harmony is completely dependent upon the history of musical instruments, just as we understand that after it was discovered that powders could be ground into oil, the art of easel painting evolved on its own, without any further technological innovation. On the other hand, it is definitely true that the evolution of architecture, at least in its major lines of development, is determined in a nearly fundamental manner by available building materials, or at least by the way these have been theoretically grasped. Hence the very same types of stones go into both Romanesque basilicas and Gothic cathedrals, but the architects knew how to deploy them in an ever more efficacious manner.

Ought we to set off the evolution of the so-called *abstract* arts, like music or literature, from that of the *concrete* arts, where materials dominate? It wouldn't seem so, since in all cases the aesthetician discerns some logic—certain internal laws—in whatever art is under consideration, thereby defining evolutions and subsequent involutions, at least in an a posteriori sense. Arguments among architects aren't really very different in essence from those that pit traditional musicians against disciples of the twelve-tone system. In these areas, the mind definitely decides how an art proceeds. It may well be that such decisions will later be inflected or reshaped by the exigencies of history, but evolution, even when foiled, maintains a hypothetical integrity and a definable direction.

Do things operate this way with cinema? If we examine its history, we can surely doubt whether the critical spirit and the will of the artist count for much in this medium's destiny. Of course cinema doesn't lack its creative souls, even some of real genius, who have helped this art advance in just as irrefutable a way as those of the traditional arts. There's no space here to be horrified by the way such artists are generally thwarted by the requirements of mass-audience consumption. In fact, these requirements are also the source of cinema's grandeur, from which it has drawn the most positive of aesthetic profits. More numerous and weighty perhaps than anywhere else, such requirements don't make cinema's situation essentially distinctive. But then its progress, though always difficult even in normal circumstances, is completely at the mercy of technological perturbations, which can interrupt the flow of things for nothing other than economic reasons. This is what happened with the silent film, which had just reached a point of admirable perfection when sound came to put it up for grabs.

But clearly no filmmaker would complain about an increase in technical resources, not even one whose personal style has little to gain from these. Producers, and only producers, are the ones who wager to introduce a new attraction. Even sound cinema had been feasible a number of years earlier. And we would have had to wait many years more for it had financial distress at Warner Brothers not forced producers there to gamble double or nothing on a brand new venture. It's not at all absurd to imagine that if this initiative, pursued in a slightly different manner, had failed with the public, the cinema might have continued to remain silent. At the end of the day it's the initial success of any new process that always determines the outcome of significant modification in exhibition. Thus Abel Gance made a film with three screens in 1927 (*Napoléon*), and Claude Autant-Lara made another with Chrétien's Hypergonar (*Construire un feu* [To build a fire]).[6] But the imperfect conditions of their projection, plus the general historical moment (attention was already focused on the talkie), aborted this potential revolution. The only difference today lies in the fact that an extensively orchestrated publicity campaign, together with massive financial resources, will possibly amortize what is really a commercial siphon, by starting a flow that may make a success out of an enterprise that failed twenty-five years ago.

Conversely, a filmmaker, by dint of the sheer force of his art, could never provoke any sort of disturbance within the technological framework that controls his medium. Naturally, he can profit quite a lot from technological advancements (the sensitivity of film emulsion, new studio equipment, etc.), but he can never determine such things.

Let's go even further. More than just these external structures of cinema's evolution are out of the filmmaker's reach; so too is the very destiny of cinema as an art. The fact that they are mortal is unquestionably and fundamentally what distinguishes the mechanical arts that have appeared since the nineteenth century from the traditional arts. The danger that television poses for cinema is thus nothing like what theater has been forced to suffer under cinema. The worst case could find that the loss of its public could reduce theater to forms that are more occasional and more modest; but its disappearance is unimaginable. Theater will always be reborn, necessarily and eternally, in children's games, in social liturgies, or in the simple need of certain young people to perform for their peers, even if they do so in the catacombs. The traditional arts were born with man and will disappear with him. In this sense cinema is not an art at all, for it is not the expression of some eternal need or some brand new one (can a radically new need even exist?), but rather is the result of a lucky conjunction between a virtual need and a particular technological and economic state of civilization. In other words, cinema is not an *art* plus an *industry;* instead it is an *industrial art,* quite susceptible of vanishing, body and soul, when the profits of this industry vanish. So if tomorrow television were to capture that fraction of cinema's clientele that still assures its profitability as an enterprise, the capital that underwrites cinema would head off to be invested elsewhere, and cinema would disappear just as suddenly as it was born. This would happen without our having to hold to some fantasy of futurist optimism, whereby television had come to the aid of cinema in a larger aesthetic evolution, the way that film indeed did come to the assistance (at least partially) of the novel and theater. Not only is television too industrial, so that its aesthetic logic plays only the feeblest role in its overall evolution, the fact is that the art of television is probably far more reduced than that of cinema. It is superior to cinema only in the realm of live reports. In everything else, television is a means of expression and transmission that is irremediably less sophisticated than film.

We must also understand that as far as their material destiny goes—and this controls aesthetic destiny—cinema and television are not really arts of storytelling or of drama at all. Such comparative aesthetics counts centrally only within a tiny given fragment of their evolution. Seen from a distance and within the capitalist world, anyway, they are industries of spectacle. Television may come to substitute for film not because it is artistically superior to it, but simply because it is more convenient to consume. In this sense television contributes to the death of cinema in the same way that sporting events do, or pastimes like bridge, which no one would dream of seeing as some new step in the dialectical development of the novel.

Hence, distinct from the traditional arts, which can never really collapse or suffer, cinema by its very principal is mortal. We should face up to this if we care to hold onto its existence. However, I announce this danger only to better establish my faith in its future. First of all, the menace has only reached Hollywood for the moment. Not that such a realization should make us happy. No matter what we think of it, Hollywood remains the capital of the world of cinema in all senses of the term. Without it, I would not say that cinema would be weak; rather it would lack some essential gland whose secretions influence everything else. But cinema would survive and no doubt finish by making up for this loss. It is certain that television will develop in Europe as it has in America, but it has yet to be proven that the French, English, or Italian public will submit equally passively to its domination. You can imagine a modus vivendi in which cheap and profitable filmed serials become increasingly divorced from quality films made on moderate budgets. The series will continue to exist for about 50 percent of today's filmgoing public, let's say, while the rest will be aimed precisely at an international public ready to escape the influence of television to go see a good film, in the same way that there exists a whole class of spectators ready to go to the theater or the cinema, it doesn't matter which, on the basis of quality alone. Naturally, the size of this kind of audience is relatively small, but with its international scale taken into account, it might be large enough for the kinds of films we love, such as those of Renoir, Rossellini, Bresson, De Sica. You can even expect television to aid the cinema later on in serving as an alternative distribution circuit, bringing in just as much as comes from distribution in movie theaters.

I could go further: not only does the death of cinema seem improbable, but the effort to solve this economic crisis through spectacle seems to be heading in the direction of substantial and desirable progress. I find it significant that this industrial art, when undergoing some economic mishap, should nevertheless always light on some technological advance that heads in the direction of aesthetic progress. Still, as much as one may naturally speak of the progress of art, from a certain perspective it will always be absurd to hold the work of Da Vinci superior to cave paintings. In this sense progress never depends on the material of a technique; more precisely, every technique or technology progresses according to its own proper evolution, whose summit is just as high as that of the evolution of the technology that comes after it. Still, we had better admit that within oil fresco there was progress quite like that which took us from the epic to the novel or from melody to counterpoint. This is not the place to defend this thesis, which you readers, I expect, will easily accept if you simply consider its opposite. To refuse the evolution of techniques is to condemn civilizations to a static life; it is to refuse to be *modern;* that is, to refuse to be at all.

Nevertheless, not every technological supplement is ipso facto a measure of progress, for they all should relate to the internal laws of the art form and to that form's specific physiology. Modern art has worked things out inversely, so as to rediscover (even with the help of highly evolved techniques) the fundamental or primitive laws buried in the undergrowth of a false historical evolution. Look at Lurçat and the history of tapestry, or at Le Corbusier and architecture.[7] Similarly, I am cautious when asserting that sound was a step forward in cinematographic progress due simply to itself and to the fact that it added an element to the image. If it was a step forward, it is only because cinema is not at all essentially an art of the exclusively visual image. It may be true that cinema's initial infirmity constrained filmmakers to create a silent language, thus contributing to the evolution of an art that by 1925 had already reached a state of classicism, and it may be equally true that sound put this language up for grabs, provoking its temporary regression; but these vicissitudes do nothing to undermine the fact that the key principle of cinema from its very birth (I have to add, even when it was a fetus in the imagination of its inventors) has been a quest for the realism of the image.

Realism, let me say, implied by the automatic genesis of the image that aims to confer on this image as many qualities as possible that are similar to natural perception. Paradoxically, the necessary abstractions of art ought to arise from the most concrete aspects of this image. Everything in it that exists as plastic convention (black and white, absence of a third dimension, the frame) can contribute here, but only provisionally. It would be the greatest mistake if we took these constraints to be exquisite, fertile principles in themselves.[8]

I should temper this assertion, which is too general to be perfectly true. It would be naïve to imagine that the cinematographic image tends toward a total identification with the universe, whose supplementary qualities it copies by successive technological additions. Perception is a synthesis whose elements interact with each other. For example, it is not true that, at least insofar as we can reproduce it, color added to the image framed in the narrow window of the screen has become a factor of pure realism. For color brings along with it an entire ensemble of new conventions that might carry cinema closer to painting than to reality. Similarly, indeed even more, stereoscopic relief provides the impression that objects are in space but inhabiting it in the state of impalpable phantoms. This contradiction at the heart of 3D, which is hardly ever mentioned, delivers at base what is an impression of unreality far more perceptible than standard black and white, flat cinema.

So you shouldn't count on the victory of stereoscopic relief in the 3D wars. Beyond the drawbacks of wearing Polaroid glasses, it is this unrealism of a universe curiously drawn back into the hole of the screen that ought to be enough to doom its future, except in those genres such as the horror film, where a certain marriage of the fantastic and reality is precisely the rule. Perhaps widescreen would make one of the major disadvantages of 3D disappear, and certain genres, like detective films and music hall revues in particular, could be made with this process.

All things considered, the truly revolutionary novelty of our era will very probably be CinemaScope; this is what you should count on. I would say right away that the attempt to assimilate 3D to the widescreen is excessive and a publicity stunt. In fact, binocular vision plays only a secondary role in the perception of depth, at least beyond a few meters, because the layout of objects that we see in space is the result of an ensemble of factors that are perceived equally well by one-eyed people. The closer a cinematographic view comes to natural vision, the more depth will appear. In this sense, the CinemaScope screen contributes more to depth by offering something beyond the standard narrow window; it gives us a greatly enlarged surface whose angle in relation to our eye is close to the angle of normal vision. But this impression of depth is not perceptible in every shot; in any case, it remains partial at best. The central question lies elsewhere, in the elongated format of the new screen.

So far, what we've been able to see projected in CinemaScope (in Paris and in Venice) have only been scenes of spectacle, including documentaries or dramatic scenes (some parts of *The Robe*), all of which were shot to emphasize the new frame. The effect is unquestionably sensational, especially in combination with the stereo soundtrack, which the enormous scale of the screen makes indispensable. You can understand that Clouzot was furious to have already made *La Salaire de la peur* [*The Wages of Fear*] before CinemaScope, a film that would have gained 100 percent from it. In the same way, we cannot doubt its affinity with genres like the Western, whose signature framing is the distinctive establishing shot that opens onto a landscape to the far horizon. Parades of horses, stagecoach chases, and pitched battles have finally found the proper room they aspire to. Yet more serious arguments arise to counter such limited advantages. What the cinema gains for its spectacular genres, doesn't it give up in psychological resources and, more generally, in its capacity for intellectual expression, which is to say precisely in its more highly evolved genres? Spread out across this bay window that now may replace the older rectangle, what will become of the sacrosanct close-up, the cornerstone of montage?

Here the challenge is declared: montage as understood since Gance and Eisenstein (as filmmakers) on one side, and since a famous critical essay by Malraux on the other side, has been the alpha of cinematographic language, the omega being the framing that organizes the contents of the image in a plastic manner. Well, the time has come to be rid of this aesthetic prejudice, which had already been disproved by many masterworks of the silent screen, like those of Stroheim and Chaplin, where montage played at best an accessory role. It is simply false that a combination of *découpage* into shots and an extended array of optical scales should be the single necessary and fundamental element of a cinematographic language that could be as subtle as you would want. It has been asserted that the evolution of the language of cinema over the past fifteen years has tended to eliminate montage. This was the great lesson we learned even before World War II from Jean Renoir, and it is also what *Citizen Kane* and *The Best Years of Our Lives* tell us, where most of the shots are exactly as long as the scenes that unroll within them. It's true that framing often helps establish a kind of virtual montage within the image. But isn't this facet of composition itself on the way out as a plastic artifice that seems foreign to the essence of mise-en-scène? *Le Journal d'un curé de campagne* [*Diary of a Country Priest*] really owes very little to its photographic arrangement [*mise en page*]; in the way it was shot I find scarcely any effects that couldn't be translated into Cinema-Scope. By contrast, I definitely see what a widescreen might have added to the meaning of the image in certain shots, like the opposition—or, better, the situation—of the priest in the landscape. A film like *The River,* whose utterly new form of beauty I have tried to describe in these pages, could only gain from the big screen. I'm waiting for someone to name me a work, at least one shot in recent years, and whose value is not trying to be aesthetically retro, that would not be able to be shot in CinemaScope. I must exclude *Othello,* whose intentions seem to have been to exhaust montage one final time, in a flurry of fireworks.[9]

On the contrary, widescreen will only concentrate what we care most about in the most modern trends of cinema: the stripping away of all artifice extrinsic to the very content of the image; the elimination of all expressionism in time or in space. Cinema will distance itself a bit further from music and from painting as it approaches its deep vocation, which is to show even before expressing, or more precisely, to express by evidence of the real, which is to say once again: not by signifying but by revealing.

NOTES

From "Le CinémaScope sauvera-t-il le cinéma?," *Esprit* 207–208 (10 November 1953).

1. Bazin here takes advantage of a homonym. The French pronounce *trois dés* (three dice) exactly as they would pronounce 3D.

2. Bazin was slightly misinformed. America's standard was 525 lines, while Europe's was 625 lines.

3. Very wide still photographs are nearly as old as photography itself. They provided sensational shots of Civil War battlefields, for instance. Cameras with the word "panorama" in their name appeared starting in the 1880s. Most involve aligning contiguous views, just as Cinerama does.

4. Rouxcolor prints are non-standard because they in fact contain four separate small images on each 35mm frame. The projectionist must attach a filtered lens atop his regular projection lens and then carefully keep the four images in alignment so that a single colored image results on the screen. Exhibitors did not relish the idea of changing their routine when such prints would arrive.

5. The catoblepas is an imaginary beast first described by the historian Pliny the Elder. Its head is so large that it seldom lifts it from looking straight down at its feet. Bazin's notion that this animal was known to eat its own feet most likely comes from Gustave Flaubert's *La Tentation de Saint Antoine* (*The Temptation of St. Anthony*), for he recounts something similar in the 1874 version. I thank Marc Cerisuelo for locating the Flaubert citation.

6. Claude Autant-Lara used Chrétien's Hypergonar anamorphic lens for his adaptation of the classic Jack London story "To Build a Fire." Purportedly shot in 1929, this short (approximately twenty minutes long) was screened in 1930 but no longer exists.

7. Jean Lurçat (1892–1966), a painter in the Post-impressionist period, turned to tapestry after World War I. In the 1930s he was inspired by the plain style of medieval tapestries, even as his work was being featured at the Musée Nationale d'Art moderne. The name Le Corbusier (Charles-Edouard Jeanneret-Gris, 1887–1965) was, and remains, synonymous with modern architecture and basic geometric principles.

8. Bazin plays on the term *gêne*, which means "irritation" (translated here as "constraints"), while its homophone *gènes* means, as it does in English, "genes." The fact that he also uses the term "fertile" here works well with his "genetic" model of evolution.

9. Bazin had written a lengthy study of Renoir's *The River* in *Esprit* 188 (March 1952). That film and Welles's *Othello* came out in France within a year of each other, in 1951 and 1952, respectively. Bazin was devoted to both directors, even if the former shot his film in color with languorous shots, while the latter used staccato montage for his high-contrast black and white images.

52

CinemaScope and Neorealism

This year the Venice Film Festival concluded with the presentation of CinemaScope, while for the first time the Golden Lion was not awarded to any film. Should we see in this circumstance more than a coincidence, the sign of something dying and something being born? I think that this interpretation would give this situation too much importance. First of all, if this year's Venice Film Festival has been the most disappointing we have ever seen, it has not been the least interesting from the point of view of film criticism. We had no works that stood out with undeniable force for the grand prize, but there were at least a dozen films with enough originality to make them worthwhile. We can't say this of all festivals. Films like *Ugetsu Monogatari, The Little Fugitive,* and *Deux Hectares de terre* [*Do Bigha Zamin*] (regrettably screened outside the festival's competition) bear witness to the fact that the cinema is alive and well, and that, before we burn Sodom and Gomorrah, it is important to value righteous films that prove cinema's purity.[1] Without a shadow of a doubt, these three films show that cinema's well-being depends on aesthetic invention rooted in either form or content! Taken as a technological innovation, CinemaScope and comparable developments can only be of temporary assistance.

Once the first reactions of surprise and wonder are gone, the audience will go back to judging films based on the stories they tell. After a certain amount of time, everything will return to the fundamental issues every art faces: what to say with the best means available. Let us not forget that if the cinema ever disappears, it will be due to a lack of imagination.

So, should we trust CinemaScope or should we doubt its future? I believe in the first option, and my sense of confidence is supported by two reasons, one general and the other specific. To argue whether a technological innovation is good or bad is a waste of time, because its justification lies exclusively in its impact. There are great silent films and there are great sound films. We already know masterpieces in color, and tomorrow we might have excellent ones in 3D. Let us not repeat the same mistake that film theorists of the silent period made, who spent all their time decrying the advent of sound, to no avail.

This is why I now want to analyze the new elements of CinemaScope, because they play into a positive evolution of cinema. To begin with, the actual format of the standard screen is a matter of chance. It is true that its proportions have a certain harmony, but this is not reason enough to justify the limits of this window that opens onto the imaginary of each film. Purely and simply, the large screen takes over the wall at the far end of the movie theatre: why should we complain about this? I am well aware that by the same stroke, the director now abandons the frame within which he was composing his image, although perhaps he was wrong in assuming that the screen is a frame. In the unfolding of film history, it has been necessary to give up other comparable means of expression. At the end of the silent period (and even in 1938 [sic] in Malraux's "Sketch for a Psychology of Cinema"), montage was considered the essence of cinematic art. Yet today montage plays a subordinate role. The notion of the shot appears and disappears during the span of ten years.[2] Likewise, the concept of framing is no longer unassailable. After all, CinemaScope does not do away with framing. On the contrary, by virtue of the additional space, it becomes possible to further develop the internal composition of the image. As a result, dramatic structure becomes stronger at the expense of plastic form. If we consider the evolution of directing during the past fifteen years, it is clear that filmmakers have become more and more interested in synthesis. Directors today follow the example of Welles and Wyler and use depth of field to organize their compositions, but they could achieve the same results by using the width of the CinemaScope screen.

Allow me to make this last point sharper by turning to Antonioni, since in directing *I Vinti* he could readily have transferred it to the widescreen. This is the case because Antonioni's filmmaking is based neither on montage nor on the plasticity of framing. Instead, everything depends on his direction of actors, and this aspect of filmmaking can only gain from an expansion of the visual field. In short, neorealism has nothing to worry about in regard to CinemaScope; indeed, the latter is likely to enhance it.

NOTES

From "Cinemascope e neo-realismo," *Filmcritica* 28 (September 1953). Angela Dalle Vacche provided the first draft of this translation.

1. At Venice in 1953, *Ugetsu Monogatari* (Mizoguchi, Japan) and *The Little Fugitive* (Ray Ashley and Morris Engel, United States) won Silver Lions, while *Do Bigha Zamin (Two Acres of Land,* directed by Bimal Roy,

India), though not in competition, as Bazin mentions, received the International Prize given out by critics.

2. Malraux, in his "Esquisse d'un psychologie du cinéma" (published in summer 1940 in *Verve*, not in 1938, as Bazin says) uses the French word *plan*, which was translated by Stuart Gilbert in the contemporaneous English edition of *Verve* as "plane" but which is generally translated in film theory as "shot." This ambiguity remains productive, but I use "shot" here because it seems to fit Bazin's concern over the rise and fall of montage, where the shot is always considered a primary unit.

53

CinemaScope: The End of Montage

Primarily for theoretical reasons, I was an enthusiast for Cine-maScope after I saw it demonstrated experimentally last summer in Paris and Venice. The tighter traditional format is an accident against which most of the best filmmakers have taken a stand. If sound had not come in to steal the public's attention, *Napoléon* and *Construire un feu* would likely have revolutionized cinema beginning in 1927.[1]

But maybe the times were not right. Abel Gance employed his triple screen less to extend the visual field than to multiply the effects of montage via space. Today, on the contrary, the interest in widescreen that I observe has to do with how it follows in the wake of depth of field; and even more than its predecessor, it has come along to definitively destroy montage as the key element in cinematic discourse. We had mistakenly taken montage to be the essence of cinema, but in effect its importance is related to the restricted size of the classic image format, which condemns directors to carve up reality. From this perspective, Cinema-Scope has marched in as the logical next step in the evolution cinema has undergone the past fifteen years, from *La Règle du jeu* to *The Best Years of Our Lives,* and from *Citizen Kane* to *Europa '51.*

Still, I have to confess that watching *The Robe* was a rude shock to my overly enthusiastic theory. Even setting aside the particular mediocrity of its scenario and direction, there remains the fact that certain of its optical faults make for a regression in the quality of what the cinematographic image has become. Must we henceforth renounce the hyper-sharp image with its bold, opaque colors? All right; supposing that these faults may be corrected (though I'd like to be reassured about this), it's still valuable to know whether the Hypergonar can work with the majority of lenses; otherwise, widening the angle of vision would be merely an illusion, and the same effect could be obtained by using a fisheye lens and an anamorphic projection. I posed this question to Professor Chrétien at Cannes without getting a very clear answer.[2] Until we're better informed, we are allowed to wonder if the aesthetic of CinemaScope might not be a drain on the ledgers of profits and losses. It is true that to assess this we will need to wait for a better demonstration than *The Robe.* While we wait, let's dream about what *La Salaire de la peur* might have been in widescreen and stereo.[3]

NOTES

From "Fin du montage," *Cahiers du Cinéma* 31 (January 1954).

1. Abel Gance's *Napoléon* was the first feature film shown in (partial) widescreen; in 1929, Claude Autant-Lara used the Hypergonar anamorphic lens to film an adaptation of Jack London's short story "To Build a Fire."

2. See note 1 in chap. 43.

3. Clouzot's *La Salaire de la peur* (*The Wages of Fear*) was one of the major French productions of 1953, featuring stunning landscapes shot in Academy ratio.

54

The Trial of CinemaScope: It Didn't Kill the Close-Up

Among the aesthetic objections brought against CinemaScope, the most frequent, and admittedly the most plausible, concerns the impossibility of this format accommodating the close-up, generally taken to be the cornerstone of montage. Even if one disputes the decisive character of montage for film art, the fact remains that the close-up is an element essential to psychological expression, and that any technological development would indeed be absurd if it resulted in depriving the cinema of this crucial resource. Indeed, at first glance, and sticking to appearances, the ideal screen format for the close-up would correspond more or less to the square within which the human face naturally fits, so the slightly rectangular proportion of the classical screen is quite well suited to a close shot of two faces. As has often been noted, if CinemaScope offers the ideal frame for landscapes, for establishing shots, and for scenes involving vast horizontal movement (as when the cavalry rides out), the director who prefers psychological analysis over spectacular effects would always be disadvantaged. In launching CinemaScope,

producers right away opted for traditionally spectacular subjects, that is, biblical or historical ones.

I was sitting next to Jean Cocteau at the last Festival de
Cannes, when, for the first time, he saw a film screened in CinemaScope. The film in question was *Beneath the 12-Mile Reef.*[1] It
was sheer pleasure to sense his enthusiasm. As with many other
directors, this enthusiasm at the discovery of widescreen must
indeed have quickly cooled, but that's another matter. I mention
this anecdote in order to note that Cocteau admired Cinema-
Scope precisely for its effective use of the close-up, contrary to
the usual prejudice against it. The author of *Les Parents terribles*
put little stock in the wide maritime panoramas, admiring
instead the eloquence of faces, isolated in the middle of this surface that was way too large and apparently useless.

I reflected on Cocteau's paradoxical view while reading *The
Public Is Never Wrong,* the memoirs of Adolph Zukor (which I've
already reviewed in *Radio-Cinéma-Télévision*). This pioneer of an
industry promoting the "star system" (that is, the commercial
cult of the movie star), having experience at the time only of
Cinerama, wrote: "I am satisfied that Cinerama can be developed in ways that *intimate* entertainment can be shown [Zukor's
emphasis]. I was speaking not so much of the technical Cinerama method as the intimacy of the audience and the players,
however it might be gained. The wide screen and the strategic
placing of loudspeakers has had a lot to do with getting the star-
tling audience effect."[2] Obviously these remarks apply equally
well to CinemaScope.

How entirely significant it is for an artist, a poet of the stature
of Jean Cocteau, to agree with a producer whose sole preoccupation is to sniff out just what the audience likes. This conjoin-
ing of such divergent spirits certainly points to an irrefutable

truth: in widescreen, it's the close-up that matters most. But this truth stops short when you realize that it constitutes a paradox. We were considering the close-up as though it were defined solely by its plastic elements, as the relationship between the size of the face and the *frame* of the screen. But this is primarily a psychological reality: the feeling of *closeness,* that is, a relationship between the face or the object in close-up and *the spectator.* So the format of the traditional screen, far from contributing to this impression of proximity, would on the contrary tend to destroy it, precisely inasmuch as it *frames* the face; the frame of a painting has no function but to emphasize the edges of an image, to set it off against the surrounding space. It may be wrong to say that CinemaScope restores depth, yet this confusion is understandable since CinemaScope does indeed make us "enter the image"! If it does not actually restore its third dimension, at least it makes us forget its absence. The "useless" space that surrounds faces is thus not as useless as all that; on the contrary, it highlights those faces, not in relation to the frame but by restoring to them a natural relation with space. Cézanne said that it was never a matter of painting perspective, but rather the air around objects. There is something of this in what Cinema-Scope gives us: the air around faces.

PSYCHOLOGICAL CINEMASCOPE

I would not have hazarded these aesthetic observations if I had not ultimately found indisputable confirmation in William Wellman's *The High and the Mighty,* which I deal with elsewhere.[3] This aviation film more or less thumbs its nose at all the spectacular effects possible with CinemaScope and with an airplane; just two or three such shots are included as a kind of minimum quota.

The bulk of the film takes place indoors. So it could be said that perhaps it's the elongated form of the fuselage that ... But three shots out of four are taken *facing the passengers,* that is, in horizontal fashion. Truth be told, this purely psychological action film is essentially based on dialogue shot in close-up. So William Wellman proves here, and does so abundantly, that the widescreen format is not at all incompatible with the close-up, at least not when one knows how to handle it with skill. He intelligently furnishes this screen's "neutral" spaces with virtually permanent close-ups. We should add in conclusion that color in this film is not inferior to that of a film in classical format and that the annoying distortions that badly adjusted lenses once produced at the far edges of the screen, have completely disappeared. Only their format distinguishes these images from those we are familiar with.

These remarks are intended not to jump to premature conclusions about CinemaScope nor about the group of artistic problems that it raises. The fact is that the variable screen remains the ideal solution, and that lacking this, for a number of reasons CinemaScope seems perhaps an awkward format to which one might ultimately prefer the "wide" screen (with dimensions of 1:1.83 or so). But in any case, whether one condemns or acquits it, it is important to listen to its defense with civility.

NOTES

From "Le Procès du CinémaScope: Il n'a pas tué le gros plan," *Radio-Cinéma-Télévision* 257 (7 November 1954).

1. Directed by Robert Webb and starring Robert Wagner, *Beneath the 12-Mile Reef* premiered in France in April 1954 in full CinemaScope and with four-track stereo.

2. Adolf Zukor, *The Public Is Always Right: The Autobiography of Adolf Zukor* (New York: Putnam, 1953) was published in French in 1954

(Editions Corée). This passage comes from pp. 315–316 of the French edition. It is Bazin who highlights Zukor's italicized word *proximité* (intimacy) in the French translation, although in fact the word is not italicized but put in quotation marks.

3. Bazin analyses *The High and the Mighty* (Wellman, 1954) in *France-Observateur* 233 (28 October 1954).

55

Massacre in CinemaScope

For two years cinema has been the object of an incredible technological swindle whose description will be enough to stupefy future historians; so too will the patience or blindness of the millions of spectators who are its victims.

The cinema is an industry before it is an art; this is a commonplace that should not scandalize us inasmuch as its economic imperatives are a guarantee of its popularity. Being indentured also makes for cinema's grandeur and its originality. Unfortunately, examined more closely, the cinema is not so much an industry as a trade. Only a mythology among critics maintains the illusion of the bull-headed producer imposing his lack of culture and his congenital prejudices on talented directors. In reality, the producer is himself nothing but a subordinate cog. The origin, starting point, and source of the cinema's evolution is the exhibitor—multiple and quasi anonymous—whose determination and money flow back up the channel of distribution to the producer, who is nothing more than his agent. This is how it is in America, in England, in France. Hence, one could say that almost all the good that has been done and that continues to be done in cinema is simply an accident in the system, or the haphazard benefit of the uncertainties remaining there. The producer no longer has the head of a bull, he is a hydra. Three times out of four, the money he collects for producing his film is advanced to him by distributors in direct contact with the exhibitors. It is definitely the latter who carry the most weight in the balance of opinions when major decisions are made, and they do so no longer sanctioned by success a posteriori, but by the a priori idea that they have derived from "their public."

You might think that this idea is the fruit of experience, hence legitimate. But this would be to credit the exhibitors with a capacity for reasoning when their behavior gives evidence to the contrary; I am not even speaking of their inability to conceive of a film as a work of art, but simply as an object that would profit from being handled with good sense and care, like an automobile or a vacuum cleaner. The history of the widescreen is proof of this.

Let me briefly summarize this history. Over the last four years, a crisis in movie theater attendance has thrown the Hollywood industry into disarray. It feverishly looks for technological novelties to outwit television and bring spectators back, even if only temporarily. With this in mind, they unearth and dust off old processes that they fix up one way or another and toss onto the market under the general advertising label of "3D." In fact, only stereoscopic projection with glasses restores the third dimension. And its failure has been so quick that films shot by this process are being projected in "flat" versions.

That leaves CinemaScope and its variants. Even if the hopes that it first engendered have turned to disappointment, its continued aesthetic interest seems certain. Two years out, one can reasonably think that CinemaScope will henceforth constitute a particular variety of films that will not substitute for all others but whose disappearance would be as aggravating as, for example, that of color films. In this way, the balance sheet of the operation could be deemed positive if it were not already forfeited by an appalling sequel, that of the panoramic screen.

Indeed, from the outset, the addled mind of the exhibitor identified the "widescreen" with the quite vague myth of films in "3D." But in fact the architecture of few theaters lent itself to the transformations necessary for the installation of a 2.55:1 screen. After all, the number of films produced in CinemaScope would have been sufficient to satisfy a general market demand. Then little by little, at the level of exhibition the idea of novelty and of progress deteriorated from the notion of genuine depth to that of the CinemaScope screen, and then, simply, to some screen that was wider than normal. At the end of this mental process, a screen of 1.66:1, 1.75:1, or 1.85:1 looked "superior" to the former screen of 1.33:1 format.

From a strictly physiological and even aesthetic point of view, the idea is not absurd a priori, for it could indeed be the case that the traditional format, likewise determined by chance (and then modified with the introduction of the soundtrack), might not be the best one possible. But it would be vain to pose this question, since in fact the exhibitors' motive had absolutely nothing in common with any concern for artistic or even technological progress. The simple stretching of the proportions appeared to them to be a symbol of luxury. Jean Renoir explained the vogue for CinemaScope and its spinoffs quite well by pointing to the prestige of the horizontal line in modern urban style. Just as a very long car is considered more beautiful than a poor little car with a more compact profile, a so-called "wide" screen is supposed to flatter the eye. In 1900, by contrast, the bourgeois dreamed of building a gothic tower on his suburban house, where he could put his study or office. The style at that time favored the vertical.

But the foolishness of prejudice gives way to a grotesque absurdity when, to lengthen the image, exhibitors simply set about chopping its height. Many of the theaters that were unable to screen films in CinemaScope were cornered into widening their screens and projecting on them films shot in the traditional format, using a mask to modify the proportions of an image whose height would thereby be sliced by nearly a third. This operation in itself demonstrates a level of stupidity that effectively suggests the idea of the infinite. More idiotic than the catoblepas, the exhibitor eats his own feet, hoping thereby to grow.[1] However, when you think about it, this is less inconceivable than his advertising plan, which actually announces on the door of the theater the existence, inside, of a truncated screen. You might read "Come back and see *La Bête humaine*, Jean Renoir's masterpiece, on a panoramic screen" (*sic*). But let's examine this disaster in greater detail.

The major catastrophe obviously lies in the excision of a variable fraction of the image, something, moreover, that is left to the discretion of the projectionist. (What will he cut in *The Barefoot Contessa*, the head or ... the feet?)[2] I will spare the reader my commentary on the evidence of this; it's enough to condemn the process. Now certain theaters, notably the exclusive ones, have the honesty and good sense not to use "panoramic" formats carelessly.[3] They project films in the aspect ratio intended during shooting. Even in this positive hypothesis, secondary disadvantages are numerous.

First, while you can argue that medium-width formats (1.75:1 or 1.85:1, for example) are aesthetically superior to the classical 1.33:1, you must also take into account some current technical consequences. Most often, panoramic formats come on a curved screen whose effect is debatable, and graver still, they come with some blurriness due to the enlargement of the image by a wide-angle lens that produces fringes and a greater instability of focus. These drawbacks, particularly noticeable in color films, set us back thirty years before the time when one of cinema's most indisputable technological advances rested precisely on the clarity of the image, for which depth of field mise-en-scène was the crowning aesthetic achievement.

On the other hand, many theaters too small to sufficiently widen their screens have in fact obtained the desired format by reducing the height. This "wide" screen, smaller than the original, is generally set too low, which makes reading the subtitles for undubbed films a tiresome exercise as you stretch your neck. Now, when we're dealing with a CinemaScope screen whose surface is clearly too small for the dimensions of the room, the reduction of its height in relation to the length actually used gives the screen the appearance of a gap in a wall, like a castle's loophole, which is exactly the opposite impression to what the process aims for. The cinema here is no longer reality seen through a keyhole, but through the slit of a mailbox. Some improvement! If only for the record, I will mention those theaters that, while possessing the necessary space, nonetheless have widened their screen just by cutting down the original. Stupidity here combines with sadism.

Another annoyance occurs quite frequently in widescreen cinemas. When a film in a smaller format is projected and doesn't make use of the whole screen, it often doesn't occur to the projectionist to mask the white margins with a black curtain or an adjustable frame, so the fringes of the image spread out flaccidly into a grayish zone that diminishes the contrast between the real universe and the film. The window (or masking) effect essential to the cinematic illusion is disrupted by the evidence of a vague stain of light projected on a white surface. Moreover, when this concave surface (again, this is an improvement) is vertically striated with visible seams in all the illuminated parts of the image, the reality of the screen's fabric has succeeded in destroying the cinematic illusion. This kind of screen is known as the "miracle screen," apparently because it brings about the miracle of preventing us from believing in the cinema.

This list still does not exhaust all the irritations caused by the "modernization" of theaters equipped with widescreens; but it should suffice ten times over to condemn, if not the process in itself, at least the incredible lack of discernment and of simple good sense with which such "modernization" has passed into the acceptable routines of exhibition. What's more, the "revolution" of widescreen, triggered by a concern to improve cinema's technology in its struggle against television, has wound up affecting countries where television does not yet exist and probably will never be a threat; yet we see everywhere a catastrophic deterioration of the cinematic image in its fundamental qualities of clarity, visibility, and lifelikeness.

But we have not yet hit rock bottom in this absurdity. We reach the crowning misfortune only when we recognize that this disaster is financed by the spectators' money and under state supervision. Yes, the Fonds d'Aide au Cinéma, sustained by a special tax on admissions, has authorized the majority of these supposed theater modernizations.[4] Now, it's true that you could have realistically attributed the public's loss of interest in cinema three years ago to the aging of worn-out theater equipment, as well as to the relative discomfort of many theater interiors. So it was fair that funds otherwise meant to support production contributed to re-equipping the exhibition sector. Still, we had to be convinced that this would be in the interest of progress and for the real benefit of the spectator. This is what the Commission Supérieure Technique would have needed to define and control. I do not at all mean to call its competence into question here, nor the perspicuity and education of its leadership. But theoretical power is not enough; you have to conclude from the situation that the oversight of the commission has been illusory, that the norms it defined or advocated have not been respected by a large number of exhibitors, and that the latter have violated these with impunity and with money from the Fonds d'Aide.

I'm not sufficiently competent to discuss who is responsible for all this; within the cinematic corporation, the power of the exhibition sector is massive, and it may well be that those who saw the danger, who described and denounced it in due course, simply do not in practice have the necessary power to avert it. It could be that the commission lacked tenacity and audacity, since public opinion has remained passive. Somehow dazzled by advertising unworthy of the most naïve fairground enterprise, the average spectator has allowed himself to be temporarily swayed by the idea that his neighborhood cinema has been modernized and that he must pay in order to come and admire this marvel. One day he will end up realizing that he is being shown films that are truncated, stitched together, blurred, distorted, and when they are in color, washed out. I could go on. The list doesn't end here.

If the technicians who are aware of this catastrophe remained silent in some state of helplessness or limited themselves to mentioning the danger in small professional gatherings, their resignation would make them complicit. I am appealing to their expertise. What are projectionists doing to fight the massacre of the images that they are forced to screen in some more or less panoramic shape? What are directors doing? In the most audacious cases, they make use of a transparent grid while shooting that enables them to leave sufficient useless space both top and bottom. Victory! But we can't leave it at that. Every week I get letters from readers who have finally become aware—and resentful—of this farce for which they are required to shell out their money. One of them—M. J. Donnamour, of Clichy—writes to me, for example, after having seen *Die letzte Brücke* [*The Last Bridge*] on a panoramic screen:[5] "I would like to warn your readers about these scandalous practices, and all those who have fallen into the trap should communicate to you the name and address of the theater so you can publish it. I do not need to tell you that upon leaving I asked to see the manager and that in his absence I created a small scandal in turning back the ten or so spectators who were going in."

This righteous indignation ought to find an echo. The time will come when people who love the cinema will start to exchange their recommendations and say among friends, "I've discovered a little theater in the thirteenth arrondissement that hasn't yet changed over. The seats are bad, you'll catch fleas, but until next Wednesday you can see *La Bête humaine* again on a good old pale blue screen. It's a dream, my dear, a dream!"

P.S.: I apologize to the small minority of exhibitors who have made the effort to correctly fit out their theaters; my severity is not directed at them. I am sure they cannot help but agree with me. Instead I hope that this article will help lead readers to the theaters they operate. Let me also note with satisfaction that the VistaVision process seems able to correct several of the drawbacks inherent in enlarging a positive copy of a standard image.[6]

It is only that much more disastrous that such improvements should be compromised in advance due to hasty and poorly designed theater renovations.

<h2 style="text-align:center">NOTES</h2>

From "Massacre en cinémascope," *Arts 525* (20 July 1955).

1. See note 5, p. 286.

2. *The Barefoot Contessa* (Joseph Mankiewicz, 1954), starring Humphrey Bogart and Ava Gardner, quickly attained a cult following among Bazin's younger colleagues at *Cahiers du Cinéma.*

3. *Exclusivité* is a designation given to top-rate first-run theaters, where—until *Jaws* and *Star Wars,* at least—films opened and remained as long as they took in enough spectators. After an "exclusive" run, a film would be distributed more widely in the country and in second-run Parisian theaters.

4. The Fund to Support Cinema was put in effect in 1948 to counteract the effects of Hollywood domination after the 1946 Blum-Byrnes accord, which opened France's market to the backlog of 2,000 American films made during the Occupation. The fund was restructured in January 1954, just a year and a half before Bazin wrote this article, and it now included not just advances for producers but money for theater owners to upgrade their facilities.

5. *Die letzte Brücke*, directed by Helmut Käutner and starring Maria Schell and Bernhard Wicki, was an award-winning German film shot in Academy ratio (1.37:1). It arrived in France in January 1955.

6. Bazin is suggesting that the area of each frame of VistaVision allows for a wide image that needn't be subject to the anamorphosis of CinemaScope; hence the aberrations of the latter are automatically avoided, even if VistaVision cannot achieve quite so wide an image.

56

Will CinemaScope Bring about a Television Style in Cinema?

Has the coming of CinemaScope, linked to the general use of color, doomed traditionally formatted films in black and white to a more or less lengthy expiration? This would be likely if the evolution of the arts were linear and uniform, and if the cinema were nothing but spectacle. However, beyond the fact that for technical reasons it is not going to be feasible to retrofit all theaters for CinemaScope for a very long time to come, thus maintaining a market for ordinary films, we can already clearly discern a reaction that is taking shape against the cinema of spectacle.

It may sound paradoxical, nevertheless a film like *Marty* very likely would never have been filmed were it not for CinemaScope. We know that widescreen was unveiled by Hollywood so as to technically outclass television and bring about a resurgence of interest in cinematic spectacle. But at the same time, television has conditioned a mass public to put up with images that are in black and white, and rudimentary in the quality of the way they look. As a result, the victory of CinemaScope is ambiguous, aesthetically at least, since a certain simplicity of mise-en-scène that had previously been considered impover-ished has once again become possible in the cinema, where the public will accept it, if the subject fits.

The films that have made the most noise in America the last two years are productions in black and white whose entire appeal lies in the originality or the social audacity of their screenplays: *From Here to Eternity, Marty,* and *Blackboard Jungle.* The most recent, whose release here we can expect, is called *The Phenix City Story* (by Phil Karlson).[1] In a neorealist style and with a very limited budget, it recounts the political and social cleaning-up of a small American city where gambling and seedy dives abound. With all the appearance of a true story, its bloody episodes indeed make for a stunning account of a certain side of American sociology.

Certainly since *Scarface,* and indeed well before, the American cinema has gotten us used to this theme, but it has always been exploited for its drama and spectacle, while the success of this new film is due more to its social daring, which is doubled by its recent topicality. The large success of films like these and the profits they guarantee for their producers, especially given the fact that their cost is relatively low, ought to contribute to keeping them from disappearing.

And so, on the margins of the major productions, directed in the heavy, complicated manner demanded by CinemaScope or other expensive processes, we can expect "small films" to prolif-erate, thriving exclusively on the moral and social interest of their stories.

NOTES

From "Le Cinémascope va-t-il assurer le succès du style télévision au cinéma?," *Radio-Cinéma-Télévision* 311 (1 January 1956).

1. *From Here to Eternity* (Fred Zinnemann, 1953) was a massively successful adaptation of the James Jones bestseller and starred Burt Lancaster, Montgomery Clift, and Deborah Kerr. *Marty* (Delbert Mann, 1955) won four Oscars. *Blackboard Jungle* (Richard Brooks, 1955), starring Glenn Ford, was a controversial film on juvenile delinquency that was nominated for four Oscars. *The Phenix City Story* (Phil Karlson, 1955) was shot on location in Alabama and without notable actors.

PART SEVEN

Finale

57

Is Cinema Mortal?

The fact that one can reasonably ask oneself such a question today, and that it requires some thinking through to come to an optimistic answer, should be enough to justify astonishment and musing. While deliberately sensational, Raymond Cartier's article published recently in *Match* on the current situation in Hollywood is fundamentally correct; the statistics he provides in support of his thesis are perfectly convincing.[1] Let us recall that, roughly speaking, Hollywood has lost some 50 percent of its domestic public over the last ten years. This massive loss (attributable especially, but not exclusively, to TV) seems, however, more or less to have stabilized. Hence we can imagine a corresponding decline in production: either 150 or 200 films per year, or a proportional reduction of the budget of each film.

But we know perfectly well that in a capitalist economy, things do not operate so simply. We have to be realistic and imagine that one fine day, the large companies will all find themselves in the red, so that from then on cinema, having ceased to be a profitable industry, will realize that the capital on which everything runs will not wait around to be further diminished, but will migrate to be invested elsewhere. In other words, having passed beneath a certain economic threshold, production will cease to adjust itself to consumption and will simply drop out of the game, just as the French agricultural sector would immediately lose interest in raising beets if the government did not artificially keep the price of French alcohol above the going international rate.

If we envision the continuation of cheap alternative production by new independent studios benefiting from the pullback of big corporate money, the situation does not necessarily get any brighter. This kind of production already exists right in the heart of Hollywood, and has for some time. In sheer number, cheap alternative films represent more than half the annual output; and they are not monopolized by second-tier production companies, for even the large studios have their Z productions. However, in this latter instance, save for a few isolated cases of unintentional poetry—which can be the paradoxical product of extreme standardization—these films suffer from total intellectual and aesthetic indigence.

Yet this hypothesis authorizes what amounts to an optimistic misgiving. In a sense, with cinema restricted to this third zone of production, it might return to its popular origins, to the quasi anonymity at work at the outset of the movies. In no longer aspiring to Art with a capital A, perhaps film will rediscover its real genius, not what the "exclusive," first-run theaters advertise. Personally, I can't quite believe this will ever happen, since the conditions would be the same only in appearance. Any turning back to reduced pretentions would be achieved without the innocence of those early years, and so would amount not to a natural evolution but to an involution, a decline. Thus, either cinema would cease physically to exist, or it would subsist in larval forms, at the level of comic strips in the big American newspapers—falling short of Art.

The fact is that cinema is not an Art plus an industry, it is an *Industrial Art.* And so we should not imagine for it the types of survival mechanisms the theater enjoys. In France theater still exists in spite of cinema thanks, on the one hand, to the devotion and sheer willpower of so many people of the theater, people ready for any sacrifice and full of the ingenuity needed to carry on the ritual of stagecraft, and thanks, on the other hand, to subventions from the state, which understands, in spite of its changing regimes and ministers, that a nation without theater would be like a dead country. In this sense the theater cannot die, for it will always be reborn everywhere, in children's games, at country festivals, out of the irrepressible need of certain young men and women to "play" for their assembled fellows.

But cinema does not enjoy this immunity. It was born not of man but of technology; it depends completely on the latter and on its evolution.

.   .   .

Perhaps it is only in some mental game, some optical illusion of history, fleeting like a shadow traced by the sun, that we have been able to believe in the existence of cinema for fifty years. Perhaps "the cinema" was in fact nothing but a stage in the vast evolution of the means of mechanical reproduction that had their origin in the nineteenth century with photography and the phonograph, and of which television is the most recent form. Perhaps it is only by way of one cluster of serendipitous technical, economic, and sociological convergences that the thing we call cinema has had the time to evolve toward indubitably aesthetic forms. Lumière, in short, had it right when he refused to sell his camera to Méliès on the pretext that it was merely a technological curiosity, at best useful for medical doctors.

It was a second birth that made cinema into the spectacle it has become today. However, you can readily imagine that the evolution of this art, proceeding through misunderstanding, might be brutally interrupted by the appearance of a more satisfying technology, such as television. This would be satisfying not, certainly, from an artistic point of view—which does not belong here—but in its capacity as an automatic means for the reproduction of reality. Indeed, it takes puerile idealism to believe that the artistic quality of its spectacle can defend cinema against the advantages of television, whose image brings about, for modern mankind, the miracle of ubiquity.

Hollywood is ready to play double or nothing with 3D, but then tomorrow television will come up with depth and color and thus everything will be called into question again.

So? So perhaps in twenty years the "young critics" of some new form of spectacle that we cannot even imagine, and which can't be guaranteed to be "an art," will be reading our film criticism from 1953 with a condescending smirk. Our views today could seem to them more naïve than the aesthetic sectarianism we find in our predecessors from the 1930s, who were properly outraged at the death throes of an art of the pure image that had finally reached maturity.

In the meantime and while waiting, let's just play dodgeball; I mean, let's go to the cinema and treat it as an art.

NOTES

Originally published as "Le Cinéma est-il mortel?," *L'Observateur politique, économique et littéraire* 170 (13 August 1953).

1. Raymond Cartier (1904–1975) was an acclaimed political writer whose books and essays on anticolonialism and World War II landed him the post as New York correspondent for *Paris-Match*. On July 18, 1953, he authored the cover story of *Paris-Match* whose title, "Le Cinéma va-t-il disparaitre?" (The cinema, is it going to disappear?), is scripted on a Doric column cradled by Marilyn Monroe.

A Selective Reference Guide to 1950s French Television

These brief entries cover most of the people and programs mentioned in André Bazin's articles on television. This is by no means an encyclopedia. Certain key figures, such as Jean d'Arcy, director of programming for most of the decade, are not included. Nevertheless, the writers and directors of the most enduring or important shows do come up here, and the decade 1949–1959 does form a coherent period, from the founding of RTF (Radiodiffusion-Télévision Française) to its reorganization under the Ministry of Information of the brand new Fifth Republic. Many changes in personnel and shows took place in 1959, when, by the way, about 12 percent of French households had receivers.

PERSONALITIES

Antoine, Jacques (1924–2012). Grandson of famed theater director André-Paul Antoine, he worked in radio and television, principally devising scores of game shows, including *Télé Match*. He would later be program director for Télé Monte-Carlo.

Antoine, Jean (b. 1930). Initiated the variety show *Place au théâtre* in 1952 before moving to his native Belgium, where he would produce many programs, most notably on art and artists, under the rubric *Styles*. His influence on Belgian television has been immense.

Barma, Claude (1918–1992). Credited with directing the first live French television show, an adaptation of Marivaux's *Le Jeu de l'amour et du hasard* in 1950, he later scripted a court trial program in 1955, *En Votre âme et conscience*. He went on to direct important adaptations, including those of several Shakespeare plays, and he oversaw a long-running series based on Simenon's Inspector Maigret novels from 1967 to 1981.

Bluwal, Marcel (b. 1925). A prolific French director of TV programs and telefilms, he got his start with episodes for children in 1952. From 1954–1960 he directed more than thirty adaptations from theater, opera, and canonical novels. He also directed the four ninety-minute episodes of *Si c'etait vous* scripted by Marcel Moussy. He directed adaptations and original teleplays over the next decades. In 2009 he received a prize for his contribution to the miniseries *A droite toute*, about the rise of rightwing sentiment in Paris during the Popular Front. As his autobiography, *Un Aller*, recounts, he experienced anti-Semitism firsthand during his adolescence and then the Occupation.

Cazeneuve, Maurice (b. 1923). After training to be a theater director, he worked in cinema (with Marcel Carné) before turning to television as a writer-director best known for his adaptations of French authors such as Balzac. In 1948 he helped found *Radio-Loisirs*, the forerunner of *Radio-Cinéma-Télévision* and thus of *Télérama*.

Chabannes, Jacques (1900–1994). Founder and editor of *Opera* from 1945 to 1955, he was a prolific and award-winning novelist, a biographer of saints, and an essayist who published topical and historical books and contributed to numerous periodicals. He composed a dozen plays and is responsible for the dialogue of nearly twenty films from 1938 to 1958, though none of particular note. He found his real calling in television, where for years he presented *Télé-Paris* and then *Paris-Club*. From 1950 to 1965 he adapted on average three plays a year for TV.

Chalais, François (1919–1996). A journalist who involved himself early on with French television, he eventually earned fame for his broadcasts from North Vietnam and later from Cannes, where a prize bears his name. His *Ciné-Panorama* ran on TV from 1957 to 1965.

Chatel, François (1926–1982). A television director who got his start in 1954 with an episode of *En Votre âme et conscience*, he brought nearly twenty telefilms to the screen. He also directed two dozen of the *Apostophes* programs beginning in 1975, the first year of that series.

Cravenne, Marcel (1908–2002). After directing a few films before and after World War II, from 1952 to 1955 he directed over two dozen episodes of the American-produced series *Foreign Intrigue* and *Captain Gallant of the Foreign Legion*. While he worked once for *36 Chandelles*, he was known for the dozens of TV movies and two miniseries he directed, including a Maigret series in the 1970s.

Darget, Claude (1910–1992). A principle voice delivering the *Journal télévisé* in the early years of French TV, he was known for injecting personal (often acerbic) opinions into the news. When in the early 1950s commentators were instructed to efface themselves, he was confined to two programs, one being *La Vie des animaux*. Bazin sharply criticized him in "Le Cas Claude Darget," *Radio-Cinéma-Télévision* 339 (21 July 1957).

Desgraupes, Pierre (1918–1993). He was a major force in French journalism, responsible for editing radio news from 1947 to 1956. With Pierre Dumayet he launched the popular *Lectures pour tous*. Soon after that, they were joined by Claude Barma for *En Votre âme et conscience* (1955–1970), which turned spectators into a jury to decide famous historical court cases. Desgraupes had a tumultuous career after 1968, when he was appointed head of news at ORTF. He was replaced in 1972 but reemerged in the 1980s to found the European station *La Sept*.

Drot, Jean-Marie (born 1929). Writer and documentary filmmaker specializing in literature and painting. At age twenty he was chosen as assistant director for the first Vatican TV program. After several interview programs in Rome with the likes of Rossellini, Visconti, and Claudel, he made a series of documentaries on art in the 1950s. Fame came to him with his series on Montparnasse starting in 1962 and his show on Giacometti (1963). In 1974 he directed a thirteen-episode series on André Malraux and art, with the great man appearing on camera.

Dumayet, Pierre (1923–2011). A writer working alongside Pierre Desgraupes in radio, he helped launch the first French TV news programs. He wrote dialogue for the first French TV serial, *L'Agence Nostradamus,* and then became very well known for *Lectures pour tous* and *En Votre âme et conscience.* Over many years his literary interview shows brought to the public writers like Borges, Ionesco, Céline, and Cocteau.

Gillois, André (1902–2004). Pseudonym of Maurice Diamant-Berger. In the 1930s he worked for his brother, a major producer, and for René Clair, but he found his niche in radio, where he interviewed Bergson and other famous writers. The radio voice of Charles de Gaulle's London-based Resistance, after the war he wrote novels as well as scripts for broadcast. He was among those who created France's first TV game show, *Télé Match,* in 1956. For decades he was associated with the director Marcel Bluwal.

L'Herbier, Marcel (1888–1979). The first established filmmaker to work in French television. Prominent in the narrative avant-garde of the 1920s, he made dozens of sound films, but in 1952, he turned completely to television, with particular ideas about its artistic and social values. From then until 1969, he produced over 200 broadcasts on cultural subjects, serving as presenter on most. Aside from a few programs on classical music and a couple of biographies, he generally explored aspects of cinema. One series of eight programs combined critical discussion and interviews with extracts from films. He also directed five television plays that were transmitted live.

L'Hôte, Jean (1929–1985). A writer for film and television, he also collaborated with Jacques Tati on *Mon Oncle* (1958).

Joubert, Jacqueline (1921–2005). Selected in a competition in 1949, she became France's first *speakerine* and was ubiquitous on TV in the 1950s. Later she produced and directed her own shows, particularly children's fare for Antenne 2 in the 1980s.

Lalou, Etienne (b. 1918). With six novels to his credit, he turned to TV in the 1950s. In 1952 he authored an early study of television that Bazin reviewed. He created a science show, *Médicales,* in 1955. His reputation was made in the early 1960s, when, with Igor Barrère, he created the highly influential *Faire Face,* which mixed prerecorded documentary and live debate.

Langeais, Catherine (1923–1998). The longest lasting *speakerine*, she presented programs until the ORTF first channel became TF1 in 1975. In the 1950s she also played roles in numerous regular series such as *36 Chandelles*, *La Séquence du spectateur*, and *Art et magie de la cuisine*. Famously, she was engaged to François Mitterand at the outset of the Occupation; she later married Pierre Sabbagh (see entry below).

Lorenzi, Stellio (1921–1990). Assistant to Jacques Becker on *Falbalas* (1945) and to Louis Daquin, he was, like Daquin, a communist. He taught at the French film school IDHEC but in 1949 turned to TV, for which he directed several "Visits to" programs, such as the one to the Musée Rodin. A force in the labor union, he was briefly suspended for fomenting a strike in 1954. But he became a top television director and producer, specializing in historical films (the series *La Caméra explore le temps*) and adaptations, and eventually rising to a high post at Antenne 2.

Louis, Roger (1925–1982). In the 1950s he created *D'hier à aujourd'hui*, a thirteen-part series dealing with the problems of rural France in an urbanizing culture, which UNESCO reported on in a 1956 study, *Television and Rural Adult Education: The Tele-clubs in France*. His investigative journalism cost him his job after May 1968, and, unlike others, he was never rehired by French television, so he turned to documentary filmmaking, going to Africa and Latin America, hotspots of political turmoil.

Lucot, René (1908–2003). A journeyman television director who got in on the ground floor at R.T.F. in 1949 and wound up with over 200 programs to his credit, many of them on sports.

Margaritis, Gilles (1912–1965). He staged the first French TV variety programs, *Music-Hall Parade* and *Chester Folies,* the circus show he produced from 1949 until 1954, when it became *La Piste aux étoiles,* on which he worked until his death. He remains most famous for his appearances in 1934 in Jean Vigo's *L'Atalante* and Robert Bresson's *Les Affaires publiques.*

Masson, Jean. Writer-director mainly of documentary shorts. From 1947 to 1964 he completed eight of these, including one on Monaco and Princess Grace in 1956, as well as *Musée Grévin* (1958), directed by Jacques Demy. His television credits in the 1950s are topped by *Place au théâtre*, which he co-created with Jean Antoine.

Moussy, Marcel (1924–1995). A novelist and English teacher, he turned to television writing in 1956, developing *Si c'était vous*, the series that caught the attention of François Truffaut, with whom he wrote *Les 400 Coups* and *Tirez sur le pianiste*. Although he worked on a couple of other films, the remainder of his career was in television. He never again found the success he enjoyed in the late 1950s, however.

Nohain, Jean (1900–1981). A songwriter and irrepressible radio personality, he created and hosted the hit variety show *36 Chandelles*, which ran from 1952 to 1958 on France's single channel.

Prat, Jean (1927–1991). Although trained at Paris's film school, he never worked in cinema but became an apprentice in television at age twenty-five, assisting Claude Barma and René Lucot. He directed twenty episodes of the juridical program *En Votre âme et conscience* and a great many episodes of *Lectures pour tous* from 1955 to 1968. He would go on to direct some thirty movies for television.

Rossif, Frédéric (1922–1990). After World War II, he participated in the existentialist café culture of Paris (along with Sartre, Camus, and Boris Vian) while holding a job at the Cinématheque Française. In the early 1950s he directed an amateur film with Jean Cocteau and co-directed Sacha Guitry's *Si Versailles m'etait conté*. His career, however, was in television from 1952 on, particularly after he directed two well-known TV series on animals. Later he served as a programmer for ORTF. Among dozens of documentaries on World War II and on art and music, his most acclaimed work is the film *Mourir à Madrid* (1963).

Sabbagh, Pierre (1918–1994). A journalist who first worked for TV in 1949, his series *Au Théâtre ce soir* would eventually present 300 plays. He also created game shows. In the 1970s he rose to the post of Director-General of the France 2 network. He was married to the *speakerine* Catherine Langeais.

Tchernia, Pierre (b. 1928). A writer with French television news from its first broadcasts in 1949, he then wrote scripts and dialogue for Marcel Bluwal's programs, such as *La Séquence du spectateur*, as well as for Bluwal's 1963 comic noir film *Carambolages*. He became a household figure as the program animator on *Monsieur Cinéma,* which lasted from 1967 to 1976. He directed a half dozen films and ten TV movies. He was a witer and voice for several *Asterix* films.

Thévenot, Jean (1916–1983). He was a key figure in radio before he turned to television in the 1950s. With an advanced degree in sociology, he wrote books on both media. Moderator for the series *Lectures pour tous*, he interviewed authors on camera. In the 1960s he developed the popular series *Le Grand Voyage*.

TELEVISION PROGRAMS (TITLES FOLLOWED BY DATES, GENRE, AND KEY PERSONALITIES)

36 Chandelles (36 candles), October 1952–1958. Variety. In 1959 it became *Rue de la Gaîté*. Jean Nohain.

A l'école des vedettes (At the school for stars), 1956–1963. Variety based on popular radio show.

A Vous de juger (You must decide), 1953. Historic events recreated.

L'Art et les hommes (Art and man), 1954–1969. Reportage, encounters with artists. Jean-Marie Drot.

Cabaret du soir (Evening cabaret), 1958. Variety. Jean Kerchbron.

La Caméra explore le temps (The camera explores the past), 1957–1966. Dramatization of historical events. Expanded from *Les Enigmes de l'histoire* (1955). Stellio Lorenzi.

Ciné-Panorama, 1956–1965. Film clips and interviews with cinema personalities. Frédéric Rossif, François Chalais.

Cinémathèque imaginaire, 1952. Film history. Marcel L'Herbier.

D'hier à aujourd'hui (From yesterday to today), 1955. Reportage and interviews. Roger Louis.

Editions spéciales, 1952. Reportage. François Chalais, Frédéric Rossif.

En direct du fond de la mer (Live from the bottom of the sea), June 1957. Jacques Cousteau.

En Votre âme et conscience (In all honesty), 1956–1977. Dramatization of court cases, followed by discussion with viewers. Pierre Desgraupes, Pierre Dumayet, Claude Barma.

Impromptu du dimanche (Sunday impromptu), 1955–1957. Poetry and performance. Jean-Louis Barrault, Madeleine Renaud.

Joie de vivre, 1952. Variety. Henry Spade, Robert Chazal.

Journal télévisé, beginning 29 July 1949. Daily 9:00 PM news broadcast (8:00 PM after 1954). Pierre Sabbagh.

Lectures pour tous (Books for everyone), 1953–1968. Literary discussion with authors. Pierre Desgraupes, Pierre Dumayet, Jean Thévenot.

Music-Hall Parade, February 1949. First variety show on French TV. Gilles Margaritis.

Musique pour vous, 1954. Educational.

La Piste aux étoiles (Circus ring), 1954–1974. Circus variety show succeeding *Chester Folies* (1949–1954). Gilles Margaritis.

Place au théâtre (A seat at the theater), 1952. Variety. Jean Antoine.

Science de demain (Tomorrow's science), 1955. Educational. Also known as *Médicales*. Etienne Lalou.

La Séquence du spectateur (The spectator's sequence), 1953–1989. One of French TV's longest-running programs. Film clips and previews. Claude Mionnet, Catherine Langeais.

Si c'était vous (If it were you), 1957–1958. Social drama. Marcel Bluwal, Marcel Moussy.

Télé Match, 1954–1961. Game show. André Gillois, Jacques Antoine.

Télé-Paris, 1947–1959. Variety show that grew out of radio's *Paris-Cocktail*. Jacques Chabannes.

Toute la télévision, 1954. Three episodes on how TV works. Etienne Lalou, Catherine Langeais.

Trois objets, une vie (Three objects, one life), 1953–1955. Interview program. Jean Thévenot.

La Vie des animaux (The life of animals), 1952–1976. Nature. Frédéric Rossif, Claude Darget.

Index

3D: anaglyphs, 232, 236–37, 248–49, 258; and color, 232–33, 238, 241, 248–49, 252; and dance, 233; and horror, 24, 251–52, 283; with polarized lenses, 232, 237–38
12 Angry Men (Lumet), 17–18, 167–69, 178
16mm film, 150, 151n6, 161, 186
35mm film, 10–11, 30, 38, 216, 218n1, 226n6, 231n1, 261, 264n6, 271, 286n4
36 chandelles, 69, 108, 321, 323–25
48-fps projection, 20
400 Coups, Les (Truffaut), 19, 28, 212n0, 324

Academy Awards. *See* Oscars
Academy ratio, 29, 293n3, 307n5
action painting, 6
Adam, Alfred, 86
Adventures of Rin-Tin-Tin, The, 134, 135n1
Agel, Henri: *Le Cinéma*, 254
Aida (Verdi): staged for Cinerama, 221, 230

Alain (Emile Chartier), 18
Alchemist, The (Jonson): adapted for television, 204
A l'école des vedettes, 52, 325
Alfred Hitchcock Presents. See Hitchcock, Alfred, and television
Allégret, Marc: *Avec André Gide*, 46, 47n2
anamorphic lens, 10, 21, 31, 231n1, 272, 286n6, 293n1. *See also* Hypergonar
anamorphosis, 227, 260, 264n6, 293, 307n6
Andersen, Hans Christian, 161
Andromaque [*Andromache*] (Racine): staged for television, 41, 87
animals: and television, 63–66, 134, 137. See also *La Vie des animaux*
animation: stereoscopic, 25, 233, 240–41. *See also* Norman McLaren
Antoine, Jacques, 319
Antoine, Jean, 79, 319–20, 323

Antonioni, Michelangelo: *I Vinti*, 31, 290
apparatus theory, 31
architecture, 276, 281, 286n7
Aristotle, 211
Around Is Around (McLaren), 233
Arrivée d'un train en gare de La Ciotat, L' (Lumière brothers), 24, 241, 242n4, 252
Art et les hommes, L', 95, 97, 325. See also "Problèmes d'un jeune artiste d'aujourd'hui"
astronomy: and television, 12–13, 49–50, 61, 130
Audiberti, Jacques, 18
Au Royaume des images, 163, 165
Autant-Lara, Claude: *Le Blé en herbe*, 117, 118n1; *Construire un feu*, 278, 286n6, 292, 293n1
auteur theory, 1, 9, 21; and television, 18, 65, 99–100, 150–51, 180–203
automobile, 10, 300
Avatar (Cameron), 26
Avec André Gide (Allégret), 46, 47n2
Avery, Tex, 233
A vous de juger, 153–54, 163, 325

Bachelor Party, The (Mann), 167–69, 170n1, 178, 183
Bal des Petits Lits blancs, 48–49
Ballet mécanique (Léger), 241
Balzac, Honoré de, 99, 133, 155, 320
Bardot, Brigitte, 197
Barefoot Contessa, The (Mankiewicz), 302, 307n2
Barma, Claude, 182, 320–21, 324–25; *Casino de Paris*, 157
Barrault, Jean-Louis, 82–83, 84n1, 183n2, 186n2, 325
Barrère, Igor, 140, 322
Baudelaire, Charles, 100

Bayeux Tapestry, 201
Bazin, André: "The Myth of Total Cinema," 23, 241n1; *Qu'est-ce que le cinéma?*, 47n2, 173n2
Becker, Jacques, 72n1, 158, 323
Belin, (Commissaire) Jean, 54–56, 56n1
Belle Hélène, La (Offenbach): staged for television, 90
Beneath the 12-Mile Reef (Webb), 295, 297n1
Beowulf (Zemeckis), 26
Bérard, Christian, 93, 94n3
Berlin Film Festival, 17, 169
Bernhardt, Sarah, 171
Best Years of Our Lives, The (Wyler), 285, 293
Bête humaine, La (Renoir), 24, 241, 242n4, 302, 306
Birth of a Nation, The (Griffith), 271
Blackboard Jungle (Brooks), 21, 151, 262, 309, 310n1
Blé en herbe, Le (Autant-Lara), 117, 118n1
Blum-Byrnes accord, 2, 307n4
Bluwal, Marcel, 58, 182, 205–6, 209–210, 320, 322, 324, 326
B movies, 268
Boudu sauvé des eaux (Renoir), 185
Boulogne-Billancourt film studios, 174, 175–76n1
Bourgeois de Calais, Les (Rodin), 100, 101n3
Brave Eagle, 134, 135n1
Bresson, Robert, 158, 280, 323; *Journal d'un curé de campagne*, 31, 285
Britain, Festival of, 232, 234n1, 237, 241, 249
bronchoscopy, 119–20, 129–130
Brooks, Richard: *Blackboard Jungle*, 21, 151, 262, 309, 310n1

Brunot, André, 82–83, 84n1, 86
Bwana Devil (Oboler), 248–49, 252

Cabaret du soir, 52, 325
Cahiers du Cinéma, 1, 12, 19, 21, 151n1,
  257n1, 307n2
"Caméra a-t-elle un cœur?, La," 124
Caméra en Afrique, 63
Caméra explore le temps, La, 323, 325
Candida (Shaw): staged for
  television, 86–88
Cannes, Festival de, 186n3, 223, 230,
  293, 295, 320
Canon City (Wilbur), 117n
Capra, Frank, 149, 157; *Why We
  Fight,* 155
Carné, Marcel, 72n1, 158, 175n1, 320
Cartier, Raymond, 313, 317n1
Cartier-Bresson, Henri, 191
Casino de Paris (Barma), 157
catoblepas, 274, 286n5, 302, 307n1
Caurat, Jacqueline, 111–12
Cavell, Stanley: *The World Viewed,*
  15
Cazeneuve, Maurice, 182, 320
censorship, 3; and television, 12,
  106, 109, 116–18, 125, 211; and
  widescreen, 21
Cézanne, Paul, 296
Chabannes, Jacques, 86, 150, 320,
  326
Chalais, François, 124, 153, 155, 163,
  320, 325
Chapiteau Pitilliata, 136, 138n2
Chaplin, Charlie, 15–16, 48–49, 284;
  A King in New York, 122, 123n2, 167,
  170n1
character
Charlot. *See* Chaplin, Charlie
Chartier, Jean-Pierre (pseud.
  Jean-Louis Tallenay), 49, 50n1,
  122–23n1

Chatel, François, 52, 92, 321
Châtelet, 220, 259, 263n2
Chayefsky, Paddy, 19, 168, 205,
  210–212
Chemise (France): staged for
  television, 90, 91n1
*Chester Folies. See La Piste aux
  étoiles*
Chevaliers de la Table ronde (Cocteau): staged for television,
  92–93, 94n1
Chrétien, (Professor) Henri, 10,
  227, 231n1, 269, 272, 275, 278,
  286n6, 293
Chronique d'un été (Morin and
  Rouch), 20
ciné-clubs, 164
Cinéma, Le (Agel), 254
cinema: as an industrial art, 6–7,
  279, 281, 315; "pure," 7, 76; total,
  23–24, 241
cinéma direct, 20
CinemaScope. *See* widescreen
Cinémathèque française, 165, 324
Cinémathèque imaginaire, 82, 325
cinéma vérité, 20
Ciné-Panorama, 69, 138, 320, 325
cinephilia, 1, 21, 147
Cinerama. *See* widescreen. *See also*
  Polyvision
Cinerama Holiday (Bendick and De
  Lacy), 27, 225n
Citizen Kane (Welles), 285, 293
Clair, René, 101n1, 158, 322
Clément, René, 158
close-up, 192, 209, 246–7; and
  tele-theater, 41; and television,
  63, 107, 191–92; and widescreen,
  29, 218, 284, 294–98
Clouzot, Henri-Georges: *Miquette
  et sa mère,* 117–18n; *Le Salaire de la
  peur,* 284, 293, 293n3

Cocteau, Jean, 25, 46n1, 223, 295, 322, 324; *Chevaliers de la Table ronde,* 92–93, 94nno, 1, 3; *Les Parents terribles,* 161, 162n1, 295; *La Voix humaine,* 194, 203n1
Cold War, 7, 247no
Colette, 155; *Le Blé en herbe* (novel), 118n1
commedia dell'arte, 80, 199–200
commentary: in television programs, 63–66, 100, 163–66, 171–72, 186, 188
Commission Supérieure Technique de l'image et du son, 305
Construire un feu (Autant-Lara), 278, 286n6, 292, 293n1
Continent perdu (Continente perduto, Gras and Moser), 223, 225n4
Cooper, Merian: *This Is Cinerama,* 225no, 230–31, 231n3
co-production, 194–95, 268
Cordion, Rolla, 79
Cousteau, Jacques: *Le Monde du silence,* 124, 125n1
Crary, Jonathan, 23
Cravenne, Marcel, 41, 146, 321
Cubism, 199
Cummings, Robert, 18
Cygne noir, Le, 233

Dante Alighieri, 100
Darget, Claude, 63, 65, 137, 156, 321, 326
Darwin, Charles, 5
Dead of Night (Cavalcanti), 177, 179n1
de Caunes, Georges, 110, 115n7
Delluc, Louis, 82
Del Ruth, Roy: *Phantom of the Rue Morgue,* 254–257, 257no
DeMille, Cecil B., 271
Denis, M. A. and Mme., 63–64
depth of field, 238, 290, 292, 303

de Rieux, Max, 86, 89n1
De Seta, Vittorio: *Isole di fuoco,* 223, 225n4
Desgraupes, Pierre, 45, 96, 128, 321, 325–26
De Sica, Vittorio, 206, 280
D'hier à aujourd'hui, 44–45, 323, 325
Dial M for Murder (Hitchcock), 25, 255–56
Diary of a Chambermaid, The (Renoir), 194
Dimanche à Pékin (Marker), 64, 66n1
Disney, Walt, 233
Do Bigha Zamin (Roy), 288, 290–91n1
documentary, 20, 64–65, 193, 255, 257n3; and 3D, 233, 246; and television, 44–45, 47n2, 96, 153, 155, 164, 186, 199–201; and widescreen, 31, 223–24, 225n4, 230–31, 259, 284
Doniol-Valcroze, Jacques, 254, 257n1
Dr. Jekyll and Mr. Hyde (Renoir), 182, 185, 187–89
drive-in theaters, 4
Drot, Jean-Marie, 95, 97–98, 127, 321, 325
Du côté des grands hommes, 153
Dumayet, Pierre, 45, 82, 96, 128–29, 321–22, 325–26
Dumazedier, Joffre, 130–31, 132n3
"Dynamic Square, The" (Eisenstein), 10–11

East of Eden (Kazan), 263, 264n8
Echec au public, 69
Ecole des parents, 116
Ecole nouvelle, 70
Ecran Français, L', 1
Edison, Thomas, 10–11, 38, 62n2, 216, 271

Editions spéciales, 69, 153–55, 325

Eisenstein, Sergei, 284; "The Dynamic Square," 10–11

Elizabeth II (queen of England): coronation of, 8, 50, 108

Empire Theater, 220, 225nno, 1

En direct du fond de la mer, 51, 325

endoscopy, 70, 129–130. *See also* bronchoscopy

En Votre âme et conscience, 69–70, 320–22, 324–25

eroticism: in film and television, 105–115, 197–198

Esprit, 6, 47n2

Europa '51 (Rossellini), 293

exquisite corpse, 125, 125n2

"Family of Images, The" (Sartre). See *L'Imaginaire*

Fanny (Pagnol), 84n3; staged for television, 83

Farrebique ou Les Quatre Saisons (Rouquier), 16

Farrow, John: *Hondo,* 256, 257n4

Father (Père) Ubu, 71, 260, 264n4

Feuillade, Louis, 150, 151–52nn5, 7

Fin de la jalousie, La (Proust): radio broadcast, 77

Flaubert, Gustave, 155, 286n5, 307n1; *Madame Bovary,* 77, 150

Florey, Robert, 148–49, 151n5, 178, 179n2

Florian, Jean-Pierre Claris de, 260, 264n5

Folies-Bergère, 27, 220, 259, 263n2

Fonda, Henry, 18, 169

Fonds d'Aide au Cinéma (Aide Law), 259, 304–5, 307n4

Ford, Charles, 165, 166n2

Ford, John, 149, 157; *How the West Was Won,* 27

France, Anatole: *Chemise,* 90, 91n1

France-Observateur. See *Observateur, L'*

François le Rhinocéros, 63

François Mauriac (Leenhardt), 46, 47n2

Frères Jacques, Les, 53n1; "Méli-Mélo," 52, 53n1

Fresnay, Pierre, 77, 77–78n3

Fromentin, Eugène, 155

From Here to Eternity (Zinnemann), 309, 310n1

Gabin, Jean, 174–176, 176n2

Gance, Abel, 10, 28, 215, 221, 225n2, 227, 229, 246, 259, 264n3, 269, 272, 277–78, 284, 292; Napoléon, 28, 43n1, 89n2, 175n1, 221, 229, 231n1, 272, 277–78, 292, 293n1. *See also* Polyvision

General Motors, 154, 177

Germany Year Zero (Rossellini), 186

Gheri, Alfred: *Sixième étage,* 57–59, 59n1

Gide, André, 18, 46, 47n2

Gillois, André, 107, 322, 326

Giono, Jean, 164, 166n1

Gir, François, 137–38, 138n3

Gish, Lillian, 198

"Glass Eye, The" (*Alfred Hitchcock Presents*), 177–179, 179n0

Gobelins tapestry, 201

Goddard, Paulette, 194

Gone with the Wind (Fleming), 271

Grand Ballet de Monte Carlo, 79, 81n1

Grande Illusion, La (Renoir), 77–78n3, 175–76n1, 184, 195

Grand Guignol style, 249, 251

Grave, Serge, 150, 151n6

Griffith, D. W., 263; *The Birth of a Nation,* 271

Gros plan, 70

Guitry, Sacha, 138n3, 151n6, 171–73, 173n1

Hamlet (Shakespeare), 77
Hessling, Catherine, 160
High and the Mighty, The (Wellman), 296–97, 198n3
hippomobile, 137
Hirsch, Robert, 80, 81n2
Histoire générale du cinéma (Sadoul), 235
Hitchcock, Alfred: *Dial M for Murder*, 25, 255–56; and television, 149–50, 157, 180–81, 187; *To Catch a Thief*, 177. *See also* "The Glass Eye"
Hitler, Adolf, 121
Hollywood: classical period, 149, 178, 268; and European cinema, 2–3, 269, 307n4
Hondo (Farrow), 256, 257n4
House of Wax (de Toth), 251–53
How the West Was Won (Ford, Hathaway, and Marshall), 27
Huffington Post, 2
Hughes, Howard, 148
Hypergonar, 10, 231n1, 275, 278, 286, 293, 293n1. *See also* Chrétien, (Professor) Henri

Ile de feu. See *Isole di fuoco*
I Love Lucy, 111
Imaginaire, L' (Sartre), 7–8, 14
IMAX, 20
Impromptu du dimanche, 82–83, 325
improvisation: and television, 64–65, 79–80, 82–85, 173
India 58 (Rossellini), 182–83, 185–86, 186n3, 187–88, 200
Invention du cinéma, L' (Sadoul), 235, 241n1
Isole di fuoco (De Seta), 223, 225n4

I Vinti (Antonioni), 31, 290

Jack the Ripper, 113n
Jazz Singer, The (Crosland), 252
Jeanne, René, 165, 166n2
Joie de vivre, 69, 325
Jonson, Ben: The Alchemist, 204
Joubert, Jacqueline, 110–12, 15n7, 322
Journal d'un curé de campagne (Bresson), 31, 285
Journal télévisé, 71, 124–25, 325

Kafka, Franz, 71
Karlson, Phil: *The Phenix City Story*, 309, 310n1
Käutner, Helmut: *Die letzte Brücke*, 306, 307n5
Kazan, Elia: *East of Eden*, 263, 264n8
kinescope, 33n8, 51–52
kinetoscope, 62n2
King in New York, A (Chaplin), 122, 123n2, 167, 170n1

Lacombe, Georges: *Leur Dernière Nuit*, 175, 176n2
La Fontaine, Jean de, 83, 264n5
Lalou, Etienne, 49, 119, 127, 139–40, 322, 326; *Regards neufs sur la T.V.*, 67–71
Langeais, Catherine, 110–112, 139, 141n1, 323–24, 326
Laren, Mac. *See* Norman McLaren
Léautaud, Paul, 136, 138n1
Le Corbusier (Charles-Edouard Jeanneret-Gris), 281, 286n7
Lectures pour tous, 44–46, 69–70, 82, 96, 122, 127–129, 321–22, 324–26
Leenhardt, Roger, 47n2; *François Mauriac*, 46, 47n2
Léger, Fernand: *Ballet mécanique*, 241
Le Mans: catastrophe at, 124

Leonardo Da Vinci, 281
letzte Brücke, Die (Käutner), 306, 307n5
Leur Dernière Nuit (Lacombe), 175, 176n2
L'Herbier, Marcel, 82, 84n2, 153, 158, 159n1, 322, 325
L'Hôte, Jean, 163, 322
Linder, Max, 203
Little Fugitive (Ashley and Engel), 288–289, 290n1
Lola Montès (Ophüls), 262, 264n7
Lorenzi, Stellio, 49, 99–100, 157, 173–74, 323, 325
Louis, Roger, 42, 44–45, 127, 323, 325
Lucot, René, 90, 323–24
Lumet, Sidney, 169: *12 Angry Men*, 17–18, 167–69, 178
Lumière, Louis, 37, 232, 237, 242n3, 251, 315–16; *Arrivée d'un train en gare de La Ciotat, L'*, 24, 241, 242n4, 252. *See also* 3D: polarized lenses
Lurçat, Jean, 281, 286n7

Macheaukis, Eugène, 86
Madame Bovary (Flaubert), 77, 150
Madame De … (Vilmorin), 46–47n1
Magazine des explorateurs, 65, 127–29
Malentendu, Le (Camus): staged for television, 41
Malladoli, (Professor) Cincinnatus, 136–38
Malraux, André, 5, 46–47n1, 284, 321; "Sketch for a Psychology of Cinema," 290, 291n2
Mankiewicz, Joseph: *The Barefoot Contessa*, 302, 307n2
Mann, Delbert: *The Bachelor Party*, 167–69, 170n1, 178, 183; *Marty*, 19, 151, 168–69, 170n2, 183, 205, 262, 308–9, 310n1

Manuel, Robert, 80, 81n2
Margaritis, Gilles, 96, 98n2, 323, 326
Marius (Pagnol), 84n3, 166n1; staged for television, 83
Marivaux Cinema, 195
Marken, Jane, 80, 81n2
Marker, Chris: *Dimanche à Pékin*, 64, 66n1
Marre, Bernard, 97, 98n4
Marshall Plan, 2
Marty (Mann), 19, 151, 168–69, 170n2, 183, 205, 262, 308–9, 310n1
Masson, Jean, 79, 323
Match. See *Paris Match*
Matisse, Henri, 18
Mauriac, François: film about, 46, 47n2
McCarey, Leo, 149, 157
McCarthy, Joseph, 122; hearings, 123n2
McLaren, Norman, 233, 234n2; 3D (stereoscopic) animation, 25, 240–41; *Around Is Around*, 233; *Now Is the Time*, 233
media ecology, 21, 32
Méliès, Georges, 37, 203, 246, 251, 316
"Méli-Mélo": musical broadcast, 52; song (Les Frères Jacques), 52, 53n1
Metroscopix, 248–49
Meurisse, Paul, 182, 183n2, 185, 186n2
Mionnet, Claude, 165, 326
Miquette et sa mère (Clouzot), 117–18n
Mizoguchi, Kenji: *Ugetsu Monogatari*, 288, 290–91n1
Monde du silence, Le (Cousteau and Malle), 124, 125n1
Monet, Claude, 171
Monogram Pictures, 268

Montaigne, Michel de, 18
Monthelrant, Henry de, 46, 47n3
Moreau, Jeanne, 80, 81n2
Morin, Edgar, 20; *Chronique d'un été*, 20
Moussy, Marcel, 19, 204–212, 320, 324, 326
Münchhausen [Münchausen], Baron, 136, 138n1
Murder in 3D, A, 249
Musée Grévin, 251, 253n1, 323
Musée Rodin. See "Visite au Musée Rodin"
Music-Hall Parade, 69, 323, 326
Musique de film, La, 164
Musique pour vous, 96, 326
Mystery of the Wax Museum (Curtiz), 24
"Myth of Total Cinema, The" (Bazin), 23, 24m1

Napoléon (Gance), 28, 43n1, 89n2, 175n1, 221, 229, 231n1, 272, 277–78, 292, 293n1
narration. See commentary
neorealism, 31, 309; and Cinema-Scope, 31, 288–91; Italian, 199; and television, 18–19, 31, 206
New Republic, 2
Newsweek, 2
New Wave: French, 19–20, 173n1, 257n1
Nohain, Jean, 107–108, 324–25
Normandy theater, 61, 62n3
nouveau roman, 6
Nouvel Observateur, Le. See *Observateur, L'*
Now Is the Time (McLaren), 233
Nuremberg, 121

Observateur, L', xvii, 2, 33n12, 66n1, 257n1, 298n3

Observateur d'Aujourd'hui, L'. See *Observateur, L'*
Observateur politique, économique et littéraire, L'. See *Observateur, L'*
Offenbach, Jacques: *La Belle Hélène*, 90
Olivier, Laurence: *Richard III*, 154
Olympic Games: live television broadcast, 8
One Thousand and One Nights, 133
On purge bébé (Renoir), 185, 186n1
Ophüls, Max; *Lola Montès*, 262, 264n7; *Madame De...*, 46–47n1
ORTF (Office de Radiodiffusion-Télévision Française), 7, 72n3, 321, 323–24. See also RTF
Orthicon camera, 100, 174–75
Oscars, 170n2, 310n1; live television broadcast, 8
Othello (Welles), 285, 287n9

Pagnol, Marcel, 218n1; *Fanny*, 83, 84n3; *Marius*, 83, 84n3, 166n1; miniseries about, 163–65
Painlevé, Jean, 129, 132n1
Païsa (Rossellini), 185
"panoramic screen," 259–60, 262, 273–75, 301–7
Paramount: 1948 divestiture decree, 3; and VistaVision, 226n6, 264n6
Parents terribles, Les (Cocteau), 295; film adaptation, 162n2; as telecinema, 161
Parisien Libéré, Le, 1
Paris Match, 313, 317n1
Paris 1900 (Védrès), 171, 173n2
Pêche au thon, La. See *Tempo di tonni*
Père (Father) Ubu, 71, 260, 264n4
Petite Marchande d'allumettes, La (Renoir), 160–61

Phantom of the Rue Morgue (Del Ruth), 254–257, 257n0

Phenix City Story, The (Karlson), 309, 310n1

photogénie, 9, 42, 82, 93, 94n2, 174

Pichard, (Father) Raymond, 121, 122–23n1

Pirandello, Luigi, 207

Piste aux étoiles, La, 323, 326

Pitilliatas. *See* Chapiteau Pitilliata

Pizella, Stéphane, 63–65

Place au théâtre, 79–81, 88, 319, 323, 326

Plato's cave, 120

poetry: pure, 99, 101n1

Polaroid glasses, 249, 252, 258, 283. *See also* 3D: glasses

Polyvision, 10, 28, 221, 229, 259, 264n3. *See also* Gance, Abel

post-impressionism, 199, 286n7

Potonniée, Georges, 235

Prat, Jean, 204, 234

problem play, 206–208

"Problèmes d'un jeune artiste d'aujourd'hui" (*L'Art et les hommes*), 95, 97–98, 98n1

Proust, Marcel, 49; *La Fin de la jalousie,* 77

Public Is Never Wrong, The (Zukor), 295, 297–98n2

Quatre cent coups, Les (Truffaut). *See* 400 coups, Les

Qu'est-ce que le cinéma? (Bazin), 47n2, 173n2

Quéval, Jean, 72n1; T.V., 67–72

Quitte ou double, 70

radio: as art, 39, 75–77; and culture, 127; "pure," 77

Radio-Cinéma-Télévision, 2, 50n1, 122–23n1, 264n6, 295, 320

Radio-Luxembourg, 127

Raimu (Jules Auguste Muraire), 164, 166n1

RCT. See Radio-Cinéma-Télévision

realism, 174, 282; and 3D, 252, 282–83; and tele-theater, 58–59; and television, 167–69; and widescreen, 27, 21, 222, 228–30. *See also* neorealism

Rebikoff, Dimitri: "torpedo," 124, 125n1

Regards neufs sur la T.V. (Lalou), 67–71

Règle du jeu, La (Renoir), 246, 293

Renaud, Madeleine, 82–83, 84n1, 325

Renoir, Auguste, 160, 171, 202

Renoir, Jean, 81n2, 280, 285, 301; *La Bête humaine,* 24, 241, 242n4, 302, 306; *Boudu sauvé des eaux,* 185; *The Diary of a Chambermaid,* 194; *Dr. Jekyll and Mr. Hyde,* 182, 185, 187–89; *La Grande Illusion,* 77–78n3, 175–76n1, 184, 195; *On purge bébé,* 185, 186n1; *La Petite Marchande d'allumettes,* 160–61; *La Règle du jeu,* 246, 293; *The River,* 285, 287n9; and television, 182–203, 183n2, 186n1; *Tire au flanc,* 185, 186n1

Resistance: French, 1, 322

Rex theater, 61, 62n3

Richard III (Olivier), 154

Ringling Brothers Circus, 27

River, The (Renoir), 285, 287n9

River of No Return (Preminger), 218

Rivette, Jacques, 18, 151, 152n8

RKO Pictures, 148

Robe, The (Koster), 225n3, 261, 267, 284, 293

Robinson, Madeleine, 175, 176n2

Rodin, Auguste, 99–100, 171; *Les Bourgeois de Calais,* 100, 101n3. *See also* Musée Rodin

Rohmer, Eric, 30

Roman Holiday (Wyler), 108, 114n3

romanticism, 197; futurist, 38

Rossellini, Roberto, 18, 151, 280, 321; *Europa '51,* 293; *Germany Year Zero,* 186; *India 58,* 182–83, 185–86, 186n3, 187–88, 200; *Païsa,* 185; and television, 182–203; *Viaggio in Italia,* 18–19

Rossif, Frédéric, 63, 124, 148, 153, 155, 163–64, 171–72, 324–36

Rossini theater, 60, 62

Rostand, Edmond, 171

Rouch, Jean: *Chronique d'un été,* 20

Rouxcolor, 216, 218n1, 254–55, 257n2, 272, 286n4

RTF (Radiodiffusion-Télévision Française), 71, 72n3, 131, 136, 184, 319. *See also* ORTF

Rue de l'université, 77, 77–78n3

Sabbagh, Pierre, 56, 111n, 127, 129, 323–35

Sadoul, Georges, 22; *Histoire générale du cinéma,* 235; *L'Invention du cinéma,* 241n1

Saint-Saëns, Camille, 171

Salaire de la peur, Le (Clouzot), 284, 293, 293n3

Sartre, Jean-Paul, 28, 136, 324; *L'Imaginaire,* 7–8, 14

Scarface (Hawks and Rosson), 309

Schaeffer, Pierre, 77, 77–78n3

Science de demain, 119–20, 326

Sciences d'aujourd'hui, 128–30

Sennett, Mack, 157, 233

Séquence du spectateur, La, 153–54, 163, 165, 323–24, 326

Shaw, George Bernard: *Candida,* 86–88

Si c'était vous, 29, 204–5, 320, 324, 326. *See also* Moussy, Marcel

Sixième étage (Gheri): staged for television, 57–59, 59n1

"Sketch for a Psychology of Cinema" (Malraux), 290, 291n2

speakerine, 12, 16, 109–13, 113n, 115nn6, 7, 141n1

special effects, 24, 122, 146, 160, 175, 179n2, 248

Spottiswoode, Raymond, 232–33, 238, 241, 241–42n2, 249. *See also* stereoscopy

star system, 295

Stendhal (Marie-Henri Beyle), 155

stereophotography, 23, 232, 235–36

stereoscopy (stereoscopic 3D), 23, 25, 222, 228, 232–33, 235–41, 245, 248, 251, 255, 267, 282–83, 300

stereo sound, 3, 25, 221, 227, 284, 293, 297n1

Stevenson, Robert Louis: *Dr. Jekyll and Mr Hyde* (novel), 182, 187

Stroheim, Erich von, 284

Tallenay, Jean-Louis. *See* Chartier, Jean-Pierre

tapestry, 201, 281, 286n7

Tati, Jacques, 158, 175–76n1, 322

Tchernia, Pierre, 52, 175, 324

Technicolor, 11, 233, 249

telecinema: and classical cinema, 180

télégénie, 9, 42–43, 44–47, 82

Télé Match, 69, 108, 319, 322, 326

Télé-Paris, 126, 320, 326

teleplay. *See* tele-theater

telescope, 12–13, 49, 61, 130

tele-theater, 13–15, 18, 40–42, 44, 57–59, 79–94, 84–85n4, 145–46, 204–05, 211–12.

television: and advertising, 16, 154, 211; audience statistics, 130–132, 244; as industrial art, 7, 279; "pure," 99, 120, 129, 147

Tempo di tonni (Sala), 223, 225n4

Temps Modernes, Les, 6

Tennberg, Jean-Marc, 97, 98n3

Thévenot, Jean, 42, 45, 55–56, 129, 325–26; T.V., 67–72

This Is Cinerama (Cooper and Thomas), 225no, 230–31, 231n3

Thomas, Lowell: *This Is Cinerama,* 225no, 230–31, 231n3

Tire au flanc (Renoir), 185, 186n1

To Catch a Thief (Hitchcock), 177

Toute la télévision, 139–41

Trois objets, une vie, 44–46, 129, 326

Truffaut, Francois, 46–47n1, 173n1, 324; *Les 400 Coups,* 19, 28, 212no, 324

T.V. (Quéval and Thévenot), 67–72

Twentieth Century Fox, 268, 273

Ugetsu Monogatari (Mizoguchi), 288, 290–91n1

United Artists, 248

Urbino pottery, 202

variable screen, 10–11, 254, 263, 273, 297

Variety, 20

Védrès, Nicole: *Paris 1900,* 171, 173n2

Venice Film Festival, 183n2, 186n2, 290–91n1; and CinemaScope, 283, 288, 292; and television, 60–62, 62n1

Vermorel, Claude, 41, 43n1, 87, 89n2

Viaggio in Italia (Rossellini), 18–19

video, 20, 30

Vidor, King, 150, 157

Vie des animaux, La, 63, 65, 137, 153–56, 164, 321, 326

Villon, François, 100

Vilmorin, Louise de, 45–46, 46–47n1; *Madame De ...,* 46–47n1

"Visite au Musée Rodin," 99–101, 173, 323

VistaVision, 11, 30, 225, 226n6, 259, 261, 264n6, 306–7, 307n6

Vitascope, 61, 62n2

voce umana, La (Rossellini), 194, 203n1

Voix humaine, La. See *voce umana, La*

Warner Brothers: and the coming of sound, 23, 243, 268, 277

Warner Color, 252

Welles, Orson, 187, 290; *Citizen Kane,* 285, 293; *Othello,* 285, 287n9

Wellman, William: *The High and the Mighty,* 296–97, 198n3

What Is Cinema?. See *Qu'est-ce que le cinéma?*

Why We Fight (Capra), 155

widescreen: and movie theater architecture, 29, 259, 273, 301

World Viewed, The (Cavell), 15

Written on the Wind (Sirk), 218

Wyler, William, 290; *The Best Years of Our Lives,* 285, 293; *Roman Holiday,* 108, 114n3

Zinnemann, Fred: *From Here to Eternity,* 309, 310n1

Zola, Emile, 155

Zukor, Adolph: *The Public Is Never Wrong,* 295, 297–98n2

Text:	10.75/15 Janson MT Pro
Display:	Janson MT Pro
Compositor:	IDS Infotech, Ltd.
Indexer:	Madeline Whittle
Printer and binder:	Maple Press